THE FRENCH
REVOLUTION

❋❋

THE FRENCH REVOLUTION

by
GEORGES PERNOUD

and
SABINE FLAISSIER

with a preface by
ANDRÉ MAUROIS

translated by
RICHARD GRAVES

London: SECKER & WARBURG: *1962*

CONTENTS

❧❧❧❧❧❧❧❧❧❧❧❧❧❧❧❧❧❧❧❧❧❧❧❧❧❧❧❧❧❧❧❧❧❧❧❧❧

CHRONOLOGICAL TABLE

1789	January	Louis XVI summons States General
	May	States General meet at Versailles
	June	States General in future called National Assembly
	July	Fall of the Bastille—National Guard formed with Lafayette as Commandant
	October	The Paris mob march on Versailles. King removed to Paris
1790	September	Necker resigns as Chief Minister
	December	King gives assent to Civil Constitution of the Clergy
1791	June	The flight to Varennes
	September–October	National Assembly dissolved and Legislative Assembly formed—Lafayette resigns from National Guard
	December	King vetoes decrees against émigrés and priests
1792	April	Assembly declares war on Austria
	August	Mob attacks Tuileries—King taken prisoner—Lafayette flees from France—Danton as Minister of Justice
	September	The Cannonade at Valmy—Assembly abolished and Convention meets—Girondins in power—Republic proclaimed
	November	French victory at Jemappes
	December	Trial of King
1793	January	King executed
	February	Convention declares war against England and Holland

1793	March	Royalist revolt in La Vendée
	June	Fall of the Girondins
	July	Committee of Public Safety formed, dominated by Danton and Robespierre—"The Terror" begins—Series of French military reverses—Assassination of Marat by Charlotte Corday
	October	Execution of Marie Antoinette
	November	Celebration of the "Feast of Reason"
1794	April	Danton executed—Robespierre all-powerful
	June	Celebration of the "Feast of the Supreme Being"
	July	Fall and execution of Robespierre—Commune of Paris abolished—end of "The Terror"

PREFACE

❦❦

THE MATERIAL of history is composed of remains, of documents, inscriptions and other objects. The Château of Versailles evokes the Court of Louis XIV: the arena of old Paris, a Roman city: the Arc de Triomphe reminds us of Napoleon's Grande Armée.

Documents provide facts and figures; they need to be checked strictly—not everything written or printed by Governments is true: far from it. Letters are often valuable but sometimes misleading. The evidence of eye-witnesses reflect at once events themselves and the prejudices of the witness. But they can be compared, contrasted and weighed, and the result brings one nearer to the truth.

Unfortunately truth is not always the historian's target. A learned man is none the less a man—a man who will take sides for or against the French Revolution. If he is for, he will paint great epic canvases, in the style of Michelet, and wash away the blood in a torrent of epithets. If he is against, he will, like Taine, reduce the great passions of the epoch to a logical, abstract design. Moreover, there was more than one internal revolution within the Revolution itself. The historian may favour the Girondins at the expense of Danton. He may be for Danton and against Robespierre: for Robespierre and against Thermidor. As Paul Valéry has said, the historians of the Revolution pelt each other with severed heads. "Monsters," cries one: "Heroes," replies another. The authors of this book and of its successors have preferred to present to the reader the evidence of witnesses, authentic, pure, uncommented and coming from every point of the compass. They leave to us the task of reading, weighing and judging. I consider this a sound method. It strips the original stories of the usual crust of useless glosses and above all it puts us in touch with living reality. Except in the rare instance where the historian is a genius, the eye-witness will be more truthful. It is a task to prove our discernment by assigning to each witness his place and his position.

At this point we should consider the notion, or rather the function of the reporter. The reporter is a witness of quality. When he comes home, he writes down his impressions, so as to preserve alive something he believes of capital importance, which has taken place before his eyes. The reporter knows how to use his eyes—he does not shrink from throwing himself into the heart of an action so as best to follow its episodes. He has the art of picking out what is important. He is able to make the reader see what he has seen himself. He achieves this by selecting his details, by the apposite quotation of something he has heard and by keeping his narrative in motion. Finally, if he is really a first-class reporter, he knows how to master his own feelings. He sees not what he wants to see, but what is there before his eyes. This objectiveness is rare, but we find it more often among the great reporters of our day, who are obedient to a strict professional ethic, than among the eye-witnesses of historical events in the past. Nevertheless, some of the latter had enough spiritual greatness to escape from the trammels of contemporary prejudice. Roederer, who is often quoted in this work, is a signal example.

When the reporter possesses talent, this form of journalism produces admirable writing. Victor Hugo excelled himself in *Choses Vues* on which this series will certainly draw in its subsequent volumes. That collection contains an account of the meetings of the Académie Française in the days of Guizot and Thiers, and visits to King Louis-Philippe—all overflowing with truth. There is no caricature and no flattery. A series of truthful profiles, of apt phrases, caught on the wing, and of attitudes recorded by the pencil-stroke of a master. It is life itself observed by a seeing eye and a noble intelligence. I would say the same of certain passages in the Memoirs of Vigny or Chateaubriand.

Men of genius have not been involved in all the great events of history and we cannot always cite a Victor Hugo as witness.

But the title of this series *There is always a Reporter* tells the truth. Whenever a group of men gathers together, to accomplish some important action, there is always to be found among them a born-spectator, curious and intelligent—in a word, a reporter. The protagonists of the drama are often too deeply involved to have the time or the inclination to observe what is happening around them. The reporter is sometimes a minor personage, whom chance has associated with the historical event, or a man whose professional duties have involved him in it, or a detached outsider, temperamentally observant, like Goethe at the battle of Valmy. A valet, a secretary, a maid of honour—all these live in the shadow of powerful persons and are very likely to find themselves present on occasions when others of greater importance are excluded. If chance has placed in subordinate posts like these men or women superior to the positions they occupy, persons, that is, who are able to keep themselves free from the pettinesses and rancours which are too often inseparable from these minor functions then their evidence becomes a thing of inestimable value. They were present at the time: they received confidences: if their spirits were noble they loved their masters and mistresses. Such persons have contributed to history more often than one supposes, and we must admit that some men *are* heroes to their own valets.

᛭

I find it an excellent thing that this series opens with a volume on the French Revolution which is at once an extraordinary adventure, a sublime epic and an occasion of bloody or sordid scenes. It is almost impossible to disentangle this network of grandeur and horror and we have already said that most historians have not succeeded in doing so. Each author in claiming to deal with the events has cut away those strands of the tapestry which have inconvenienced him. That is why this epoch more than any other lends itself to the present method of treatment which is objective by definition, consisting as it does in presenting the evidence of witnesses, nothing else, to the reader's judgement.

All these "reporters" were no doubt at the time passionately involved in the drama as you and I would doubtless have been, had we been in their place, but it is only by the comparison of so many views taken from different angles that we can form a credible image of the French Revolution. As many as fifty thousand pieces of first-hand evidence for this period are known to exist. It would of course have been possible to select other "reporters"—there is no lack in numbers or variety. No one could claim to have chosen the best texts, but it is fair to say that those which have been collected in this volume have been selected without bias and that it is impossible to read them without emotion and without interest.

In the case of each witness the reader should ask himself to what extent his character and his functions may have coloured his views. Let me give a few examples. The authors have quoted largely and rightly from the memoirs of Gouverneur Morris (Gouverneur was his baptismal name) for the early part of the Revolution. We need to know what sort of a man this was. Morris, who came to France for business reasons did not become the representative of the United States in our country until 1791. He was a friend of Washington, whose liberal ideas he shared—liberal with a strong conservative tinge.

At Paris and Versailles, Morris was introduced by La Fayette to the first leaders of the revolutionary movement and also to the aristocratic families connected with the La Fayettes—those of Noailles, Poix, Tessé, d'Aguesseau and Ségur. With his ample fortune and aristocratic temperament Morris was more at home in salons than in the clubs. He thought that France needed reforms, but hoped that these could be introduced in a peaceful atmosphere. Violence horrified him and so he could not accept the doings of the 14th July or the 6th October. Towards La Fayette he always acted as a friend (as will be seen, when the family was in great trouble and Morris became the generous protector of La Fayette's wife and children), but he could not conceal his pain at seeing a man, whom he admired, associated with movements which he despised and condemned. One must keep this attitude in mind, if one wishes to estimate Gouverneur Morris's judgments at their true value, and it is thus that we should criticize each piece of reportage.

Another example—that of Roederer. Here we have a first-class

eye-witness. Roederer was born at Metz in 1754, the son of
a lawyer. A young Frenchman belonging to the enlightened
bourgeoisie, he had his period of enthusiastic idealism in the
manner of Rousseau. But soon he revealed qualities of firmness
and strength, supported by ambition. From the early days of
1789 he got into the way of writing something every day about
the events which interested the public at Metz. In short he was a
natural journalist—a reporter if you will—and as long as it was
possible he reconciled this kind of publicity with his duties as an
official. He was associated in the work of the Constituent Assembly
and was appointed Public Prosecutor for the Department of the
Seine. At first he tried to fulfil these functions as an honest
administrator, but politics soon overwhelmed him. Though
obliged to put up with demagogy, he notes its progress in his
Chronicle of Fifty Days, and in writing about 20th June and
10th August he tells the truth "without art or contrivance,
without any ambition for effect, oratorical, dramatic or romantic".

Invariably cool, but by no means devoid of courage, Roederer
was an ideal reporter. It was he who wrote in the Journal de Paris
the account of the trial of Louis XVI. This he did with humanity.
A solid basis of culture is a valuable asset for a journalist. It
enriches all that he says with the fertile humus of style and
wisdom. Roederer writes very well, like a man who has read his
Tacitus. The keenness of his impressions, the horror of his
memories added to his knowledge of the great authors often lend
his articles or his books not only force but beauty. And what an
eye-witness is the man who could say after the 18th of Brumaire
with a mixture of pride and melancholy, "I was with Louis XVI
throughout the last night of his reign, and with Bonaparte
throughout the first night of his." Here is a reporter conscious of
the nobleness of his mission and the soul of honour in his reports.

The authors deserve commendation as much for having un-
earthed a multitude of obscure witnesses, who give a lifelike
flavour to their evidence, as for having resuscitated and reprinted
the admirable journalists I have mentioned. How strange it is to
read, in connection with la Marseillaise, a letter from Madame
Dietrich, the wife of the Mayor of Strasburg about Engineer
Captain Rouget de Lisle, "a charming poet and composer".

"His piece was played in our house to the great satisfaction of all present. I send you a copy of the music. The band of little *virtuosi* you keep round you will only have to read the notes and you are sure to enjoy the piece." Thus was born the battle-hymn which swept the world.

We find here a valuable document by the lawyer Maton de la Varenne on the subject of the September massacres. This time the reporter is on the side of the victims. He actually saw the butchers dip their bread in the blood of the slaughtered. His narrative, studded with details which no one invents, is at once terrible and beautiful.

And how interesting it is to read in the passage on the 9th of Thermidor, the story of the famous gendarme Méda (or Merda), who fired his pistol at Robespierre with a report which has echoed down two centuries. Méda was twenty. Having run to the Committee of Public Safety to find out what the Commune were up to, he suddenly found himself ordered to attack the latter. It was then that he shattered Robespierre's jaw. The gratitude of the Convention was such that they contemplated promoting the brave gendarme to the rank of General. Then they forgot him. Bonaparte had no wish to remember Thermidor. So Méda had to win promotion step by step on the battlefields. He had finally reached the rank of Brigadier-General, when he was killed by a round-shot at the Moskowa—What a career and what a witness, into the bargain!

Henri Bergson liked to say that there are ready-made ideas just as there are ready-made overcoats. He preferred his philosophy made to measure in an endeavour to fit it to reality which was always on the move, rather than making do with formulas and doctrines pulled at haphazard from the shelf. Ready-made history also exists, which makes do with certain stock legends. The pseudo-historians who write it do not seek to ally it to the mysterious history once consisting of life itself. Here we shall find history in the making and borrowing from life those elements without which it could not exist. These are no sidelights on history but history itself, living and breathing.

ANDRÉ MAUROIS
de l'Académie Française

PREFATORY EXPLANATION

AN EVENT occurs: a revolt or a feat of arms, a disaster or a discovery, a crime or a coup d'état. Someone was present. He saw it. Returning home he notes down what he saw in order to keep alive this thing, which happened under his eyes. So the witness becomes a reporter.

This book is constructed from reportages. The diverse events which it reports together make up a single event—the French Revolution. But they make it up gradually and, as it were, unconsciously, for the reporters are more often passionate partisans than objective observers, just as no doubt we should have been, had we been there.

About fifty thousand contemporary reports on the Revolution are known to be in existence, which means that a hundred volumes like this one could be compiled without any text being repeated. We do not claim to have made the best possible selection.

From the texts we have chosen we have retained those which corresponded most closely with our title. General ideas, personal considerations, in fact, anything which did not report some event has usually been cut out. The reader can easily consult any of the texts, which may interest him, by referring to the list published at the end of the volume which gives the author, the title and the number of the source at the National Library or in the National Archives.

We have retained the original spelling of the texts quoted. So here we present the story of the French Revolution told by men and women each of whom could say, "I was there".

THE FOURTEENTH OF JULY

⚜⚜⚜⚜⚜⚜⚜⚜⚜⚜⚜⚜⚜⚜⚜⚜⚜⚜⚜⚜⚜⚜⚜⚜⚜⚜⚜⚜⚜⚜⚜⚜⚜

URING THE last days of April 1789 Versailles saw a varied assortment of travellers descending from dusty stage-coaches: country gentlemen, lawyers and doctors from the provinces, clergymen and peasants. Together with the noblemen and the prelates who came in their own carriages the total number of new-comers was 1,165. These were the members of the States General. This assembly, of which Prime Minister Necker had made a present to France, was going to meet for the first time. The whole of France was asking, "What are they going to do?". Meanwhile, the King had placed a pillared hall, La Salle des Menus Plaisirs, at their disposal.

The Assembly opened its proceedings with a procession of the Holy Sacrament in which the King took part. His Majesty was, however, not the highlight of the spectacle. More people stared at the Queen, the Royal lady smirched by the Affair of the Necklace, whom the new deputies refused to applaud. An American tourist, who witnessed the scene, sympathized with Marie Antoinette. This was Gouverneur Morris, a future Senator of the United States, who was at Versailles as the guest of M. de Flahaut, the Intendant of the Royal Gardens.

MAY 4TH:

At six this morning I set off for Versailles. Am overtaken on the Road by M. Le N^d and M. La Caze. We alight together and walk tho the Streets till the Procession commences, except a little while that I sit with Mme de Flahaut who was so kind as to send and offer me Part of a Window. M. de Villefranche speaks to me about the Bal d'Opéra and he tells us a Story somewhat characteristic of national Manners. His Wife and a Lady, her Friend, went thither together. After a while they seperated, and meeting again conversed, the Lady being perfectly ignorant who the Person was which he had picked up, for she was with him. After the Bal was over and all three had got home they rallied the Friend on being so taken in. She could give no other Reason for being so much deceived but that Madame was in Company with Monsieur and therefore she could not possibly suppose that it was his Wife.

The Procession is very magnificent, thro a double Row of Tapestry. Neither the King nor Queen appear too well pleased. The former is repeatedly saluted as he passes along with the Vive le Roi but the latter receives not a single Acclamation. She looks, however, with Contempt on the Scene in which she acts a Part and seems to say, "For the moment I submit but I shall have my Turn." . . . Return to Paris and dine. Walk to the Palais Royal & see Mme de Chattelux. Find I was right in my Conjecture as to the Queen's Temper and the King's. He was vexed that the Duke of Orleans should walk as Representative and not as Prince of the Blood, and also that his Consort received no Mark of public Satisfaction. She was exceedingly hurt. Her Conversation at meeting the Dutchess of Orleans, who as well as the Duke had been repeatedly applauded, was reported to me. I cannot help feeling the Mortification which the poor Queen meets with for I see only the Woman and it seems unmanly to break a Woman with Unkindness. Mme de C. tells me a sprightly Reply of Madame Adelaide, the King's Aunt, who when the Queen in a Fit of Resentment, speaking of the Nation said: "These unworthy French" (*Ces indignes Français*) exclaimed: "Should you not say indignant (*indignés*), Madame?"

Next day, at the opening meeting of the States General, Morris was to see the hero of the hour, M. Necker the most popular man in France because he was reckoned to be a liberal, and the Duke of Orleans, who, like many of the nobility, but making more of a stir because he was the King's cousin, had adopted the ideas of Voltaire and Rousseau. The American went home mollified. At last the Queen had been acclaimed.

MAY 5TH:

Go to Versailles and a little after eight get into the Hall. Sit there in a cramped Situation till after 12, during which Time the different Members are brought in and placed, one Baillage after the other. When M. Necker comes in he is loudly and repeatedly clapped and so is the Duke of Orleans, also a Bishop who has long lived in his Diocese and practised there what his Profession enjoins. Another Bishop is applauded but those near me say that this Applause is unmerited. An old Man who refused to dress in the Costume prescribed for the Tiers and who appears in his Farmer's Habit, receives a long and loud Plaudit. M. de Mirabeau is hissed, tho not very loudly. The King at length arrives and takes his Seat, the Queen on his left, two Steps lower than him. He makes a short Speech, very proper and well spoken, or rather read. The Tone and Manner have all the *fierté* which can be desired or expected from the Blood of the Bourbons. He is interrupted in the Reading by Acclamations so warm and of such lively Affection that the Tears start from my Eyes in Spite of myself. The Queen weeps or seems to weep but not one Voice is heard to wish her well. I would certainly raise mine if I were a Frenchman, but I have no Right to express a Sentiment and in vain solicit those who are near me to do it. After the King has spoken he takes off his Hat and when he puts it on again his Nobles imitate his Example. Some of the Tiers do the same, but by Degrees they one after the other take them off again. The King then takes off his Hat. The Queen seems to think it wrong and a Conversation seems to pass in which the King tells her he chuses to do it, whether consistent or not consistent with the Ceremonial; but I would not swear to this, being too far distant to see very distinctly, much less to hear. The Nobles uncover by Degrees, so that if the Ceremonial requires these Manœuvres the Troops are not yet properly drilled. After the King's Speech and the coverings and uncoverings, the Garde des Sceaux makes one much longer but it is delivered in a very ungraceful Manner and so indistinctly that nothing can be judged of it by me untill it is in Print. When he has done, M. Necker rises. He tries to play the Orator but he plays it very ill. The Audience salute him with a long and loud Plaudit. . . . This will convince the King and Queen of the National Sentiment and tend to prevent the Effects of the Intrigue against the present Administration, at least for a while.

After this Speech is over the King rises to depart and receives a long and affecting *Vive le Roi!* The Queen rises, and to my great Satisfaction she hears for the first Time in several Months the Sound of *Vive la Reine!* She makes a low Curtesy and this produces a louder Acclamation, and that a lower Curtesy.

However, within the Assembly, the deputies of the Third Estate (those who represented neither the nobility nor the Clergy but the Commons) sought to attract their colleagues to their benches in order to constitute a Legislative Assembly capable of imposing a constitution on the Monarchy, on the English model. But the nobility refused to mix with the Third Estate (though they ended by doing so). The Clergy, who also eventually gave way, sought for the moment to play the part of mediators and with that object endeavoured to draw the deputies of the other two orders to their benches. On this occasion a Swiss named Etienne Dumont heard a speech by an unknown person who would not always be unknown. He says:

The Clergy wishing to bring about unexpectedly the union of the Three Orders, sent as their representative to the Commons the Archbishop of Aix, who delivered a pathetic speech on the miseries of the people and the wretched state of the rural districts. He produced a piece of black bread which animals might have disdained and to which the poor were reduced. He invited the Commons to send some deputies to confer with those of the Clergy and the nobility regarding methods of relieving the distress of the poor. The Commons, who did not wish to be dislodged from their positions, scented the trap, but did not dare openly to reject the proposal for fear of compromising themselves in the eyes of the public. A deputy rose to speak and outdid the Prelate in his appeal in favour of the poorer classes, but he cleverly threw doubt on the intentions of the clergy. "Go and tell your colleagues," he said to the Archbishop, "that if they are so eager to relieve the sufferings of the people they should come to this chamber and join forces with the friends of the people. Tell them not to delay our operations by intentional dilatoriness; tell them not to employ niggling methods to induce us to abandon the causes on which we are resolved; better still I exhort you, ministers of religion, to be worthy followers of your master, to renounce the luxury which surrounds you, to give up your splendour so wounding to the poor and to return to the modest ways of your first founders. Dismiss these proud lackeys who form your escort and spend your vile superfluity on food for the starving."

After this speech which chimed in so well with the passions of the moment, there followed not a burst of defiant applause, but a confused murmur which was infinitely more flattering. Everyone asked who the speaker was. He did not seem to be known and it was only after enquiries had been going on for some minutes that a name went round the Chamber and the Galleries, which three years later caused the whole of France to tremble—that name was Robespierre. Reybaz, who was sitting by me said "that young man has not had much practice; he is too verbose and does not know when to stop, but he has a fund of eloquence and bitterness that will set him apart from the crowd."

But it was not at Versailles, it was in Paris that great events were happening. Paris was starving: extract from the diary of Morris.

JULY 8TH–11TH:

The Doctor says I must stay eight Days longer in Paris . . . I should more readily adopt this Opinion if I were anywhere else than in so large and so stinking a City as Paris. (As soon as I have finished my Business I shall go to London.) Go to Romainville to bid Adieu to the Maréchal de Ségur and his Daughter in Law. Mme Lebrun is there, the famous Painter. Approaching the House we find Mesdames de Ségur and Chattelux and are presently joined by Monsʳ de Pusigneu. He assures me that the Scarcity of Corn is excessive, which he is the better able to judge of as his Regiment of Chasseurs are employed in the Escort of Provisions and Protection of the Grain now standing. Take a walk with Mme de Ségur and converse on the Situation of their public Affairs, which she understands as well as any Body. Take leave with Promises to return speedily. Promise also to write to her. Return to Town. I observe that the Potatoes which I see growing are what we consider as the worst Kind, at least if one may judge from the Tops. . . . The King, in Answer to the Address of the States respecting his Troops, has told them that he had no Intention to affect them and if their Apprehensions continue he will remove the Session of the States to Soissons or Noyons and go himself to Compiègne. This is an artful Reply. If he can get them far from Paris he will weaken that Impulse which at present creates such Alarm. But the Evil lies deeper than his Counsellers are aware of and the Business now broached must have its complete Course. While at Club receive a Message from Mme de Flahaut who begs I will come to Supper to tell her the News. Go. A Partie Quarrée when I arrive and make the fifth. Stay till eleven and reconduct an Abbé, one of her Favorites. He is humpbacked and far from an Adonis in other Respects, it must therefore be a moral Attachment.—This Day has been hot but the Evening is very pleasant and I feel no small Pleasure to smell the ripening Grain. There are now in and about this City above a Million of human Creatures whose only Resource for Bread is in the Vigilance and Attention of Government, whose utmost Exertion however can but just keep Pace with the Necessity.

General de Besenval, entrusted by the Duc de Broglie, Minister of War, with the Defence of Paris.

Eight years previously the King had appointed me to the command of the following provinces of the interior—the Île de France (not including the city of Paris, the Soissonnais, the Berry, the Bourbonnais, the Orléannais, Touraine and Maine. The administration of such a large area was made more difficult in April 1789 by the shortage of grain, which was already noticeable and which foreshadowed a famine in the near future. The dearth of this essential produce and fears for the future caused panics and produced a general agitation. Stormy scenes took place in the markets and the convoys which the Government directed to the places most in need of supplies were sometimes intercepted. This obliged me to break up the troops under my orders into small groups in order to put detachments in the large number of markets I was obliged to supervise, and to maintain order in them, as well as to assure the movement of cereals and to tranquillize the districts, in which daring brigands, encouraged by the general fermentation, were likely to disturb the peace. Up to July the twelfth, when the revolution broke out, I had the satisfaction of maintaining orderly conditions throughout the whole of my command. Not a single regrettable incident occurred, not a single inhabitant was molested and not a single complaint was submitted regarding the conduct of my troops, although the large number of detachments I had to furnish made it impossible to place each one under the command of an officer. The precise orders that I had issued were carried out to the letter, so perfect was discipline at that time.

I have already said that I had no orders to give in Paris where the state police in normal times were under the control of Parliament and all the administrative details were the responsibility of the Minister of the Household. The agitation which had begun to manifest itself, in addition to the scarcity of foodstuffs, obliged the authorities to have recourse to the methods usual in such cases, that is to say to employ the two regiments of Guards, French and Swiss, to maintain order.

The Colonel of the French Guards is almost always a Marshal of France and in circumstances like these, the command of all the troops has fallen to him. This time, however, the Duc du Châtelet, who was appointed to this command, was only a Lieutenant-General, as was the Comte d'Affry, who commanded the Swiss Guards. Consequently the command was shared equally by these two officers, who both assumed responsibility for maintaining order in the different quarters of the city, in proportion to the number of troops at the disposal of each.

Towards the end of April M. d'Affry sustained a serious accident which brought him to death's door and from which he was not expected to recover. In my capacity as Lieutenant-Colonel of the Swiss Guard, I was obliged to replace him and to add the duty of looking after Paris to all the other duties with which I was already overloaded. This meant that I had no time at all for rest. My days were taken up with the job of looking after Paris and keeping in touch with my own command, and during most of the night I attended meetings convened at police headquarters to assure the arrival of the grain necessary to sustain Paris.

"As long as Necker is here everything will be all right," said the people. Then suddenly the uneasy quiet of this sultry July in which Parisians trembled for their daily bread and their lives was broken by a crash of thunder: Louis XVI had dismissed Necker. "A victory for the Queen," cried the Minister's son-in-law, when he heard the news. It was also a triumph for the Comte d'Artois, Louis XVI's younger brother, who was held to be an enemy of reform and who one day called Necker, who was Swiss, "a fornicating foreign bastard."

MORRIS:

JULY 12TH:

Dine with the Maréchal de Castries who enquires very kindly the State of my Business. As I am going away he takes me aside and informs me that M. Necker is no longer in Place. He is much affected at this Intelligence, and indeed so am I. Urge him to go immediately to Versailles. He says he will not; that they have undoubtedly taken all their Meassures before this Movement and therefore he must be too late. I tell him that it is not too late to warn the King of his Danger which is infinitely greater than he imagines. That his Army will not fight against the Nation, and that if he listens to violent Counsels the Nation will undoubtedly be against him. That the Sword has fallen imperceptibly from his Hand, and that the Sovreignty of this Nation is the Assemblée Nationale. He makes no precise Answer to this but is very deeply affected. . . . all agreably to my Promise on Mme de Flahaut. Learn that the whole Administration is routed and M. Necker banished. Much Alarm here. Paris begins to be in Commotion, and from the Invalid Guard of the Louvre a few of the Nobility take a Drum and beat to Arms. Monsʳ de Narbonne, the friend of Mme de Stahl (Necker's daughter), considers a civil War as inevitable and is about to join his Regiment, being as he says in a Conflict between the Dictates of his Duty and of his Conscience. I tell him that I know of no Duty but that which the Conscience dictates. I presume that his Conscience will dictate to join the strongest Side. The little hunchbacked Abbé Bertrand, after sallying out in a Fiacre, returns frightened because of a large Mob in the Rue St Honoré, and presently comes in another Abbé who is of the Parliament and who, rejoicing inwardly at the Change, is confoundedly frightened at the Commotions. I calm the Fears of Madame, whose Husband is mad and in a printed List, it seems, of fiery Aristocrats. Offer to conduct the Abbés safely Home, which Offer Bertrand accepts of. His Terror as we go along is truly diverting. As we approach the Rue St. Honoré his Imagination magnifies the ordinary Passengers into a vast Mob, and I can scarcely perswade him to trust his Eyes instead of his Fears, Having set him down, I depart for Mr Jefferson's (the American Ambassador); in riding along the Boulevards, all at once the Carriages, Horses, and Foot Passengers turn about and pass rapidly. Presently after we meet a Body of Cavalry with their Sabres drawn, and coming Half Speed. After they have passed us a little Way they stop. When we come to the Place Louis Quinze observe the People, to the Number of perhaps an hundred, picking up Stones, and on looking back find that the Cavalry are returning. Stop at the Angle to see the Fray, if any. The People take Post among the Stone which lies scattered about the whole Place, being hewn for a Bridge now building. The Officer at the Head of this Party is saluted by a Stone and immediately turns his Horse in a menacing Manner towards the Assailant. But this Adversaries are posted in Ground where the Cavalry cannot act. He pursues his Route therefore and the Pace is soon encreased to a Gallop amid a Shower of Stones. One of the Soldiers is either knocked from his Horse or the Horse falls under him. He is taken Prisoner and at first ill treated. They had fired several Pistols without Effect, probably they were not even charged with Ball. A Party of the Swiss Guards are posted in the Champs Elisées with Cannon. Proceed to Mr Jefferson's. He tells me that M. Necker received yesterday about Noon a Letter from the King, by the Hands of M. de la Luzerne, in which he orders him to leave the Kingdom, and at the same Time M. de la Luzerne is desired to exact a Promise that he will not mention the Matter to any Body. M. Necker dines and proposes to his Wife a Visit to a female friend in the Neighbourhood. On the Route he communicates the Intelligence and they go to a Country Seat, make the needful Arrangements and depart. M. de Montmorin immediately resigned, and is now in Paris. In returning from Mr Iefferson's I am turned off to the left by the Vidette posted on the Road to the Place Louis Quinze. Go to Club. A Gentleman just arrived from Versailles gives us an Account of the new Administration. The People are employed in breaking open the armorers' Shops, and presently a large Body of the Gardes Françoises appear with Bayonets fixed, in the Garden, mingled with the Mob, some of whom are also armed. These poor Fellows have passed the Rubicon with a Witness. Success or a Halter must now be their Motto. I think the Court will again recede, and if they do, all farther Efforts will be idle. If they do not, a Civil War is among the Events most probable. If the Representatives of the Tiers have formed a just Estimate of their Constitutents, in ten Days all France will be in Commotion. The little Affray which I have witnessed will probably be magnified into a bloody Battle before it reaches the Frontiers, and in that Case an infinity of Corps Bourgeois will march to the Relief of the Capital. They had better gather in the Harvest.

The people of Paris march along the boulevards carrying the busts of Necker and the Duke of Orleans. They have borrowed these waxen effigies from the Curtius Gallery, the Musée Grévin of the period. A college professor, Beffroy, is present at the scene.

During the morning of Sunday, July 12th, one of the leading actors of the boulevard brought me several tickets for a new play, which he had written. Being prevented by business from going out on that date, I gave the tickets to some ladies who went out at half past four in order to arrive early at the show. They had hardly walked a few steps along the street, when they returned to the house, breathless and troubled, with the tidings, uttered in a broken voice, that all the places of entertainment were closed, that M. Necker had left, that the people of Paris had risen and all the citizens were running in a panic to shut themselves up in their houses.

I immediately went down to ascertain the truth and I certainly saw a lot of people running precipitately along the streets. It was in vain that I asked them what was happening; no one would reply. I walked as far as the Boulevard du Temple. There I saw perhaps five or six thousand men marching rather quickly and without much order. They were armed, some with guns, others with swords, lances and pitchforks. They were carrying in triumph the wax busts of the Duke of Orleans and M. Necker, which they had borrowed from M. Curtius. Beside them they carried two standards in black and white as a sign of mourning for the disgrace of an idolized Minister.

This little army threatened to burn all the theatres if they did not close immediately, saying that the French people had no right to enjoy themselves in the midst of public misfortunes and that they no longer had any reason to amuse themselves. All theatres were duly closed: moreover no actor would have the courage to appear on the stage in the midst of the general alarm inspired by the certain prospect of tragic events.

The concourse of armed men grew greater in every street, as the persons they met were forced to march with them. Later I saw in my house a journeyman carpenter with a wife and child, who had been one of the leaders of this troop of rebels. I questioned him more than once. In telling the story of his expeditions he had lost none of the fire which had inspired him to go on them. I permitted myself to make a few just comments which calmed him down. Then he said to me with perfect composure, "No, sir, we have no intention to cause the slightest damage; we only want to give the citizens the courage necessary to drive away the troops, whom they insist on leaving at the gates of Paris. And to animate everyone with the same spirit, we asked Curtius to lend us these two busts, promising to return them intact. But, sir, think of the dangers which threatened us. We knew everything that was happening and what was still being concealed from us was quite easy to guess. Why, without the first outbursts of the populace, whom they are good enough to call 'canaille', who would have had the courage to arm himself? Where would we be? And what would have happened to the town of Paris?"

I could not but applaud this man's motives and the arguments he used. In spite of his violence he seemed to me to be a good father, a good husband and a good workman. While carrying the bust of M. Necker, he was killed by a musket ball, but the bust suffered no damage and, like that of the Duke of Orleans, was brought back safe and sound to Curtius' gallery.

"To Arms," cried a young man standing on a chair in the gardens of the Palais Royal. *"Tonight the Swiss and German battalions are going to massacre the people of Paris."* The battalions of foreign mercenaries that surround the capital have got on the nerves of the people. Those that heard the young orator—Camille Desmoulins—swear to defend themselves. But they need a token by which to know one another. Someone pulls off a leaf from a chestnut tree and pins it on to his hat. They all imitate him and in a moment the green cockade has conquered Paris.

JULY 13TH:

Martin, my servant, comes in and tells me that the Hôtel de France is forced and all the Prisoners out. Presently after a Letter is brought to him, enclosing one to me from Mr. Nesbitt who is at the Temple and wishes to see me, but my Cocher tells me he cannot bring my Carriage, having already been stopped and turned back. In Effect, the little City of Paris is in as fine a Tumult as any one could wish. They are getting Arms wherever they can find any. Seize sixty Barrils of Powder in a Boat on the Seine. Break into the Monastery of St Lazar and find a Store of Grain which the Holy Brotherhood had laid in. Immediately it is put into Carts and sent to the Market, and on every Cart a Friar. The Gardemeuble du Roi is attacked and the Arms are delivered up, to prevent worse Consequences. These however are more curious than useful. But the Detail and Variety of this Day's Deeds would be endless. Dine at Home and La Caze dines with me. After Dinner dress and walk to the Louvre, having previously ornamented my Hat with a green Bow in honor of the Tier, for this is the Fashion of the Day which every Body is obliged to comply with who means to march in Peace. It is somewhat whimsical that this Day of Violence and Tumult is the only one in which I have dared to walk the Streets, but as no Carriages are abroad but the Fiacres I do not hazard being crushed, and I apprehend nothing from the Populace. Mme de Flahaut is under great Apprehension, which I endeavor to appease.

On the eve of the fourteenth of July, Besenval, who is responsible for public order, is embarrassed.

... The insurrection of the 12th assumed an alarming aspect. Fearing that the different cavalry posts detailed to maintain order in the faubourgs might be insufficient or that under provocation they might infringe the express orders they had received, I sent them word to proceed to Place Louis XV (Place de la Concorde). A strong detachment of Swiss Guards with four pieces of Artillery was already in the Champs-Elysées.

I also ordered Berchiny's hussars, M. de Choiseul's dragoons and Salis-Samade's regiment to assemble there. Two considerations caused me to take this decision. In the first place all the troops in my command would be under my eyes and under my control, whatever might happen; and secondly I was able to show the insurgents an imposing force. This attitude might restore calm, and my dispositions permitted me to put extreme pressure on the disaffected mobs once they were reduced to their own resources. In this critical moment no other calculation was permitted to me.

On their way to Place Louis XV the troops were the target of insulting cries, stone-throwing and pistol-shots. Several men were severely wounded, but not a single menacing gesture was made by the soldiers, so great was their respect for the order that not a drop of their fellow-citizens' blood was to be shed.

The disorder increased hourly and with it my misgivings. What decision was I to take? If I engaged my troops in Paris, I should start a civil war. Blood, precious from whatever veins it flowed, would be shed without achieving any result likely to restore calm. The crowds were tampering with my men, almost under my eyes, seeking to seduce them with the usual promises. I received alarming reports concerning their loyalty. Versailles ignored my cruel situation and persisted in regarding a rising of three hundred thousand men as an unlawful assembly and the revolution as a riot.

With all these considerations in mind, I thought the wisest course was to withdraw the troops and to leave Paris to itself. And I decided at one o'clock in the morning to do this.

Three Swiss regiments were camping on the Champ-de-Mars, comprising eight hundred mounted men, hussars and dragoons. I visited this camp and held a council at the Military School where several general officers were waiting for me. The unfortunate Intendant of Paris took refuge there during the morning. I was surprised at his freedom from apprehension, which bore witness to his blindness rather than his courage. On the evening of the 13th I was at the Invalides. M. de Sombreuil, the Governor brought me deputations from two districts, who came to ask me to leave them the fifty-two thousand muskets stored in the hospital. They expressed the liveliest alarm saying that they were surrounded by brigands who threatened their homes with fire and pillage.

I replied that I could not take the responsibility of handing over such a large store of arms, but that I would write for instructions. They insisted and I continued to refuse.

I had no intention of satisfying their expectations.

Although the spokesmen of these deputations had prepared their arguments cleverly, it was easy for me to see that they had been put up to it and that they wanted the arms rather for the purpose of attacking us than defending themselves.

I wanted to have a look at the armoury, so M. de Sombreuil, took me into the basement, where it was situated. He told me that the night before, being apprehensive of the use to which the muskets might be put, it occurred to him to have the triggers and ramrods removed, but in six hours twenty pensioners whom he had detailed for this job had only put twenty muskets out of action. He said that a spirit of sedition was rife in the hospital and that for the past ten days the soldiers had their pockets full of money. A legless cripple, whom no one suspected, had introduced into the establishment bundles of licentious and subversive songs. In a word, he concluded, it was hopeless to count on the pensioners, who, if they received orders to load their cannons, would turn them on to the Governor's apartment.

Writing that night to Maréchal de Broglie, I mentioned these facts and the conclusions to which they pointed.

I received no reply.

On the 14th at 5 a.m. a man came into my room. This man (whose name I learnt later) with his fiery eyes, his swift incisive speech, his bold demeanour and rather handsome face, made a striking impression on me. He said, "M. le Baron, I must warn you to avoid a useless resistance. Today the carriers of Paris will be burnt. I am sure of this and neither you or I can do anything to prevent it. Do not try to do so. You will sacrifice your men without extinguishing a single torch.

I don't remember exactly what I said to him, but he grew pale with rage and left hastily. I should have had him arrested, but I did nothing.

☙

July 14th. "I took the Bastille."
Keversau, a man of law, who, as we shall see in the chapter on The Terror, was to become estranged by the Revolution.

Veteran armies inured to War have never performed greater prodigies of valour than this leaderless multitude of persons belonging to every class, workmen of all trades who, mostly ill-equipped and unused to arms, boldly affronted the fire from the ramparts and seemed to mock the thunderbolts the enemy hurled at them. Their guns were equally well served. Cholat, the owner of a wine shop, who was in charge of a cannon installed in the garden of the Arsenal was deservedly praised, as was Georger, a gunner who arrived from Brest that same morning and was wounded in the thigh.

The attackers having demolished the first drawbridge and brought their guns into position against the second could not fail to capture the fort. The Marquis de Launay (Governor of the Bastille) could doubtless have resisted the capture of the first bridge more vigorously, but this base agent of the despots, better fitted to be a gaoler, than the military commander of a fortress lost his head as soon as he saw himself hemmed in by the enraged people and hastened to take refuge behind his massive bastions, where he hoped to be able to await in safety the relief promised for that evening by Baron de Bezenval and M. de Flesselles.

The drums were beat for a parley and the white flag was raised on the tower of la Bazinière. It was too late. The people infuriated by the treachery of the Governor, who had fired on their representatives, took these offers of peace for another trap and continued to advance, firing as they went up to the drawbridge leading to the interior of the fort. A Swiss officer addressing the attackers through a sort of loop-hole near the drawbridge asked permission to leave the fort with the honours of war. "No, no," they cried. He then passed through the same opening a piece of paper, which those outside could not read because of the distance, calling out at the same time that he was willing to surrender, if they promised not to massacre his troops. A man ran to fetch a plank which was placed on the parapet. Several persons stood on it to keep it firm, and the brave unknown walked along it towards the loop-hole; he was on the point of taking hold of the paper, when he fell into the moat, struck by a ball, said some, and died a victim of his own zeal. Then Maillard, son of a mounted process-server at the Châtelet de Paris, or else (according to others) a gallant fellow called Reole, undismayed by the death of the first man, advanced boldly along the narrow plank, took the paper and delivered it to Sieur Hulin or Sieur Elie, who read it aloud to the people. This is what it said. "We have here 20,000 kilos of powder and we shall blow up the garrison and the whole quarter if you will not accept our surrender." "On my word as an officer, we accept," said Sieur Elie; "lower the bridge." But the people cried out fiercely against the suggestion of capitulation and brought up three pieces of artillery.

They were just going to fire and the ranks of the crowd had already opened to give passage to the canonballs, when the enemy seeing that we intended to demolish the big bridge let down the small drawbridge on the left of the entrance to the fortress. In spite of the new danger arising from this manœuvre the Sieurs Elie, Hulin, Maillard, Reole, Humbert, Tournay, François, and several others swarmed across it having secured the drawbridge by pushing home the bolts.

The French Guards, who kept their heads in the hour of danger, formed a human barrier on the other side of the bridge to prevent the crowd of attackers from getting on to it. This prudent manœuvre saved the lives of thousands of persons who would have fallen into the fosse.

About two minutes later one of the Invalides opened the gate behind the drawbridge and asked what we wanted. "The surrender of the Bastille," was the answer, on which he let us in. At the same time the besiegers lowered the great bridge on which the brave Arné leapt while it was still in motion, to prevent anyone from trying to raise it again.

The Invalides were drawn up in line on the right and the Swiss on the left. They had stood their arms up against the wall. They clapped their hands and cried "bravo" to the besiegers, who came crowding into the fortress. Those who came in first treated the conquered enemy humanely and embraced the staff officers to show there was no ill-feeling. But a few soldiers posted on the platforms and unaware that the fortress had surrendered, discharged their muskets whereupon the people, transported with rage, threw themselves on the Invalides and used them with the utmost violence. One of them was massacred, the unfortunate Béquart, the brave soldier who had deserved so well of the town of Paris, when he stayed the hand of the Governor at the moment when he was on the point of blowing up the Bastille. Béquart, who had not fired a single shot throughout the day suffered two sword thrusts and had his hand cut off at the wrist by the stroke of a sabre. Afterwards they carried in triumph round the streets this very hand to which so many citizens owed their safety. Béquart himself was dragged from the fortress and brought to la Grève. The blind mob mistaking him for an artilleryman bound him to a gibbet where he died along with Asselin, the victim, like him, of a fatal mistake. All the officers were seized and their quarters were invaded by the mob, who smashed the furniture, the doors and the windows. In the general turmoil the people in the courtyard fired on those who were in the private quarters and on the platforms. Several were killed. The gallant Humbert received a musket ball as he stood on the platform and one of his comrades was killed in his arms. Then Arné, a brave fellow, fixed his grenadier's headdress on the point of his bayonet and showed himself over the top of the parapet, risking his life in order to stop the firing.

Maillard, Cholat, Arné, the grenadier, and several others contend for the honour of having arrested the Marquis de Launay. He was not in uniform but wore a grey tail-coat with a red ribbon. He had in his hand a sword-stick which he wished to drive into his breast, but the intrepid Arné tore it from him. Hulin, Elie and a few others undertook to guard him and succeeded in getting him out of the Bastille, though he was roughly handled by the people, who were calling for his death. They proceeded in the direction of the Hôtel de Ville escorted by a strong detachment. Elie, in uniform, led the party carrying the text of the capitulation on the point of his sword. After him came Legris, a collector of Royal taxes, who on that and the following days distinguished himself by various deeds of heroic valour. Maillard followed him, bearing the standard and then came the Governor held up by Hulin and Arné. They were immediately followed by de l'Epine, the clerk of M. Morin, procurator to the Parliament.

Such was the escort of M. de Launay. Almost all the persons who composed it expected to be the victims of the mob's relentless hatred of their prisoner and of their own zeal in defending him against the rage of the populace. Some of the crowd tore out his hair, others threatened him with their swords and tried to run him through. The wretched man, feeling the agony of death coming over him, said in a faint voice to Sieur Hulin, "Ah, Monsieur, you promised not to leave me, stay with me till we get to the Hôtel de Ville." And sometimes he addressed Sieur Elie saying, "Is that what you promised me? Ah, Monsieur, do not leave me now."

But the fury of the crowd continued to increase and their blind wrath did not spare de Launay's escort. L'Epine received a blow on the head with the butt of a musket, which would have stretched him out dead, if he had not been wearing a hard round hat which saved his life. But he had no strength left and was obliged to leave the escort at St. Gervais' Elm. Hulin, himself, in spite of his vigour and his powerful frame, could no longer resist the violence of the mob. Exhausted by his efforts to defend his prisoner and overwhelmed by the rough treatment he had himself received, he had to separate from M. de Launay at la Grève in order to take some rest. Hardly had he sat down when, looking after the procession, he saw the head of M. de Launay stuck on the point of a pike. His last words had been, "Oh, my friends, kill me, kill me at once and don't keep me suffering like this!" The people fearing that their victim might be snatched away from them, hastened to cut his throat on the steps of the Hôtel de Ville.

M. de Losme-Salbrai, his major, a man full of goodnesses and humanity, who seemed to have been sent by heaven like an angel to bring consolation to these gloomy caverns full of suffering and tears—M. de Losme, who was as much beloved by the prisoners as M. de Launay was hated, shared the latter's tragic fate. But his last moments were signalized by a spirit of heroism and gratitude, consonant with the countless virtuous actions of his past life.

M. de Miray, the Assistant-Adjutant, was killed in the Rue de Tournelles, and M. de Persan, the Lieutenant of the Company of Invalides, on the Port-au-Bled. It was in this officer's pocket that was found the Cross of St. Louis which was assumed by Sieur Dubois, then a fusilier in the French Guards, and now Captain of the regular company of the Barnabites district. Believing that noble actions and not decorations confer honour, it was enough for Dubois to have deserved the Cross, which he returned on September 3rd, through his district office, to M. de la Fayette. M. de Launay's Cross was found next day in his quarters by Sieur Alexandre de Baran, who did not take part in the siege of the Bastille, but had the good fortune to render signal service to his fellow citizens on July 15th.

The remainder of the garrison tremblingly waited for their lot to be decided. The Swiss had escaped the first wave of popular fury. They were clad in cloth smocks and the mob took them for prisoners. During the fighting they had remained in the courtyard from which they had kept up a continual fire through loopholes and openings they had made in the drawbridge. But they had not gone up on to the towers and had not been seen during the action, so that the anger of the people was concentrated solely on the Invalides, who were far less guilty than the Swiss. These did not lose a man during the attack and only one afterwards. As luck would have it this was the man who had loaded and aimed the terrible rampart gun, which did so much damage. This soldier, who probably felt himself guiltier than the others tried to flee as soon as the drawbridge was lowered, but was killed in the court-yard by a blow from a sword or a bayonet. All the others were led off to la Grève. The Pensioners, horrified by the sight of two of their comrades dangling from the gallows, overwhelmed with insults and worn out with humiliations had recourse to an officer of the city, who said to them: "You have fired on your fellow-citizens—You deserve to be hanged, and you will be immedi-ately." The people confirmed this sentence on the defenders of the Bastille by calling unanimously for their execution. But the French Guards, as humane in the hour of victory as they were terrible in combat, begged the people to reward their service by sparing the lives of their prisoners. Their generous appeal was applauded and the call for vengeance disarmed. The people yielded to the voice of the soldiers of the country, and the Place de la Grève rang with cries of "Spare them! Spare them!"

Sieur Marqué, then a sergeant in the Grenadiers of the Guard, and today a second lieutenant in the company of regular Grena-diers, in barracks at the Porte St. Antoine, crowned this act of clemency with a new display of human kindness. He placed in the middle of the detachment he commanded twenty-two Pensioners and eleven Swiss Guards of the de Salis company, and in order to withdraw them from the insulting clamour of the mob, he led them by way of the Place des Victoires to the Nouvelle-France barracks, although the people wanted to have a show made of them in the Palais Royal. These unfortunates found in the tents of their conquerors food, protection and rest, and were drafted off next morning to rejoin their respective corps. Since then, a dozen Swiss Guards have enlisted under the colours of the patriots.

In the intoxication of victory the unfortunate inmates of the dungeons of the Bastille had been forgotten. All the keys had been carried off in triumph and it was necessary to force the doors of the cells. Seven prisoners were found and brought to the Palais Royal. These poor fellows were in transports of pleasure and could scarcely realize they were not the dupes of a dream, soon to be dispelled. But soon they perceived the dripping head of their tormentor stuck up on the point of a pike, above which was a placard bearing the words: "de Launay, Governor of the Bastille, disloyal and treacherous enemy of the people." At this sight tears of joy flowed from their eyes and they raised their hands to the skies to bless their first moments of liberty.

The keys were handed to M. Brissot de Varville, who, a few years before, had been thrown into these caverns of despotism. Three thousand men were sent to guard these hated towers pending the issue of a decree ordering their destruction in accordance with the will of the people.

In the Place de la Bastille one can still see on the ground a line of white paving stones (especially in front of No. 4 Place de la Bastille and No. 49 Boulevard Henri IV). This line shows the outline of the towers of the old fortress. Built during the Hundred Years War, this stronghold had eight towers each 23 metres high (the equivalent of a seven storeyed house). "The Gouvernement" as the Governor's quarter was called was defended by three gates, two of which had a drawbridge. The old prison, where Mme de la Motte had been lodged and which in 1789 housed only seven prisoners, was in fact impregnable. That was the view of the Swiss officer Louis de Flue. He is one of those who could say, "I defended the Bastille."

In accordance with the orders I had received the previous day from le Baron de Bezenval, I marched at 2 a.m. on July the 7th from the Champ-de-Mars with a detachment of thirty-two men and a Sergeant. I had no difficulty in getting across Paris and when I reached the Bastille, I was admitted with my troop, although I was not recognized. My people were quartered in an armoury above the rooms of the Invalides giving on the first court-yard.

During the first few days after my arrival, the Governor showed me over the fortress, pointing out the places, which he thought the most vulnerable and where he expected to be attacked. He also let me see the measures he had taken to strengthen the defence. These were as follows: he had blocked up certain loopholes and apertures both in his house and in the Bastille, thus preventing the entry of bullets which he feared might kill members of the garrison. In places suitable for defence he had made fresh apertures. He had reinforced a wall in the cheek of the bastion in the Governor's garden. He had brought in several cartloads of paving stones which he had caused to be carried on to the towers. He had also had some crowbars made with which to demolish the chimneys, so as to be able to throw the debris on the heads of the besiegers. He often complained of the smallness of the garrison and said it would be impossible to defend the place if he were attacked. He allowed me to express my views regarding all these precautions. I tried to make him understand—and M. du Pujet did the same—that his fears were groundless and that the fortress was immensely strong in itself and that the garrison was adequate, if every soldier did his duty, to defend the Bastille until help could arrive.

On the twelfth of July, towards evening, it was learnt in the Bastille that the people were preparing to attack the powder magazine in the Arsenal. M. du Pujet, the Lieutenant of the Bastille, who was at the same time Commandant of the Arsenal, being unwilling to abandon the powder and judging that the Garrison of the Arsenal—a company of Invalides—was not strong enough to defend the magazine, asked permission of M. de Launay to transport the powder into the Bastille. This was granted. In consequence my detachment was employed during the night of the 12th-13th in carrying the powder from the magazine to the Bastille, where it was stored in the courtyard, where the well is situated, without adequate covering. The same night the Governor ordered the garrison to retire into the interior of the castle, being unwilling, in case of attack, to defend the outlying portions of the fortress, in spite of what had been agreed and the dispositions he had taken previously in conjunction with the staff and the officers of the garrison. To dissuade him from doing this, it was also explained to M. de Launay that he had no supplies in the fortress as my detachment had only a two days' ration of bread and a single day's ration of meat. The Pensioners had no food at all. He then got in two sacks of flour. As regards ammunition he had about three thousand rounds of musket ammunition and a few hundred for the guns, which he had had made.

During the day of July 13th we saw from the towers of the Bastille a number of conflagrations which had been started round about and we feared similar occurrences in our neighbourhood, which would endanger our stock of gunpower in the fortress. I accordingly set to work to find a safer place to store it in. I managed to find an underground chamber and showed it to M. de Launay and M. du Pujet, who thought it suitable. My men spent the morning of the 14th moving the powder into this cellar. M. du Pujet gave them two louis for their trouble.

During the morning we learnt that the people living near the Bastille and the citizens were alarmed at seeing our cannons trained on the city. We were supposed to know that a force of citizens had taken over the responsibility for public safety and it was conveyed to us that this force could not perform its functions with confidence, as long as it was threatened by the guns of the fortress. When this intimation reached us, the Governor ordered the guns to be withdrawn and had the embrasures blocked with planks and blocks of wood.

Towards three in the afternoon a band of citizens including a few French Guards started an attack on the Arsenal. They had no trouble in getting into the first courtyard of the Governor's house and cut the counter-weights to which the chains were attached, causing the bridge to come down. This operation was carried out all the more easily because the Governor had ordered that the besiegers were not to be fired on before they had been summoned to retire, which could not be done by reason of the distance. However, it was the besiegers who fired first at the men on the towers, as indeed passing bodies of men had done on the previous day.

Having brought down the bridge, the crowd easily broke open the door with axes and flooded into the courtyard of the Governor's house and on to the stone bridge leading along the kitchens to the central block, and prepared to demolish the next gate in the same manner as the first. When asked what they wanted, there was a general cry calling for the bridges to be lowered. They were told that this was impossible and that they must retire or they would be attacked. They shouted with redoubled violence "Lower the bridges, lower the bridges." At that point orders were given to thirty Invalides, posted at the slits on both sides of the gate, to fire. The Governor had gone up to the towers with thirty men. The besiegers in reply fired at the loop-holes and at the men on the platforms. When fired on they retired to the kitchens on the right of the drawbridge and took cover in the Governor's Courtyard behind the wall, where the watch go their rounds, and continued to fire through the slits in this wall and the kitchen windows. They returned once more to the attack and were again repulsed. I, with my detachment and ten Pensioners, was posted in the courtyard of the Bastille facing the door. I had behind me three guns firing two-pound balls. These were to be served by a dozen of my soldiers to prevent the besiegers rushing in, should they break down the gates. In order to checkmate the plan which the besiegers seemed to wish to carry out, after the second attack I caused two holes to be made in the raised drawbridge through which I intended to point my guns. However, being unable to get near enough owing to the tilting of the bridge, I replaced the guns by two siege guns loaded with grapeshot. We could not make much use of them, because only a few of the besiegers showed themselves. Moreover they had brought up a cart full of burning straw, with which they had set the Governor's house on fire, and placed it directly in front of the drawbridge, thus preventing us from seeing them. They had also brought up three cannon firing eight-pounder balls and a mortar, which they had posted in the garden of the Arsenal. Towards evening they fired a few rounds from this weapon, but did no damage. The fort replied with a few rounds of cannon fire. The besiegers seeing that their own artillery was ineffective, reverted to their original plan of storming the gates. With that object they brought their guns into the courtyard of the Governor's house and placed them in front of the drawbridge, aiming them at the gate. M. de Launay oberved this manœuvre from the top of a tower and without consulting his staff or warning the garrison, he ordered a drummer who was with him to beat the cease-fire. On this I went myself into the great room and to the loop-holes to stop the firing. The crowd approached and the Governor offered to surrender. The besiegers, would not accept his surrender, and merely called for the drawbridges to be lowered.

During this time I had withdrawn my men from their position behind the gate, in order not to leave them exposed to the enemy's gunfire with which we were menaced. After that I went to find the Governor, to asertain his intentions. I found him in the Council-Chamber engaged in writing a note in which he pointed out to the besiegers that he had 20,000 pounds of powder in the fortress and that if they would not accept his surrender, he would blow up the fortress, the garrison and the surroundings. He handed me the note with an order to deliver it. I then took the liberty of pointing out how little need there was to proceed to such extremities. I told him that neither the Garrison nor the fortress had suffered any damage, and that we still possessed the means of defending ourselves. Up to then we had only one In-valide killed and two or three wounded. He seemed not to appreciate my reasoning, so I had to obey. I passed out the note through the hole I had previously made in the drawbridge. I handed the note to an officer, or at least someone wearing the uniform of an officer in the Queen's Infantry Regiment, who had approached the gate walking on a plank which they had brought up. But it was all to no purpose. They continued to cry "Lower the bridges" and "no capitulation".

I returned to the Governor and reported how things were, after which I at once rejoined my troops, whom I lined up on the left of the gate. I was waiting for the moment when the Governor would put his threat into effect. But what was my surprise to see a moment later four Invalides opening the gates and lowering the drawbridges. The crowd at once poured in. We were at once disarmed and a guard was set on each one of us. The mob broke into all the quarters and threw everything into confusion: they seized all the arms they could find, threw the archives out of the window and plundered everything. The soldiers, who were not carrying their sacks, lost all their effects, as I did. We received every sort of ill-treatment and were threatened with massacre and slaughter in all its forms. Finally, the fury of the besiegers abated a little and they took me, together with part of my detachment, who had remained near me in the mêlée, to the Hôtel de Ville.

The streets through which we passed and the houses flanking them (even the roof-tops) were filled with masses of people insulting and cursing me. Swords, bayonets and pistols were being continually pressed against me. I did not know how I should die but felt that my last moment had come. Those who had no arms threw stones at me and the women gnashed their teeth at me and threatened me with their fists. Already two of my men had been murdered behind me by the savage crowd and for my part I am convinced that I should never have reached the Hôtel de Ville alive but for the protection of my escort, an arquebusier named Ricart and a man called Favereau, who urged the people to respect their prisoners. I finally arrived in the midst of cries of "hang him" to within a few hundred paces of the Hôtel de Ville, when they brought me a head stuck on a pike to look at, saying that it was the head of M. de Launay. As I crossed the Place de Grève, they led me past M. de Lorme, the Major of the Bastille, lying on the ground bathed in his blood. Further on, someone told me they had killed M. de Miray, the Assistant-Major, while in front of me they were engaged in hanging an officer and two privates of the Invalides on a lamp-post.

My own prospects seemed no less desperate as I walked up into the Hôtel de Ville. I was brought before a committee which was in session and accused of being one of those who had resisted at the Bastille and had been the cause of shedding of blood. I defended myself as well as I could by saying that I had been under orders and that if I had caused harm they should blame the orders I had been obliged to carry out. Then, seeing no other way of saving myself and the unfortunate remnant of my troop from a bloody death, I declared my desire to join the town and the nation. I do not know if they were tired of killing or if my explanation appeared convincing; anyhow, they were greeted with applause and cries of bravo, bravo, brave Swiss! which made me hope they had accepted my offer and that I would be reprieved. They immediately brought wine and we had to drink to the health of Paris and the Nation. From there we were led to the

Palais Royal and made to walk round the garden to show ourselves to the people, who did not yet appear completely appeased.
However, a lucky chance established us in their affection. It
happened that at this moment a former prisoner, newly delivered
from the Bastille, was also being walked round the garden.
The crowd took us also for newly rescued prisoners and everyone
began to pity us. Some people even thought they could detect on
our hands the marks of the fetters with which we had been
loaded. At last the misunderstanding was so complete, that after
they had made us go into an upper room, a speaker, standing at
a window, made us stand by him in order to show us to the
people in the garden whom he was haranguing and whom he
told that we were prisoners just rescued from the Bastille. He
said we had been shut up there in the cells because we had refused
to fire on the citizens, that we were people who deserved their
respect and that he recommended us to their good graces. Immediately someone was sent round with a basket to make a
collection for us. He soon returned with some ten écus (five franc
pieces) which he had collected and from which he paid for the
supper they had brought us in the interval. By this time we were
on friendly terms with everybody.

I was urgently begged to try to persuade some of my comrades
in the regiment to come over and join the citizens. In order not
to appear half-hearted in my support, I had to yield to their
demands and to write to the camp asking comrades to join me.
So I wrote, in pencil, a note addressed to M. Dimart, a captain
in the regiment, knowing that he would understand me and
appreciate the situation. I told him that I had gone over to the
townspeople and invited him to come and join me at the Palais
Royal. One of my soldiers named Schmitt was ordered to carry
my note to the camp. They dressed him in civilian clothes, so
that he should not be recognized as a soldier, and took him to the
Champ-de-Mars, but as the camp had been moved elsewhere, he
could not deliver my note. The fact that he was not in uniform
enabled him to escape and rejoin the regiment. After supper an
order came for us to be brought back to the Hôtel de Ville.
When we arrived we were quartered in different districts. I was
sent with my sergeant and a corporal to Saint-Jean en Grève,

where we passed the night in the church, which was being used as a guard-house.

I then thought I was quite safe and that I had no reason to fear for my life. Wrapped in this sweet illusion I lay down on a bench in the hope of a good sleep, as I had not slept for several nights. On that same evening they had released several of the Invalides who with us had formed the garrison of the Bastille. But before they sent them off to their hostelry, they questioned them about the defence of the Bastille and asked them about the manner in which each individual had conducted himself. These fellows, accordingly, in their depositions charged me with having forced them to fire and said that I was responsible for the resistance of the garrison and that without me the place would have been surrendered without a blow struck. They talked like that in the presence of the French Guards and many other people. This revived the animosity of the people against me to such a degree that some persons immediately came to the place where I was detained to tell me what had happened and to threaten and insult me afresh, adding that my case was not yet finished and that my fate would be decided on the next day. Other members of the detachment of Invalides who had been released on the morning of the 15th were interrogated and these also taxed me with being the cause of the troubles of the previous day. They would have succeeded in having me hanged on the same day had not a person, whom I have never been able to identify, but who exercised authority over them, imposed silence, telling them that there had been enough misery and that it was useless to shed more blood. He ended by ordering them to drop my case.

N.B. The cannons which the King of Siam had presented to the King and which were kept in the *Garde-Meuble* were used in the attack on the Bastille.

❧

MORRIS:
JULY 14TH:

Am stopped twice to see if there be any Fire Arms in the Carriage. . . . Go to M. Le Couteulx's. While sitting here a Person comes in and announces the taking of the Bastile, the Governor of which is beheaded and the Prévost des Marchands is killed and also beheaded; they are carrying the Heads in Triumph thro the City. The Carrying of this Citadel is among the most exraordinary Things that I have met with. . . . Yesterday it was the Fashion at Versailles not to believe that there were any disturbances at Paris. I presume that this Day's Transactions will induce a Conviction that all is not perfectly quiet.

⚜

In the diary of Louis XVI (344 pages written by the King's own hand and preserved in the National Archives) one can indeed read "July 1789: 13th, Nothing. 14th, Nothing."

However, the British Ambassador, the Duke of Dorset wrote on the 15th to the Secretary of State after a description of the events that had occurred.

"Thus, my Lord, was accomplished the greatest revolution recorded in history, and, relatively speaking, considering the importance of the results, one which has been achieved with very little bloodshed."

During the night of the 14th-15th the King was awakened by the Duke of Liancourt. As Grand-Master of the Wardrobe the Duke had the right to enter the King's bedroom at any time. His visitor related what had happened. Louis XVI was astonished. "It's a revolt," he said. "No, Sire, it's a revolution." Louis XVI was deeply moved and decided to go to Paris on the 17th.

Meantime the Parisians appointed a Mayor, the astronomer Bailly, and created a militia, the National Guard, entrusting the command of this force to La Fayette, an aristocrat, who had given proof of his liberal views by going to America to fight with "the rebels" against the English.

Bailly, the new Mayor (unlawfully appointed) was instructed to receive the King at the gates of Paris. This is what he says in his diary:

At eleven o'clock at night M. Herwyn, a deputy from the National Assembly, brought the news that the King was coming to Paris on the next day. He also announced the arrival of a large delegation from the Assembly to communicate the news to the

Hôtel de Ville. The delegation arrived at one a.m. and was received with suitable honours.

FRIDAY—JULY 17TH:

I rose early in the morning as I wished to leave for town at seven o'clock, and go over what I would have to say to the King, when I received him at the Gates of Paris. It depressed me to leave Versailles. I had been happy there in the midst of an Assembly with an excellent tone, which was worthy of the great tasks which it was called to perform. I had seen and taken some part in its great achievements. Now I was leaving these memories behind and I felt my happiness was at an end. If there have been brilliant days and moments of satisfaction in my life before this I can truly say that I have not been happy since.

I had sent to call a carriage, but was kept waiting. I couldn't guess why. When I went out I was met by the coachmen of the royal carriages, who offered me a tree loaded with flowers and ribbons. I was sorry to leave Versailles, and Versailles was sorry to see me go. I was obliged to submit to this tree being fixed on to the front of the carriage. All the coachmen accompanied me, firing off crackers, although it was broad daylight, down to the end of the Avenue. It was impossible to prevent them. At last I parted from them at the end of the Avenue, grateful for their friendly send-off and very pleased to be able to pursue my journey, which had been somewhat delayed. I was highly praised in the newspapers, who found that the Chief Officer of the Capital had displayed great simplicity in driving to Paris in one of those conveyances vulgarly called chamber-pots. Since then the lampoonists have censured my luxury. For my part I have thought that the First Officer of the greatest city in the world should be simple in his habits and in his person, as a magistrate representing the people, and at the same time that he should maintain in his public appearances a style worthy of the city, of whose dignity he is the custodian.

I had ordered a hired carriage which I found at Place Louis XV where I deposited Mme Bailly. I drove in this to the Hôtel de Ville, arriving at ten o'clock. There I found everyone busy with preparations for the King's reception. The Aldermen asked to be separated from the electors and wished to appear in their municipal robes, which were of velvet. Nothing could be more absurd. The answer given them was "if you wish to distinguish your-selves from the electors, who saved Paris, you are of course free to do so". It seems that they also asked if they should address the King kneeling. To which it was replied that they were still free to perpetuate this degrading custom, but, if they did, the electors would demand to be separated from them. However, I ought to say that the first request was submitted to me as chief of the Municipality and that I had no knowledge of the second. In point of fact the Aldermen were not free to perpetuate this usage, for the Spokesman of the city was myself and no power would have induced me to speak otherwise than standing upright. I had won this right at Versailles for the whole nation and I was not going to come to Paris to lose it for my fellow citizens.

At last we left to go and meet the King. The procession was composed of twenty-five chosen electors, twenty-five members of the Municipal Council, and the City Guards in full force. I marched at the head preceded by the Colonel of the Guards and two Aldermen, Messrs. Buffault and Vergue, who took it in turn to carry the keys of the City in a silver-gilt basin. On the way I asked certain questions regarding the ceremony of the keys. What would the King do with them when I had handed them over to him. They said, "He will hand them back." "And what shall I do with them?" "You will keep them." "Do you think I am going to carry these great heavy keys all the way back? I'll pitch them into the first convenient corner." "Don't do that, please. These keys are precious. They are the ones that were presented to Henry IV." That at once gave me an idea of an opening for my speech, to which I hastily added a few lines in pencil.

Usually the old city received the King in Place Louis XV, because its boundary was there, at the gate called La Conférence, which was long ago demolished. We marched beyond this point until we reached Chaillot and the fire-station opposite it. There we met about three hundred deputies on the way to Paris as part of the King's escort. The King arrived. I presented the keys to him and said:

"Sire, I bring to Your Majesty the keys of his good town of Paris: they are the very keys presented to Henri IV. He had reconquered his people, and today the people have reconquered their King. . . ."

M. de la Vigne spoke.

The King replied that it was with pleasure that he received the homage of the town of Paris and the electors.

The procession passed through Place Louis XV, Rue Saint-Honoré, Rue du Roule and the quays as far as the Hôtel de Ville. The route on both sides was lined by men of the National Guards and behind them stood the crowd, three and sometimes four deep armed with muskets, swords, pikes, lances, scythes, sticks and whatnot. Among them one saw women, monks, friars with guns slung over their shoulders. It was estimated by some that two hundred thousand armed men were there. I think, myself, this is an exaggeration although, at a pinch Paris could have produced this number. My belief is that the route could well have been lined four deep by sixty thousand persons, which permits one to suppose that there were a hundred thousand armed men in Paris on that day.

When the King was passing through Place Louis XV, a ball from a carbine fired from near the Palais Bourbon, killed a woman not far from his carriage. We had reason to suppose that this unfortunate incident was due to an accident, but it was a strange thing to happen. . . .

I was the first to arrive at the Hôtel de Ville and it was suggested that I should present to the King the three-coloured cockade which the Parisians had adopted since the revolution as an emblem and in order to be able to recognize one another: I did not quite know how the King would take this and wondered if there was anything improper about the suggestion. I came to the conclusion that I ought to present the cockade and that the King ought not to refuse it.

When the King got out of his carriage I walked a few steps in front of him. And then, turning, I offered him the cockade, saying, "Sire, I have the honour to offer to your Majesty the distinctive emblem of the French." The King took it in very good humour and fastened it on to his hat. He then went up the steps leading into the Hôtel. He was guarded and surrounded by a number of citizens representing the town. They were all carrying swords which they crossed over his head making a trellis of steel, but the clashing of the swords, the hubbub of voices and even the cries of joy, reverberating through the vaulted building, sounded somehow frightening. I should not be surprised, if at that moment the King had felt somewhat alarmed. But thronged as he was by the crowd, he marched along with the assurance of a good King in the midst of a friendly people. They say that, when the Maréchal de Beauvau wished to keep the crowd away from him, he said, "Leave them alone, they love me well."

As he entered the council-chamber, there was a burst of applause and cries of *Vive le Roi* were heard everywhere. The people with tears in their eyes turned to look at him and stretched out their hands towards him. And when he had taken his seat on the throne which had been prepared for him a voice from the back of the hall uttered this heartfelt cry: "Our King! Our Father!" at which the applause, the transports of enthusiasm and the cries of *Vive le Roi* became even more intense.

M. de Corny demanded that a statue should be erected to Louis XVI, the restorer of public liberty and father of the French nation, and immediately, by universal acclamation, it was voted that this statue should be set up on the site of the Bastille.

❖

MORRIS:

It is a magnificent Procession in every Respect. After it is over go to Dinner at the Traiteur's and get to a Beef Steak and Bottle of Claret. A Deputy from Bretagne, whom I met with formerly at a Table d'hôte at Versailles, comes in and we seat him at our little Table. He tells me that the King Yesterday sent the Assembly a Letter of Recall for M. Necker. That the Ministers have all resigned except the Baron de Breteuil, who says he never accepted. That the Count D'Artois, the Duke and Dutchess of Polignac, Monsʳ de Vaudreuil, and in short the whole Committee Polignac, have decamped last Night in Despair. I tell him

that travelling may be useful to the Count D'Artois and therefore
it would be well if he visited foreign Countries.

※

*Mme de Polignac was the intimate friend of Marie-Antoinette and
Vaudreuil of the Comte d'Artois. The whole of this cabal—the no-
compromise party—was beginning to lose ground. The emigration was
about to begin. It was being discussed in the salons. This is what was
being said in Mme d'Amblimont's salon, for instance. The daughter
of the house is speaking.*

Mme de Laugeron is more like Diana than any of the Dianas.
Yesterday evening, didn't she want to kill M. Necker and the
Duke of Orleans with her own hands! "And what would they
do to me?" she said. "I would go to the King and say: 'I have
rendered you the greatest possible service, not like all these people
round you, who act as though they were walking on eggs and
spend all their time being tactful to the *canaille*.'" Her mother
cried, "Diana, be quiet." "But, mother, what *would* they do to
me? And besides that just think of how I should be serving the
King and how my name would go down to posterity. And I'd
take a strong line with skin-flints like Mirabeau and Siéyès and
boobies like M. de la Fayette. Take from this scum the gold of
the one and the reputations of the other two and they soon would
fall into the hands of the executioner." I agree with her. She
wanted to show me how well she could handle a pistol, so she
went to her husband's room to fetch one and was amused at my
nervousness and her sister's. I didn't feel at all comfortable, as she
played all sorts of tricks and the pistol was loaded. Being afraid
of nothing and being really capable of doing what she said, she
laughs at Albertine and me. We left her to revel in her fantastic
dream of solving simply and speedily the affairs of state.

※

*The nobles hesitated between the party of the Comte d'Artois, more
royalist than the King and that of the Duke of Orleans, more revolu-*

tionary than the Revolution. Sometimes they returned to the land, the source of their existence.

The Duchesse de Gontaut:

After she married Lord Edward Fitzgerald, Pamela and her husband adopted the most democratic ideas. It is even said that at her wedding she wore "the red bonnet".

At Bellechasse (Mme de Genlis' place) there was talk of a sleigh party and Mademoiselle offered me a place in her sleigh, which the Duke of Orleans, her father, was to drive. The idea was to have a children's dinner at Mousseaux and to play blind-man's-buff afterwards. I looked forward tremendously to this party. If my father had not been very kind and yielded to my prayers, I should never have got the consent of my mother, who had not been invited.

It was a delightful party. After dinner Mme de Genlis, who was looking after the children of the Duke of Orleans, withdrew to her apartment in the château with the Duke, leaving us to be looked after by teachers and tutors and various persons belonging to the Prince's household, among whom were the Marquis de la Valette, the father of Mme de Juigné. Though a young man at that time he undertook to be our mentor and he was certainly worthy of the role by reason of his perfect breeding and amiable manners. The Duke of Orleans often entrusted his children to him and got him to take them out riding.

At the most exciting moment of our game a hunt-servant came and said it was time to go, to everyone's great regret. We held a consultation and it was decided to send me with M. de la Valette on a deputation to ask Mme de Genlis for one hour's grace. There were a number of salons through which we passed moving in the direction from which we heard many voices. I was so frightened that when we entered the room and I found myself in the middle of a group of men, I could not pick out Mme de Genlis. But she had seen me and the Duke of Orleans, observing my embarrassment, took me by the hand and led me to her. I carried out my commission very clumsily, being disconcerted by her cross expression.

She unwillingly granted me the favour I had come to beg

from her. The only face I could recognize in the room was that of the Duc de Biron. I had seen him sometimes in my mother's house. He spoke to me kindly and tried to reassure me. At that moment he was engaged in a lively conversation with a fat ugly man who paid me many compliments. I have seen him since then at Versailles at a dinner in the house of M. de Saint-Priest, then Minister of the Household—a cousin of mother's. I still retain the memory of the fat man's face, which was distasteful to me. It was M. de Mirabeau.

A comedy, written for the occasion—the birthday of Mme de Genlis—was to be played at Saint-Leu. We were earnestly begged to attend, so my mother went with the Dowager Countess of Gontaut and me. Everyone seemed restless and my mother was anxious. The Duke of Orleans was expected, but he did not come. During the evening someone said to my mother in a low voice that they were fighting in Paris. She and the Comtesse de Gontaut wished to go there. The latter was very anxious about her son, the Marquis de Saint-Blancard, who was a captain in the French Guards. Mme de Genlis insisted that their fears were imaginary, but her arguments did not stop us from going. When we got to the Rue Royale we had difficulty in getting into my father's house, owing to the great crowd. Berchiny's Hussars were preventing the mob from breaking into the Tuileries. During the scuffle, a man of the people was killed on the Swivel-Bridge. The turmoil continued far into the night. The French Guards began to mingle with the insurgents, deserting their barracks and turning against their officers, who themselves were obliged to leave their posts. The mob chased M. de Saint-Blancard who took refuge in our house just as we returned from Leu. The next day was horrible: we saw the French Guards arriving in the Rue Royale from the boulevards, all mixed up with the people and shouting, dancing and dragging along women disguised as nuns. And there were men dressed like friars forcing trembling women to march with them while everyone cried, "Hang the aristocrats" and such like slogans.

These brigands came from the Faubourg Saint-Antoine where they had already burnt and pillaged Réveillon's.

The mob stopped in front of our house and broke through the

gate of the royal furniture repository, expecting to find arms there. After an hour of pillage, priests, women, soldiers and nuns came out, loaded with loot, in a dreadful state of drunkenness and excitement. We thought we were lost. My father was determined to defend us and had barricaded the doors and windows of the house. Three carriages blocked the main entrance manned by three of our men, who were almost mad with rage, while my father stood at the top of the staircase with a pistol in each hand. He made me stand behind him and was resolved to defend us to the death. Ah! never have I been so terrified!

Two days afterwards we went to Versailles with my father, who, in spite of his age, wished to offer his services to the King.

To give an idea of the frenzied condition people were in, I shall mention that a hunt-servant wearing the livery of the Comte d'Artois, who was carrying a note to my mother, was set upon, beaten and stripped of his clothes in Place Louis XV. He could only deliver a fragment of the letter that had been entrusted to him.

Next day my mother went to Versailles to enquire what this missive was about. The Comte d'Artois knowing my father's high-spirited and loyal character and realizing our anxiety on his behalf advised my mother to take him on a short voyage, which would distract him and calm his sometimes unwise impetuousness. My mother followed this advice and spoke to one of her friends, Mme de Montesson, who was herself intending to spend some time in her splendid château at Berny. She suggested that my mother should go with her and should take me and arrange for my father to meet us there, so that we should all be on the high road for the South of France, where he had agreed to go.

It is known that Mme de Montesson had secretly married the old Duke of Orleans, the father of the present duke (Egalité). She enjoyed the privileges of a Princess and had a fine house in the Rue Grange-Batelière. She used the Orleans livery and the arms of this branch of the Royal House were added to her own. She was pleasant, gentle and kind-hearted, her house an agreeable one to be in and her friends witty and select.

We set off in a two-horse carriage with a groom in livery in front. A curious way of travelling incognito! When we arrived at Saint Roch the crowd surrounded us, stopped the carriage and forced us to get down and wait on the steps of the church, while they ransacked the carriage hoping to find treasures. After searching in vain for an hour they let us get back into the carriage and go back to the Montesson Mansion. I had a painful surprise on seeing among the crowd who had been goaded to attack us my wet-nurse, who lived on a pension paid her by my mother. Her ingratitude was such that, not content with the insults which were hurled at us, she added an obscene gesture, which I will not describe.

After this false start it was thought advisable to wait until the popular excitement had calmed down, and a short time afterwards, we set out in a coach with servants, maids, etc., and reached the place appointed by my father, which happened to be his birthplace, without the slightest incident.

Near Nérac there stands a great old manor house called the Château du Lys. There my father spent his childhood. At the time of which I am writing his elder brother was no longer alive. He had left a son, who had twelve children, eight boys and four girls. Our arrival at the Manor was positively mediaeval. We found the peasants drawn up in line, and the eight sons of the seigneur standing with their hats off. In the place of honour were eight soldiers who had fought with my father in the Seven Years War. One could still see under their white hair the scars of honourable wounds.

Our coach drove over the old bridge, which spanned a broad moat, and came to a stop under a dark, vaulted archway. The women and girls were assembled there and the Lady of the Manor with her daughters.

My father's emotion had communicated itself to us and at his first words my mother and I shed tears.

"Come nearer, comrades," he said to his old companions. "I have come here to die amongst you, for I can do no more to serve our King."

The Manor had the reputation in the country of being very beautiful, but the first sight of it depressed me. The great coach with its six horses could not turn in the square courtyard overshadowed by high towers, whose windows, few and small, looked to me like those of a prison. I had never seen any château but Versailles or any great walls but those of Paris. But soon I grew accustomed to the old-fashioned ways and habits of this ancient manor and appreciated the simplicity and goodness of this worthy family so much that I became deeply attached to the place. My high-spirits returned and I felt so happy at Lys that for a whole year the successive phases of the Revolution hardly made any impression on me.

✦

Gracious God, what a People!
JULY 22ND:

At three I go to the Club to meet the Gentleman with whom I engaged to dine at Table d'Hôte. We go thither and have a good Dinner for 3; Coffee &c., included the Price of the Dinner is 48 Francs. After Dinner walk a little under the Arcade of the Palais Royal waiting for my Carriage. In this Period the Head and Body of M. de Foulon are introduced in Triumph. The Head on a Pike, the Body dragged naked on the Earth. Afterwards this horrible Exhibition is carried thro the different Streets. His Crime is to have accepted a Place in the Ministry. This mutilated Form of an old Man of seventy five is shewn to Bertier, his Son in Law, the Intendt of Paris, and afterwards he also is put to Death and cut to Pieces, the Populace carrying about the mangled Fragments with a Savage Joy. Gracious God, what a People!

THE FIFTH AND SIXTH OF OCTOBER

❧❧❧❧❧❧❧❧❧❧❧❧❧❧❧❧❧❧❧❧❧❧❧❧❧❧❧❧❧❧❧❧❧❧❧❧❧❧❧

THE REVOLUTION continued and with it the famine. In the Assembly the Nobles abandoned their game rights and the Clergy renounced the tithe. Privilege had ceased to exist, but there was still no bread to eat. The troops continued to intimidate the public. Early in October the King's bodyguard trampled on La Fayette's three-coloured cockade and replaced it with the Queen's black one. Seven thousand rioters—mainly women—then marched on Versailles.

A young officer of the French Guards, Thiébault, was on duty at the time. Here is what he says:

An order came to prevent the people from invading Versailles and immediately afterwards some sixty frightful women appeared announcing with loud cries that they were looking for the King and calling on everyone to join them. Seeing these harpies, who, coming from the direction of the Palais Royal increased their numbers and their intoxication at every drinking-shop they visited and many of whom brandished bludgeons and cutlasses, I made the few men remaining with me stand to arms. I posted them in battle order in front of the gateway of Les Feuillants and I sent a corporal with four men to drive back the rabble. The only result of this was to exasperate these females and my sort of vanguard was showered with abuse and driven back. I at once supported them with the rest of my troops, which was barring the Rue Saint-Honoré, and charged these creatures. We used our butt-ends on them and kicked them and went so far as to prick them in the stomach and the side with our bayonets. And so we drove them back fighting as far as the hill of Saint-Roch, where they threw themselves down uttering horrid imprecations and threats against us.

While I was cleaning up Rue Saint-Honoré, all the drummers at Les Feuillants were beating the call to arms, as I had instructed them. Our companies reformed fairly quickly and in the belief that we had received orders we could carry out, we blocked all communications with Versailles, as far as our sector was concerned, in such a way that no one could get through. However, it was too late to achieve our object, for in the other sectors the orders of which I have spoken were not sent or were regarded as a dead letter with the result that our efforts only caused some of these bands to make a détour, every step of which was signalled by abominable acts. The mob stopped all carriages, pulled out their occupants and made them march with them.

At six in the evening an aide-de-camp of M. de la Fayette arrived at Les Feuillants. We at once stood to arms. Our right half-battalion set off for Versailles. Eight or ten hours before they ought to have sent 20,000 men to occupy Meudon Wood and the gates of Sèvres and Saint-Cloud.

We had still not reached Point-du-Jour, when there was a block, caused by the slowness of a night march and the absurd decision to arrange in battle order sixty half-battalions of infantry and a number of batteries of artillery. We advanced in short stages interrupted by long halts. Moreover, it had begun to rain: there were frequent heavy showers and the mud was horrible. Our march, which became more and more painful, lasted more than six hours and it was half an hour after midnight when we deployed on the Place d'Armes at Versailles, where we were ordered to bivouac.

After we had piled arms, M Doazan, senior, a fermier-général and my captain, took me aside and said: "I have ordered them to prepare supper for two at the Hôtel des Fermes. Come along and let us eat it. To set a good example we'll leave my brother here with these other gentlemen, who will have to look after themselves as best they can." Never was a proposal more timely. We were hungry, soaked and frozen, but we had a marvellous supper in front of a fire which served the double purpose of warming and drying us. When the meal was over, we threw ourselves down on one bed. At dawn they woke us up and we at once left to join the company. We were still on the staircase when we heard them sounding the call to arms. That was the moment when, through a gate left open accidentally or on purpose, the mob surged into the courtyards of the Palace, penetrating as far as the Queen's quarters, and when the attack began on the Bodyguard, who were saved by the French Guards, just as they had saved the Royal Family.

We ran at full speed to rejoin our unit, whom we found had just got under arms. Cries were heard on all sides. While some of the rioters were stealing the horses from the royal stables, others were preparing to slaughter the Bodyguard. Our centre three companies were ordered to go after the horses and succeeded in getting nearly all of them back. My company of grenadiers with some others, was ordered to go to the help of the body-guard who were attacked by the mob, as they tried to enter the Château. We saved them all and I, for my part, was very happy to have rescued three of them from these fanatics, who had disarmed them and were just about to cut their throats. I entrusted these three members of the Bodyguard to my half-company and marched them back with my men to Paris. As we were passing in front of the Garde-Meuble, I saw my father, my mother and my sister at a window, so I left the ranks with my three body-guardsmen, who had been overwhelming me since the morning with expressions of gratitude, and took them into the main entrance of the house, having signalled to my father to receive them. To complete the story they remained with my father, who kept them to dinner, until nightfall. Then they changed their clothes for riding-dress, which was procured for them, and taking a hired carriage they drove to the house of the family of one of them, who lived in Paris. As soon as they arrived they sent back the garments they had borrowed by a servant, who brought them their uniforms which were no longer of any use to them.

The transfer of the King to Paris, announced as a triumph and considered a victory, resulted in peace being re-established for the time being. The first essential was to get these frightful hordes back to Paris.

Behind them marched several battalions of soldiers. All along the route the mob kept shouting that the King was coming— they called him the Baker in view of the abundance that was now to reign in Paris. Instead of banners they carried the heads of two luckless members of the Bodyguard and accompanied these ghastly trophies with hideous songs.

After Versailles had been pretty well stripped, the King and his family set off for Paris accompanied by a hundred deputies and escorted by thirty thousand men of the National Guard from Paris. In front of the carriages marched the half-battalions of the three first divisions, and the half-battalions of the three last divisions marched behind them, independently of the men who marched beside them. From the toll-gate of the Bonshommes to the Hôtel de Ville via the Rue Royale, the Rue Saint-Honoré, etc., the whole procession marched between two lines of national guards and it was the same thing from the Hôtel de Ville to the Tuileries, which had not been inhabited for a century. Although the soles of my court shoes had given out by the time we got to the Palais Royal, I marched the whole way, but when I reached home my feet were so swollen, that I was unable to walk for two days.

❧

Dumont, the Genevan, a great friend of Deputy Mirabeau was at Versailles, at the Assembly: this is what he says:

We were dining with M. de Servan, in the palace called "*Les Petites-Ecuries*", where he has an apartment as Governor of the Pages.

From the windows which command the whole of the great square, we saw multitudes arriving from Paris including fishwives and bullies from the markets, and all these people wanted nothing but bread. The Flanders Regiment and the National Guard of Versailles were drawn up outside the precincts of the Château, while the King's Guards, foot and mounted, were inside the great and the little court. There was some violent commotion but we could not see clearly what was happening. Mirabeau did not stay long with us, in fact I have an idea that he was not dining with Savner.

Although the crowd was dense and we did not know exactly what might happen, we walked about freely and saw the King's carriages driving along by-roads, which made me think there was some idea of getting the Royal Family out of the way. Tired of wandering about, I went into the Assembly at about 8 p.m. It presented a strange spectacle. The Chamber had been invaded by the people of Paris and the surroundings were crowded. The galleries were full of women and men armed with scythes, sticks and pikes. The sitting had been suspended but someone came on behalf of the King to request the President to send a deputation to the Château and to keep the Assembly in session. I went to look for Mirabeau, whom I found already in bed although it was not eleven o'clock. When we got back to the Assembly where the President was wasting his strength trying to keep order, Mirabeau raised his masterful voice and called on the President to see that the Assembly was respected and to call for the withdrawal from the Chamber of all strangers. It needed all his popularity to achieve this. Gradually the crowd withdrew and the Deputies began to discuss calmly certain aspects of the Penal Code. I was in a gallery, where a harridan was directing the movements of about a hundred women and a number of young people who shouted or kept silence as she ordered them. She addressed the deputies with coarse familiarity: "Who's that talking down there? Make the chatterbox shut up. That's not the point: the point is that we want bread. Tell them to put our little Mother Mirabeau up to speak. We want to hear him." Then everyone shouted for our "little Mother Mirabeau" (a form of affectionate expression employed by people of this class). But Mirabeau was not the man to waste his energy on occasions like this and his popularity, as he said himself, was not that of a mob-orator.

Towards midnight an aide-de-camp announced that M de La Fayette had arrived at the head of the National Guard from Paris and people felt themselves in safety under his auspices. His soldiers had renewed their oath of allegiance to the law and the King and the multitude began to grow calmer after the pledges the King had given and which had been carefully circulated. At about 2 a.m. we left, with the house still in session. When I woke up I was given a confused account of what had happened

—the invasion of the Château and the disarming of the bodyguard. My informant attributed the violence to misunder-
standings, imprudent actions and chance quarrels.

✤

*A deputy of moderate views, the Marquis de Ferrières (who favoured
a constitutional monarchy) relates what he saw and "things which
persons worthy of credence have assured him took place". He was
himself present at the Assembly.*

La Fayette arrived. He asked Mounier (the President) to come
with him into one of the offices. Mounier fearing that they might
take advantage of his absence to divide the Assembly sent Lally-
Tollendal and Clermont-Tonnerre. La Fayette protested that the
intentions of the militia from Paris were loyal and said that there
was no reason for anxiety about the way the posts were manned.
"I will answer for everything," he added, "and now I must take
some rest. I suggest that the President should do likewise." Such
a positive assurance satisfied Mounier. He adjourned the meeting
and as he went out saw La Fayette who confirmed what he had
just told Clermont.

It was then three o'clock in the morning. At six a crowd of
women and armed men assembled in the square summoned by
the beating of drums. They rallied round a standard with red
flames on a blue ground. At first the multitude moved about in
different directions but afterwards formed into several columns,
as if obedient to the orders of different chiefs. Shouts of rage
against the Bodyguard were heard. One of these columns marched
up to the Royal Gate, but found it locked. Another got through
by the gate of the chapel, which was open. One of the National
Guards of the Versailles Militia led the way to the King's staircase.
Miomandre de Sainte-Marie and some of the Bodyguard ran up:
"My friends," cried Miomandre, "you love your King and yet
you even come into his palace to disturb him." No one answered.
The column continued to advance. The Bodyguard mustered in
their hall. The doors were soon broken down, and they were
forced to evacuate it. The conspirators approached the Queen's

apartments crying, "We are going to cut off her head, tear out her heart, fry her liver and that won't be the end of it." Miomandre flew to the door of the first ante-room, opened it hurriedly and called to a lady whom he saw: "Save the Queen, they mean to kill her. I am alone facing two thousand tigers. My comrades have been obliged to quit their hall." After these few words Miomandre shut the door and bravely waited for the conspirators. One of them tried to stab him with his pike: he parried the blow. Another taking the pike by the head, struck him a blow with the butt which felled him to the ground. "Stand back," said he—he was the man of the National Guard who was leading the column. The crowd made room for him. Then measuring the butt of his musket against Miomandre's head, he struck him with all his force so that the trigger penetrated his skull. Miomandre, streaming with blood was left for dead.

The conspirators poured into the great hall. Meanwhile, the Duke of Orleans in a grey frock-coat and a round hat, with a riding whip in his hand, was walking cheerfully about among the groups, who filled the parade ground and the courtyards of the Château. He smiled at some and talked in free and easy manner with others. All round him the air resounded with cries of "Our father is with us: Long live King Orleans". Encouraged by these striking tributes to his popularity the Duke marched for a while with this group, but on reaching the top of the stairway, he did not dare to traverse that redoubtable gap which, in the definition of crime, separates intention from execution. He contented himself with pointing towards the Queen's apartment and, turning towards the King's quarters, disappeared.

Meantime, Mme Auger, first Lady of the Bedchamber, got the Queen into a petticoat and threw a cloak over her shoulders. The Queen then ran up the private staircase leading to the King's apartment and knocked at the door of the ante-chamber. In the noise and confusion her knocks were not heard and she waited for a few moments in fearful anxiety. At last the door was opened. The Queen entered and burst into tears calling, "Save me, my friends, my dear friends."

The conspirators now in possession of the hall of the bodyguard broke down the doors leading to the Queen's apartment and burst into her bedroom. Approaching the bed they stabbed it with their pikes. The men of the Bodyguard who had barricaded themselves behind tables and stools could not hold out for long. The tops of the tables were being knocked to pieces by repeated blows. The Duke was going to enjoy the fruit of his crimes. Then the Grenadiers of the old French Guards rushed up and, putting the conspirators to flight, occupied the inner posts.

While the conspirators, then masters of the Château, were flooding through the apartments, men dressed as women were spreading word among the people that M de La Fayette was a traitor and that they must get rid of him. One of the leaders wearing the uniform of an officer of the National Guard with the Cross of Malta in his buttonhole, was advising a group of men and women who thronged round him and to whom he was handing money, to spare no one except the Dauphin and the Duke of Orleans. "We want the heads of the Queen and M de La Fayette. That man is a traitor." He left Paris against his will and very late. When he was crossing the Bridge of Louis XVI he said, "Is it possible that I should betray my King? They only made him go on by firing shots in the air." At these words a man with a frightful face disguised as a woman, displayed a sort of sickle and swore that he would be the one to cut off the old bitch's head. The women applauded and said the man who had harangued them was quite right and that they wanted the Duke of Orleans on the throne and to kill M de La Fayette. Let them have money for this.

The parade ground and the courtyards offered a still more hideous picture of popular fury. Troops of women and men armed with pikes and guns were everywhere hunting the men of the Bodyguard. M des Hutes and M de Varicourt were brought to the King's Gate, where they were thrown on the ground. A man with a great beard beheaded them with an axe. The barbarous horde broke into manifestations of savage glee. Some of them bathed their hands in the blood of the two men and rubbed it over their faces: others danced round their bodies. Several persons proposed to bombard the quarters of the Bodyguard with cannon but most of them thought it would be more amusing to hang them. Then they all scattered in search of men of the Bodyguard, as though they were chasing game. More than thirty of them, caught in different places, were led to the parade ground, where they were to be slaughtered. The man with the great beard, brandishing his dripping axe, summoned the victims in a loud voice. Then La Fayette appeared with a company of Grenadiers. Indignant at the sight which greeted his eyes he addressed his men and said: "Grenadiers, I have given my word to the King that none of the gentlemen of the Bodyguard would be harmed. If you cause me to break my word of honour, I shall no longer be fit to command you and I shall leave you. Have at them!" The Grenadiers pounced upon the band of murderers and tore their prey from them.

The whole Château presented a picture of the deepest consternation. The Queen and the Royal Family had retired to the private apartments. The Queen standing at an open window had on her right Madame Elisabeth and on her left Madame Royale, while standing on a chair in front of her was the Dauphin, who, as he ruffled his sister's hair, kept saying, "Mama, I'm so hungry." The Queen, with tears in her eyes, told him he must be patient and wait till the turmoil was over. Suddenly she perceived the Duke of Orleans, arm in arm with Adrien Duport. "They are going to kill my son," cried the Queen, carried away by an involuntary spasm of fear. She took the Dauphin in her arms and got up hastily. Then someone came to tell her that the people were calling for her. She hesitated a moment. La Fayette explained that she had to show herself in order to calm the people. "In that case," she said with spirit, "I'll do it, even if it costs me my life." Then, holding the hands of her two children, she advanced to the balcony. "No children!" cried a man in the crowd, so the Queen handed over the Dauphin and Madame Royale to Mme de Tourzel and advanced on to the balcony alone. One of the conspirators aimed his piece at her, but, shocked at the enormity of the crime he had planned, he did not dare to consummate it.

Several persons insisted that the King should come and live in Paris and the mob repeated loudly "We want the King in Paris—the King in Paris." La Fayette remarked that the only way to calm the disorder was for the King to agree to the wish of the people to see him residing in the Capital. The King accordingly

promised to go to Paris on the same day on condition of being
accompanied by the Queen and his family. He begged the people
to spare the lives of his Bodyguard. La Fayette added his entreaty
to that of the King. The members of the Bodyguard showed
themselves on the balcony in the midst of a group of Grenadiers belonging to the Paris militia. They threw their bandoliers
down to the people, gave their hats to the Grenadiers and
borrowing forage-caps from the latter, put them on their heads.
The people applauded crying, "Long live the Bodyguard!"
Rapturous joy succeeded the intoxication of fury. Peace was
solemnly proclaimed. Frequent salvoes of artillery and musketry
announced the victory of the people of Paris and the King's
departure.

The sitting of the Assembly was fixed for nine o'clock but
various factors which I shall enumerate prevented the Assembly
from meeting before eleven: these were the exhausting experiences of the night, the general confusion and disorder, the
very legitimate anxiety arising from the invasion of the Château,
the personal fears of President Mounier and a number of deputies
publicly threatened by brigands in the pay of the Duke of Orleans
and the treacherous behaviour of various other deputies, who had
played a secret but not inactive role in these tragic scenes. Most
of the deputies kept coming and going between the Château and
the Salle des Etats, a prey to painful thoughts.

Mounier observed that the King seemed to want the deputies
to come over to the Palace to visit him, but Mirabeau said, "It
does not befit the dignity of the Assembly to move over to the
Palace. It is impossible to debate there."

. . . The King left at noon. The heads of M. des Hutes and M. de
Varicourt on two pikes led the procession. Following them were
forty to fifty members of the Bodyguard on foot and unarmed,
escorted by a body of men armed with sabres and pikes. After
that came two of the Bodyguard, wearing high boots, with neck
wounds, blood-stained shirts and torn garments, each held by
two men in the national uniform with drawn swords in their
hands. Further back one could see a group of the Bodyguard
mounted on horses some riding pillion and others in the saddle
with a member of the National Guard riding behind them.

c

They were surrounded by men and women who compelled them to shout *Vive la Nation* and to eat and drink with them. A mixed multitude of pikemen, Swiss Guards, soldiers of the Flanders Regiment, women plastered with cockades and carrying poplar branches and other women sitting astride on the guns, preceded and followed the King's coach. Every musket was wreathed in oak leaves in token of the victory and there was a continual discharge of musketry, while the people cried, "We are bringing the baker, Mrs. Baker and the baker's boy"—a slogan interlarded with gross insults to the Queen and threats against the priests and the nobles. Such was the procession, barbarous and blackguardly, in the midst of which the King, the Queen and the Royal Family arrived at the Hôtel de Ville after a drive lasting more than six hours.

The same episodes seen from the Palace at Versailles. Here is a letter from the young Madame Elisabeth, Louis XVI's younger sister to her friend Angélique de Bombelles, the daughter of her governess. Mme de Bombelles had emigrated.

October 13th, 1789.

To Madame de Bombelles:

Goodness, dear heart, how long it is since I wrote to you! I had calculated that if I wrote to you by the last post, you would receive my letter almost as you arrived. But for a long time past I should have known from experience not to count on the future. But there I am, wrong again. On Monday I rode out to Montreuil, where I meant to spend the day and from where I would have written to you. I was just sitting down to table when I saw a man come into the courtyard. He told me that fifteen thousand men were arriving from Paris and that he was going to find the King who was shooting at Châtillon. You may imagine that your princess was in Versailles almost as soon as it takes me to tell you. Before I started I was told that there were two thousand women, armed with bits of rope, hunting knives and whatnot, arriving at Versailles. They actually appeared about five o'clock. They came to ask for bread of which, according to them, there was none at all in Paris. So they had come to the King to ask him for it. His reply seemed to satisfy them. They went and quartered themselves in the hall of the States General. We still did not know if troops were coming from Paris or not. Meanwhile the people of Versailles, who were already very hostile to the Bodyguard, joined the bandits in order to destroy them. The King had forbidden the Bodyguard to fire, so no one thought of doing so. Only one of them, an officer, tried to defend himself when attacked by a man with a sabre. The mob thought this such a crime, that a man shot him at point-blank range and broke his arm. But wanting to blame the Bodyguard for the incident, they accused one of the gentlemen, whose horse had been killed under him and who himself had received numerous wounds, of having fired his pistols. That was one of the tricks of these people from Versailles to show that the gentlemen of the Bodyguard had attacked, when in fact they had shown great moderation and courage. They were very often shot at during the remainder of the evening. Those that were in the hostels were wounded with blows from wooden clubs. Between that day and Tuesday morning there were eleven killed and many wounded. At eleven o'clock at night M. de La Fayette, who had been forced to come to Versailles at the head of thirty thousand men, entered the King's presence after having made his troops swear once again the oath of allegiance to the King. He said that the people wanted the Flanders Regiment removed and the French Guard given the duty of looking after the King. They all occupied their posts and everyone went quietly to bed. For my part, not having gone to bed till three, I slept soundly till seven-thirty, when someone came to say that the King wanted me and that a detachment of twelve Grenadiers would take me to him. They told me also that the people had continued to pursue members of the Bodyguard. Their rooms had, in fact, been forced open. Two guards had been decapitated and others horribly wounded by the women. The Queen had been obliged to fly to the King's quarters in her nightgown, when her own rooms were invaded. All the courtyards had been crowded with women, ruffians and men of the National Guard. The latter tried to keep some order. But for the Grenadiers, all the men of the Bodyguard would have been massacred.

They saved an enormous number and took them under their protection for the march to Paris, during which they made them embrace the people One can say they saved the lives of most of those who had come to Versailles. The mounted Bodyguards retired during the night to Rambouillet and were pursued almost the whole way. The King, two days after he had settled in Paris disbanded them. We are now accompanied by officers of the National Guard. But, to return to my account of Tuesday, the women and the people in the courtyards demanded that the King should come to Paris and this was decided upon at eleven o'clock. Then the King and the Queen showed themselves on the balcony of the King's room. There were shouts of *Vive le Roi! La Reine! La Nation! Le Roi à Paris,* and others I could not distinguish.

M. de La Fayette in an eloquent address to the people made them renew their oath of allegiance in the presence of the King. At last, at one o'clock we got into our carriages. Versailles greeted our departure with demonstrations of joy. We went on our way, surrounded by the whole of the National Guard and by several gentlemen of the Bodyguard on foot, who had exchanged their hats with the forage caps of the Grenadiers. I forgot to say that after the King had appeared on the balcony of the Palace, they had also shown themselves and had thrown away their bandoliers and their hats as a sign of peace. The King had asked the people to leave them alone and not to chase them any longer. I keep on thinking of them and always with pleasure, for no troops could have behaved themselves better. They really acted like angels. The shouts of *Vive le Roi! Vive la Nation!* and down with the priests began at dawn and continued until we had reached the Hôtel de Ville. At Paris there are only the King, the Queen, Monsieur, Madame, the children and I. My aunts are at Bellevue. My rooms look on to the courtyard. On Wednesday a crowd assembled beneath my windows calling for the King and the Queen! I went to fetch them. The Queen spoke with the charm you know so well and the way she conducted herself that morning did her good with the people. The whole day they had to show themselves at the windows, for the courtyard and the garden continued to be crowded. At present there are fewer people and the

National Guard are keeping order. On Thursday there was some excitement at the Mont-de-Piété, because the press had published something about the Queen having promised to pay for all pawned objects on which less than a louis had been advanced— that would have been a matter of three million francs. You can guess the motive for spreading this rumour. It would be impossible for anyone to show more grace and courage than the Queen has done during the last week. All is quiet here and I like the people much more than those of Versailles. M. de La Fayette has behaved perfectly and so have the National Guards. Everything is quiet. There is plenty of bread. The Court is established almost on the old footing. People are received every day. On Sunday, Tuesday and Thursday there is gaming. Public dinners on Sunday and Thursday (perhaps a banquet on Sunday). All that, my love, does not displease me. You know how adaptable I am. I was very glad you were not here last week and I can't help feeling that the mere news of what has been happening may have upset your milk. You can be sure that I am not deceiving you when I tell you that your Mother, your Aunt, I and all the people you are fond of are well. Tell your husband from me not to worry. We could not have done better than to come and live in Paris and we shall always be better off here than anywhere else.

I don't write like this because my letter is sure to be read. No, dearest, it is because I honestly think so. Remind your husband that he told me in July that I was practically the only person to take a right view of things at that time. Remind him of this so that he may have confidence in the things I write to you, which express my real views. Goodbye, my heart, send me your news at once. I embrace you and love you with all my heart.

THE FLIGHT TO VARENNES

✦❖✦❖✦❖✦❖✦❖✦❖✦❖✦❖✦❖✦❖✦❖✦❖✦❖✦❖✦❖✦❖✦

JUNE *21st*, *TUESDAY*, left Paris at midnight, reached Varennes in Argonne and were arrested there at 11 p.m.

22nd—left Varennes at five or six in the morning: lunched at Saint Menehoul: reached Châlons at ten at night: had supper and slept at the old Governorate.

23rd—at half-past eleven they interrupted the mass to hasten our departure: lunched at Châlons and dined at Epernay: found the Commissioners of the Assembly at Buisson: reached Dormans at eleven: supped there and slept for three hours in an arm-chair.

24th—left Dormans at 7.30: dined at la Ferté-sous-Jouarre: reached Meaux at eleven: supped and slept at the Bishop's Palace.

Saturday 25th, left Meaux at 6.30, reached Paris at 8 p.m. without a stop.

26th—nothing of interest. Attended Mass in the gallery. The Commissioners of the Assembly met in Conference.

28th: Took some whey.

This extract from the diary of Louis XVI summarizes one of the most dramatic episodes of the Revolution—the flight to Varennes.

On June 21st at seven in the morning, the valet-de-chambre Lemoine, on entering the King's bedroom, found the bed empty. He gave the alarm. In the Queen's apartment and in the children's rooms, not a soul was to be found. The news spread like wildfire: "The King has fled." At eight o'clock the tocsin was sounded in Paris.

The Parisians were not wholly surprised. Everyone expected the King to flee the country. Two months earlier some demonstrators and national guards in spite of orders to the contrary from their chief La Fayette, had stopped the coach which was conveying Louis XVI and his family to the Château of Saint-Cloud for the Easter holidays. The Tuileries, of which only two wings remain extant today—the Pavilions of Flora and Marsan—had become the King's prison. Though all the gates were left open, the people of Paris were the King's gaolers.

Louis XVI wished to escape. The Assembly, after having confiscated the property of the Church to back a new issue of paper-money—the assignats—had decreed that in future priests and bishops should be elected by the citizens, whether Catholics or not. The Pope condemned the schism. Louis XVI, who was very religious, then decided to make for the frontier, where he would find loyal troops and march as their head on Paris.

Those in the secret were: Mme de Tourzel, governess of the children (these were the Dauphin Louis, aged six and "Madame Royale", otherwise Marie Thérèse, aged thirteen), Madame Elisabeth the King's sister, aged twenty-seven, Axel de Fersen, a young colonel in the Royal Swedish regiment of mercenaries and a passionate admirer of Marie Antoinette and lastly the Duc de Choiseul who commanded a squadron of hussars on the frontier and his chief General de Bouillé, the Governor of Lorraine. The essential thing was to escape from the surveillance of La Fayette, the Commander-in-Chief of the People's Army.

Mme de Tourzel:

We meant to leave on the night of Sunday-Monday, June 20th, but the date was postponed till the next day for fear lest one of the maids who looked after the Dauphin's room and was on duty on the 20th and who was known to be attached to M. de La Fayette, should report to the latter the departure of the Royal Family. This woman was replaced on the following day by another maid on whom one could count. It was feared that if the first maid was moved on the Sunday, that would give substance to the rumour that was current, even in the Tuileries, that the Royal Family were shortly leaving. M. de Bouillé was informed of the change of plans and if M. le Duc de Choiseul had been less flighty and had had more presence of mind, the postponement would have done no harm.

In order not to arouse suspicion, the Queen took the children to Tivoli herself and walked them about the garden of M. Boutin on Monday evening. On her return she gave orders to the officer commanding the battalion saying that she meant to go out on the following day. I notified him that the Dauphin would be going out too. After that, in order to banish from the minds of my people all idea of our departure, I told them to prepare me a bath for the next day at the hour when I would be leaving the Dauphin's room. At ten o'clock I went up to the Dauphin's room, according to my custom, with my maid, whose room was next to the Dauphin's.

A moment afterwards the Queen came into the Dauphin's room and awakened the young Prince, who was fast asleep. As soon as he heard that he was going to the wars, where he would command his regiment, he jumped out of his bed crying, "Quick! quick! give me my sword and my boots and let's be off." The idea of imitating Henry IV, who was his hero, excited him so much that he didn't close an eye during the journey.

The Queen on giving notice of her departure instructed Mme de Neuville, the Dauphin's first chambermaid, to follow the Dauphin in a post-chaise with Mme Brunyer, Madame Royale's first chambermaid.

She told Mme de Bar, the woman I mentioned just now as perfectly trustworthy, that she was sorry not to be able to take her with her, but that she would arrange for her to be taken to her own home and that she counted on her loyalty and discretion. This poor woman behaved most touchingly. She fell on her knees in front of the Queen, kissed her hand and said that she prayed for the success of the journey, which meant much more to her than the persecution she might have to endure or the arrangements that might be made to bring her safely to her own home.

We went down to the Queen's floor to which the King had already gone. Their Majesties told me that they would be accompanied by three gentlemen of the Bodyguard, one of whom would give his arm to the Queen and lead her on foot to her carriage. The other two would drive the coach, which would be waiting for the King at some distance from the barrier. The whole of the Royal Family except the two children would leave the Palace on foot. The King, addressing me, added that I would only be told the details of the journey after we had started, so as to save me from the embarrassment of inventing answers to questions in case I was unlucky enough to be arrested/ He then gave me a note declaring, in case of accident, that it was by his orders that I was accompanying M. le Dauphin and Madame. He also gave me permission to take with me M. de Gouvion, if we met him and he agreed to help their Majesties' departure. I had also marked two gold pieces, meaning to give one to a man of the National Guard, if we should chance to meet one, with a promise to make his fortune and to give him a good sum of money on producing a gold piece with similar markings to one I was keeping in my possession, to compare with his.

A long time before, I had taken the precaution to have a little cloth dress and bonnet made for my daughter, in which I could dress up the Dauphin, if circumstances made the disguise advisable. We made use of it successfully. When our carriage arrived the Queen went to see that all was quiet in the courtyard and then, seeing that no one was there, she kissed me and said, "The King and I are entrusting to you, Madame, with complete confidence, that which we hold most dear in the world. Everything is ready. Now go." We went down through the apartment of M. de Villequier, where there was no sentinel and going out through a little used door, we got into a venerable old conveyance, looking like a hackney-carriage, with the Comte de Fersen as our coachman.

In order to give the King time to catch us up, we drove for a while along the quays and returned by way of the Rue Saint Honoré to wait for the King and Queen opposite the house then called the Hôtel de Gaillarbois. Here I waited for three-quarters of an hour without seeing any member of the Royal Family. M. de Fersen played the part of a hackney-coachman to perfection. He whistled, gossiped with a so-called "pal" who was there by chance, and took snuff from his snuff box. I was on tenterhooks, though I did not show my anxiety, when Madame Royale said to me, "There's M. de la Fayette." I at once hid the Dauphin under my skirt, telling him and his sister not to be alarmed. I certainly was alarmed, myself. M. Bailly was following him at a short distance. They both passed us without paying any attention and after an anxious wait of three-quarters of an hour I had the relief of seeing Madame Elisabeth and began to hope again.

That was at half-past eleven and it was not until after twelve that we saw the King coming. We heard that M. Bailly and M. de la Fayette, who had come for the *coucher* had started to talk and that the King in order to avoid suspicion had shown no eagerness to go to bed. Eventually he had to undress, go to bed, get up again and put on fresh clothes including a wig, as a disguise. Then he had to walk from the Tuileries to pick up his carriage. The Queen could not leave the Palace until after the King and the latter showed his deep affection for her by the manner in which he expressed his anxiety. When she at last arrived and was in the carriage, he hugged and kissed her and said, "Oh, how glad I am that you've come. There were kisses all round and the whole of the Royal Family did me the same honour. Convinced that we had surmounted the most difficult obstacle we began to hope that heaven would smile upon our voyage.

The King told us that after getting rid of M. Bailly and M. de La Fayette, he had gone out through the main gate of the Tuileries with a feeling of perfect assurance, acquired from the fact that he had taken the precaution to get M. le Chevalier de Coigny, wearing a costume precisely similar to His Majesty's, to leave the Palace every night by this same gate, so that the sentinels were accustomed to let him pass without any misgivings at all. The King felt so much at his ease, that remarking that his shoe-lace was undone, he stopped to do it up without arousing the attention of the sentries or feeling uneasy himself.

The Chevalier de Coigny was one of the King's most faithful and affectionate servants. The King had confided to him the secret of his journey and if he had taken the advice that de Coigny gave him, there is every reason to suppose that the enterprise would have been successful. "No one," he said to the King, "appreciates more than I do the valour and the loyalty of the gentlemen of the Bodyguard. Nevertheless, on such an important occasion, one must employ persons used to travel and accustomed to take quick decisions. Priol, the commandant of the Gendarmerie, an intelligent man, who is accustomed to keep his eyes open would be of great value and so would a certain retired posting-master with a perfect knowledge of all the roads in the Kingdom, who is full of intelligence and infinitely loyal to your

Majesty's person." He also named a third person whose name and style I have forgotten.

The King, who wished to show his confidence in the Bodyguard, unfortunately did not follow this good advice, and persisted in his original resolve. He had asked M. d'Agout, the assistant major of the Bodyguard to find him three persons to carry letters to the Princes, his brothers. Not knowing where they were going to be sent, he took the first three who came to hand. These were M. du Moutier, M. de Maldan and M. de Valori. It would be unfair to them to cast doubts on their courage or their loyalty, but seeing that their subordinate rank had accustomed them to a rigid obedience to orders and never having been in a position of authority, they found themselves unequal to a mission of this kind. They did not dare to take any responsibility and simply asked for the King's orders which they would have carried out, even at the risk of their lives, but they lacked the enterprise necessary to cope with unexpected circumstances.

The Queen had taken into her confidence Madame Thibault, her first Lady of the Bedchamber, a person of merit and utterly devoted to her Majesty's person. She had made all necessary preparations for the journey and had taken a travel-pass for Tournay, where she was supposed to join Her Majesty as soon as she heard of her arrival in the town, where she was staying temporarily. She had been told to take my maid with her. The terror and simplicity of this poor creature, though a subject of laughter for the Royal Family, prevented them from leaving her to look after herself.

We experienced a number of small incidents, which went to show how the smallest causes influence great issues. M. de Fersen, fearing that the gentlemen of the Bodyguard had taken a different route from that which he had indicated to them, and realizing that if he wanted to catch them up, going by the shortest way, he would have to go through the gates of Paris once more, preferred to go by a longer way to avoid this danger. Thus we lost half an hour which, added to the extra three-quarters of an hour occupied by the King's *coucher* put us back an hour and a half. After that we found a wedding going on among the tollmen at the gate, with bright lights and a large crowd, but fortunately we were not recognized and got through without difficulty.

But our chief misfortune was that the King's horses came down twice between Nintré and Châlons breaking all the traces, which it took more than an hour to mend.

It has been said, quite incorrectly, that the King stopped for dinner. He and the Family had all their meals in the coach, and there were no stops anywhere. The King got out of his carriage only once the whole way and went into an empty stable, spoke to nobody and was back in the carriage in a very short time. The children only got out twice and that was when the postilions dismounted as we climbed steep gradients; I put them out to take the air, but this little walk did not delay us at all.

Near the gate of Clichy we found the coach waiting for us, so we left our old carriage and horses without worrying about what might happen to them. M. de Fersen drove the King as far as Claye, where we took the post-coach. The King, as he parted with him, displayed his gratitude in the most affectionate manner, expressing his hope of giving tangible proof of it and counting on a speedy reunion.

We were now travelling in a large, comfortable berline— nothing extraordinary, in spite of what was constantly repeated after the sad ending of an unfortunate journey. Now I was supposed to be the mistress, under the name of the Baronne de Korff: the King was my valet-de-chambre and the Queen my lady's-maid. It was known that the Baronne, whose name I now bore, had travelled from Paris to Montmédy by the same route which we took in a carriage like ours and that her passport had nowhere been asked for. They had gone so far as to calculate how many hours she had taken to reach Montmédy, and the sad result of this last precaution will become evident later.

When we had passed through the barrier, the King, who had begun to think well of the future, began to talk about his plans. He would go first to Montmédy to show the decision he had taken and which be believed to be right. He was absolutely determined not to leave the Kingdom except when circumstances made it necessary for him to pass through certain frontier towns in order to arrive more directly in the French town in which he wished to reside, and he did not wish to stay for a moment on foreign soil,

"Well, here I am," said the kindly sovereign, "at last out of Paris where I have been drenched with so much bitterness. You can be sure that once in the saddle again, I shall be quite different from the man you have seen up to now." He then read us the memorandum he had left in Paris to be taken to the Assembly and he was full of pleasure at the thought of the happiness which he hoped to bring to France, and of the return of his brothers and faithful servants, and of the possibility of re-establishing the faith and repairing the damage which the sanctions he had been forced to impose on the Church might have caused. Then, looking at his watch, which showed eight o'clock, he said, "La Fayette must be feeling very much embarrassed just now."

It would have been difficult for the King to share the general's anxiety or to have felt anything but happiness in having thrown off the yoke of subservience.

We felt quite differently when we thought of the position of those we had left behind us in Paris. We were far from supposing that the brutal audacity shown by the Parisians at all times in the Revolution would now be replaced by a stunned consternation and we had good reason to fear the excesses they might commit against those whose attachment to the King and the Royal Family was well known. But the farther we progressed on our way, the more hopeful we became: "When we have passed Châlons, we shall have nothing to fear," said the King. "We shall find the first detachment of troops at Pont-de-Sommevel and then we shall be out of danger." We got through Châlons without being recognized. From then onwards we felt perfectly secure and had no misgivings or fears that our happiness would soon end and would be replaced by a terrible catastrophe.

When we reached Pont-de-Sommevel we learnt with grief and anxiety from the couriers that they had found no trace of the soldiers and had met no one who could give them any information. They had not dared to ask questions for fear of arousing suspicion. We should have to hope that at Orbeval, the next post, we should be more fortunate. But our happiness was at an end.

We were no more lucky at Orbeval than at Pont-de-Sommevel. The same silence, the same anxiety. By the time we reached

Sainte-Menehould we were in a state of violent agitation. This was increased when M. d'Andouins, a captain in the regiment of the Duc de Choiseul, approached our carriage for a moment and said, "The arrangements have been bungled: I must move off, so as not to attract suspicion." These few words pierced our hearts, but there was nothing to be done, but to continue on our way and we did not allow ourselves to indulge in the smallest hesitation.

We reached Clermont without a hitch, but on our arrival in this town, Comte Charles de Damas, Colonel of the Dauphin's Regiment of Dragoons, who had not left his post in spite of the warning of the Duc de Choiseul, told us that the country was in a ferment and that he was going to do his best to turn out his regiment and escort the King's carriage. He tried to do this, but failed, as the authorities joined with the inhabitants in preventing the regiment from leaving the town and the troops refused to obey M. de Damas. He was tempted to see if he could carry them with him by telling them that they were going to escort the King and his family, but he did not dare to do this, fearing a refusal which would have resulted in the King's arrest. All he could do was to send an officer at full speed to warn de Bouillé and de Raigecourt that the King was arriving. But the bad luck which attended all the efforts of the King to escape from his cruel situation prevailed once more and the officer, who did not know the way properly, took the road for Verdun instead of that which led to Varennes and was too late to fulfil his mission. On a slope above this latter town we saw a man, who seemed to be hiding himself. Our disquiet increased. We believed ourselves betrayed and drove on in a mood of trouble and distress easier to imagine than to describe.

Our position was terrible and it became worse when on arriving at Varennes we found no relays of horses nor anyone who could tell us what had become of them. We knocked at a door and asked the people of the house if they knew anything about the fresh horses that should have been awaiting us. After failing to get any information that interested us, we tried, as a last resort, to get the postilions to undertake the next stage. We offered them money, if they would do this but they refused saying that their horses were too tired. So we told them to drive us to the last inn in the town, meaning to commence our journey as soon as the horses were rested.

The carriages continued on their way, but as that containing the women, which preceded the King's carriage, was passing in front of the house of a certain Sauce it was stopped and the occupants obliged to get out and show their passports. It was then eleven-thirty at night. We were told by the men of the Bodyguard what was happening but we had gone too far into the town to be able to turn back and so we drove on.

An officer approached the King's carriage and told the King there was a ford and offered to try to get him across it. But the King seeing that the number of persons round the carriage was continually increasing and noting their ill-temper, feared to occasion a gratuitous massacre of the party, and did not dare order the officer to proceed with his proposal. He merely told him to urge M. de Bouillé to make every effort to rescue him from his cruel situation.

In Varennes and the neighbourhood the tocsin was sounded and it was impossible not to realize that we had been recognized. The King held out for a good time and refused to say who he was or to leave the carriage, but so much pressure was put on him and promises given that we should be allowed to leave after our signatures had been examined that he could not resist any longer. The King entered the house of Sauce, who was the Attorney of the Commune, and went into an upper room, where the children were laid on a bed. Thoroughly exhausted they immediately fell into a calm and peaceful sleep, which provided a heart-rending contrast with the situation of their unhappy parents.

❧

Statement of the Duc de Choiseul, Colonel of the Royal Dragoons instructed to await with his men the berline of "Baroness de Korff" at Pont-de-Somme-Vesles, and to escort it as far as Stenay where Bouillé with his regiments would take it over.

The King who was due to leave at midnight had decided to send me on ten hours ahead of him and it was agreed that the

Queen should send me her groom-in-waiting, Léonard, a little before two o'clock in the afternoon with a letter from her and instructions to do everything I told him to do. My horses were ready and only one of my men was at my door and he thought I was returning to Metz. I had just sent another man on to Bondy on horseback and I awaited Léonard.

He duly arrived at two o'clock, wearing a round hat with the brim covering his eyes and a long riding-coat over his livery. He handed me a very long letter from the Queen, which she ordered me to burn. At the end of it she said, "I have ordered my valet to obey you, as he would me, and I now repeat that order."

After reading the letter over twice and reflecting on its contents I said to Léonard: "What did the Queen say to you?" He replied: "She sent for me at a quarter past one, shortly before sitting down to luncheon with the King. At that moment the King was talking in one of the windows with Madame Elisabeth, while M. le Dauphin and Madame were playing together. The Queen, leaning against the chimney-piece, said to me in a low voice: 'Léonard, can I count on you?' 'Ah, Madame, dispose of me as you will. I am your devoted servant.' 'Yes, and I am sure of your loyalty. Here is a letter. Take it to the Duc de Choiseul in the Rue d'Artois. Don't give it to anyone else but him. If he is not at home, he will be at the Duchesse de Grammont's. Put on a riding coat and a big round hat, so that you will not be recognized. Do exactly what he tells you, as though it were me—unthinkingly and without the slightest argument.' The Queen spoke very feelingly and added, 'Go quickly and give him many, many greetings from me.' I went at once," he added, "put on this riding coat and this hat and here I am ready to obey the Queen's orders."

"Are you quite sure," I asked him, "that the Queen meant you to do everything I should tell you to do?" "Yes, sir." "Now read these last lines which repeat the order." He read them and said, "Sir, it was not necessary to show them to me." Then I took a candle and burnt the letter. The man looked at me, wondering what it was all about. The doorkeeper came in to tell me that the carriage was waiting. "Let us go down," I said to Léonard. "I am going to drive you very quickly to a place a few leagues from

Paris to perform a special service." "Yes but, Sir, what shall I do? I have left my key at the Palace. My brother won't know what has become of me and I promised Mme de l'Aage to do her hair. She is expecting me. My cabriolet is waiting in the courtyard of the Tuileries to take me there. My God! How can I get all that straight?"

I laughed and assured him that orders had been given that his servant was not to worry and was to look after the horse, and that his brother had been told not to be anxious. He could dress Mme de l'Aage's hair another day. As I said this I made him get into the carriage, pulled down the blinds when we crossed the streets parallel to the boulevards, and we were soon driving at a smart pace on the road to Bondy.

When we got there we found post-horses ready and I continued on my way to Meaux. Léonard's astonishment increased every moment, and in order to make him forget his misgivings, as it was still too early to confide in him I talked to him about the domestic arrangements in the Queen's household and the women in her service. But he kept on worrying about his key, her servant and and Mme de l'Aage's hair-do and saying, "But, Sir, where are we going?" It was worse when we had passed Claye and he saw that I was going beyond Meaux. Then, looking very serious, I said to him: "Listen to me, Léonard, I am not taking you to a house near Paris. I am taking you to the frontier to a place near which my regiment is quartered. There I shall find a letter of the utmost importance addressed to the Queen. As I cannot deliver it myself, I had to find some trustworthy person to send it by. Her Majesty has chosen you as the man most worthy of her confidence."

"Oh! Sir, I surely will prove worthy of it: but how am I going to get back? As you see, I'm wearing white silk stockings and silk breeches. I have no linen and no money. My God! What shall I do?"

I said, "I have here in the carriage riding-boots, clothes, linen, money, everything you will need and you'll lack for nothing." After that his mind was only occupied with the problem of how to carry out his mission, with happiness at having been chosen for it, and with his own feelings of devotion to the Queen, who was so good that everyone should be ready to sacrifice himself for her.

Before we got to Montmirail, I told my courier that I would spend the night at the next posting house and ordered him to have supper got ready for us. I had more than one object in view. By this arrangement I could only arrive at Pont-de-Sommevelle on the Tuesday a little before noon and if I dined there, that would give me an excuse for staying there for as long as I wanted without attracting attention. Whereas, if I travelled through the night and arrived there early in the morning, I should have to wait there for eight or ten hours, which would not appear natural, seeing that I should only be three leagues away from Châlons, where all travellers stop. Besides, in this way, if I left Montmirail at four in the morning, I should be nearer to the King's carriage, and a courier could get in touch with me sooner in case of trouble.

After supper we lay down, but not to sleep. My mind was busy with calculations, and I reckoned, on the basis of the start which I had had from the first courier, each minute after one o'clock brought him nearer to me. I had ordered the horses for four o'clock. The room I had taken was just above the entrance gate. At three o'clock I heard the loud crack of a whip and a carriage drew up. I ran to the window and saw two persons wearing the uniform overcoats of the National Guard in a cabriolet. They were asking for horses and seemed in a violent hurry. Their urgency and their uniforms aroused my suspicions. I sent for my servant and told him that he was to have my horses harnessed as soon as the two travellers had started, but not to show himself till then. I wakened Léonard and as we had lain down in our clothes we were ready to start in a moment. I reached the next posting-station at the same time as these gentlemen. After which we drove in company until, between Etoge and Chaintry, they branched off down a side road leading towards Jalons or Epernay and so put an end to my early apprehensions. I learnt that these were two individuals who had a house in this neighbourhood and that they had come from la Ferté. No longer harassed by mis-givings about them, I continued on my way, passing through Châlons at six o'clock. All was quiet in the town. At eleven I arrived at Pont-de-Sommevelle. A short time before I had said to Léonard, "It is time to tell you the truth. I know that you are an honest man and a loyal one—the fact that the King and Queen have chosen you rather than anyone else is a proof of that. You are devoted to your Master and your Mistress?" "I would give my life for them—" "I believe you would. Well, in two hours' time they will be here." "Oh God! Is that possible?" "Yes, yes (as I spoke he burst into tears) they will be here with the children and with Mme Elisabeth. They are going to Montmédy, and they will be saved. Now, pull yourself together and remember that the slightest trace of anxiety or emotion might ruin everything. Dry your tears and take heart; we are just coming into Sommevelle. We shall remain here. In a few moments a detachment of hussars will arrive. I shall order them to halt here, and we shall prolong our dinner as much as possible so as to give us a pretext for remaining here. Now mind you don't look excited." With these words I soothed this faithful servant, who was in a touching state of emotion. We reached the door of the post-house, where I found M. Aubriot with my two saddle horses. I went into a room to put on my uniform.

The hussars had not yet arrived but they appeared an hour later and M. de Goguelet came into the room where I was changing. He gave me a bundle of papers from M. le Marquis de Bouillé. There were some orders in blank and a duplicate of a formal order from the King to all officers, of whatever rank or seniority, to obey me.

I had the horses picketed. The hussars knew nothing of what was happening. I had them supplied with bread and wine and we all ate and drank what I had been able to procure.

According to our calculations and the agreed plan, the courier would arrive at least one hour in advance of the King's carriage. We expected him at two and the carriage at three. But at three there was no sign of the courier or the carriage. We walked along the road one of us always going ahead and climbing on to high ground beside the road from which one could see to a distance. At four o'clock there was no news. I cannot describe the agony it caused me to have to master my emotion, to disguise my thoughts and to assume a mask of indifference, while all the time I was consumed with anxiety.

During these dreadful hours of waiting a new drama full of scenes of violence was beginning to be enacted around us. Chance or destiny had decreed that the peasants who cultivated a property belonging to Mme d'Elbeuf, near Pont-de-Sommevelle, had refused to pay those dues, which they could not redeem by work. They had been threatened with enforcement by the soldiery and the peasants of the neighbourhood had promised to come to their help. When they saw the hussars at Pont-de-Sommevelle, they thought they had come to execute the judgment, and the tocsin was sounded on our account throughout the countryside. The peasants collected in a crowd and we became an object of general distrust. Moreover, the people of Châlons had taken umbrage on seeing that a detachment of hussars had approached so close to the town for no known reason, and that late in the afternoon, as if they wished to wait till it was dark to start something. Some horsemen of the national gendarmerie were sent to identify us and to endeavour to find out for what purpose we were there. Furthermore, there was much traffic on the road with carriages coming and going all the time and, no doubt, the postilions mentioned the fact that the hussars were still at Pont-de-Sommevelle.

The hussars were the object of particular suspicion. They were distrusted alike by the authorities, the committees and the clubs. We were the target of ill-conditioned remarks and overt signs of dislike from a whole neighbourhood. The peasants said in our hearing, "The hussars are very smart, but we are smarter."

People had already begun to whisper that we were waiting for the Queen. Four o'clock struck and there was no sign of a courier and no news. All around us in the gathering crowds the popular disquiet increased every moment. I insisted on remaining where I was, but I decided to send my cabriolet to Stenay and told Léonard, whom I sent with it, to explain to M. de Damas, the young Bouillé and the General, as he passed through Varennes, that I was still in the same position and still waiting for news. I kept with me Madame Elisabeth's diamonds and I told my servant—who was going in the cabriolet—that if I was not in Stenay in the following morning he must go at once to Luxembourg. I gave him a short note for M. Dandoins at Sainte-Menehould, in which I spoke of the anxiety which this extraordinary delay was causing me and said that I might be obliged to move my detachment whose presence in the district was disturbing public tranquillity. However, the unrest increased visibly at Châlons. They talked of sending forward patrols of the National Guards as outposts against us and doubling the guards in the town and perhaps even shutting the gates of the town. In the midst of all this agitation and the movement of people in the streets would one not have good cause for alarm if a heavily-laden coach with two couriers and followed by a cabriolet appeared in the streets of Châlons? Would not this coach provoke the curiosity and attention of the whole town? Would it not be at least inspected considering the current rumours that we were expecting the Queen? And, quite independently of the formal orders I had received to preserve the King's incognito up to the last moment and to maintain by every possible means public order on the highway, would it not be a capital blunder on our part to create by our presence a situation dangerous to the King and not to put a stop to the popular ferment if we could do so by moving away from our present positions. My whole duty was summarized in the words "do everything possible to ensure that the coach continues on its way without interference". A prey to the most lively and cruel anxiety we heard the clocks strike five and our position became more and more fatal to the execution of our plan. Crowds gathered in even greater numbers and the national gendarmes who had been sent from Châlons scoffed openly at our explanations regarding a vehicle carrying bullion and called on us to tell the true reason why we were bivouack-ing there. Finally we became convinced that if we stayed, our presence in this place would inevitably result in the arrest of the King. There was no reason to hesitate any longer, since our de-parture seemed certain to restore calm. It was about half-past five, which meant that the courier was more than four hours late. I took advantage of the fact that there were a number of towns-people and gendarmes within hearing to ask if it was long since convoys of bullion had been despatched to Metz. He replied that one had gone through that morning carrying 100,000 écus in the stagecoach, according to traditional practice, with an escort of two national gendarmes. A gendarme, who had come from

Châlons, told me that he had been one of the escort. Then I turned to M. de Goguelat and said calmly: "No doubt that's the convoy we were waiting for. M. de Bouillé could not have known that it would be despatched in this manner. There is no point in our being here and the best thing we can do is to move off."

I ordered the hussars to bridle their horses. This order, which I gave with an air of indifference, had a sudden calming effect on the people. A gendarme wheeled his horse round and rode off to carry the news to Châlons. At a quarter to six my hussars were in the saddle and I gave orders to move off in fours and we set off at walking pace towards the short cut which leads to Varennes, avoiding Sainte-Menehould, and lies at a distance of one league from Orbeval, the next posting-station. I hoped that on our way there we might be caught up by the first courier.

I have already mentioned the arguments that M. de Goguelat, supported by M. Boudet, employed in urging me not to return through Sainte-Menehould. He repeated them before we arrived at the short cut. He said that a riot and perhaps a conflict would be inevitable if the hussars passed through the town again, where they would be sure to rouse to fury the people already ill-disposed towards us. I had to yield to these arguments, which I knew were sound. Moreover, I had every confidence in M. Dandoins who commanded my dragoons at Sainte-Menehould. M. le Comte Charles de Damas was with his regiment at Clermont. Thus we followed the short cut to Varennes, passing through all the woods in the Clermont district. At each village we had to take a guide, but as the villagers had much earlier been warned against us by the tocsin, I was several times obliged to force my way through by threatening to use sword or pistol.

At the village of Neuville the people went so far as to try to seize four hussars posted as a rearguard fifty yards behind the main body, and I was obliged to charge in order to get them away.

The way through these woods is extremely difficult and dangerous, with precipitous gradients up and down. Moreover, the distance was between nine and ten leagues. Darkness overtook us in the woods, where the going was most difficult, so that we often had to dismount and walk ahead to reconnoitre the ground and avoid falling into deep holes. A hussar did fall into one of these. His comrades did not want to leave him. He had to be found, picked up and restored to consciousness and this singularly unlucky accident put us back three-quarters of an hour. At last, after overcoming all sorts of obstacles, we reached the first house at Varennes between a quarter and half-past twelve, an hour and a half after the arrest of the King.

❧

Drouet, the son of the Posting-Master at Sainte-Menehould (the posting-station was the stage where carriages on long journeys changed postilions and horses) made the following statement, a few days later, to the members of the Paris Commune:

"Gentlemen, my name is Jean-Baptiste Drouet, and I am the Posting-Master at Sainte-Menehould. I was formerly in Condé's Dragoons. My comrade, M. Guillaume, is a clerk in the district-office. He formerly was in the Queen's Dragoons. On Tuesday the 22nd at half-past seven, after dinner, I saw two carriages in front of my door, namely a coach with six passengers and a cabriolet with two. These vehicles were accompanied by three couriers. In all they had eleven horses. In the coach there was a woman, whom I thought I recognized as the Queen, and on the seat in front of her to the left was a man. I was struck by the resemblance of his face to the likeness of the King printed on an assignat which I had with me at the time. Since the morning a detachment of about fifty dragoons had been stationed at the Inn nearby. The officer in charge went up to the carriages and spoke in a low voice to the couriers accompanying them. I noticed that the couriers took a lot of trouble to move the postilions away. They looked quite confused and kept repeating what they had said. My suspicions increased, but, being unwilling to cause a false alarm and having no one by me to consult, I let the carriages go. This I did most unwillingly. I was furious and ran about the place telling everyone that I believed the King was going away. I thought I had noticed that his face was pimply, but one of my uncles said I must have made a mistake. Perhaps I should have believed him if I had not seen the dragoons preparing to mount their horses. I then gave the alarm and made the drummer beat the call to arms. The National Guards armed themselves, and threatened to fire on the dragoons, forcing them to retreat to the inn. One of them got away and rode straight off towards Clermont, where he probably warned the King that he had been recognized at Sainte-Menehould. I then took a chance and sent some of my people to barricade the Bridge. I then looked about for a trustworthy person. M. Guillaume came forward and I urged him not to let the dragoons pursue us. So we went off swearing to our fellow citizens that we would catch up the King.

I met my postilions who had accompanied the King and who were coming out of Clermont at the moment that we were going in. They told me that instead of following the road to Metz, as the couriers had proposed at my posting-station, the carriages had driven towards Varennes after leaving Clermont. We went by a side-road through the woods and reached Varennes at the same time as the carriages which were drawn up alongside the houses at the top of the town. It was then about half-past eleven and the night was very dark. However, in order not to be recognized or suspected, we took off our cross-belts and only kept our swords and then, as we passed by the carriages at a walk, we said in a loud voice. "Good Lord! we'll be very late getting to Grandpré: perhaps we shan't get there with our horses dead-beat": thus trying to pass ourselves as merchants bound for the fair at Grandpré. The carriages had stopped because there is no posting-stage at Varennes, and the postilions would not go through without resting the horses. Further down the street we found an inn, where the people were still up. I took the landlord aside and said to him, "Are you a good patriot?" He replied. "You may be sure I am." "Very well, then," I went on, "the King is at the top of the hill. He'll be passing through soon. Go quickly and collect all the good citizens you know to prevent him getting away." He went off without a word. My comrade and I wanted at first to sound the alarm, but we thought that if we did so, the King might turn round and go off at a gallop before anyone could get there to prevent him and in that way would elude us. We went to the bridge, the only place where he could get through and fortunately found there a van full of old furniture.

We used it and other vehicles we found in the neighbourhood to
block the bridge. We did all this in less time than it takes to tell
you about it. On this side of the bridge we saw some dismounted
hussars whose horses were on the other side. Then we ran to the
Mayor and the Commandant of the National Guards. In less than
five minutes we had collected eight or ten armed men . . . and
then we marched in front of the coach which was coming down
the street. We stopped it. The district attorney questioned the
travellers—who were they and where were they going? A lady
replied that she was the Baroness de Korff (the name appeared
to be German). She said she was a foreigner and that she was on
her way to Frankfort. She was in a hurry and hoped that she
would be allowed to pass. Asked if she had a passport, she said yes,
but that she did not think it necessary to have it examined.
We insisted. The passport was brought into the inn by two ladies
in attendance on her. It was read and several persons thought it
was in order. I maintained that it was worthless because it was not
countersigned by the President of the National Assembly. While
the passport was being examined, I said to the two ladies that
I could not believe that the "baroness" was a foreigner, because
if that were so she would not have the privilege in France of
being escorted by detachments of dragoons and hussars. I pre-
sumed that it was the King and the Queen who were in the berline.
My remarks caused the others to discuss the advantage of keeping
the travellers until the next morning. The Mayor and the
Attorney asked them to leave the coach, which they did without
resistance. They then went to the house of the district attorney
where they confessed who they were. The King said, "Here is
my wife, here are my children, we adjure you to show to us the
consideration which Frenchmen have always shown to their
King." They were assured that they were under the protection
of the law and that they had nothing to fear. This was related to
me because during the conversation I was down below talking
to the hussars, who were coming up with drawn swords and
occupying the street. They numbered perhaps 150. Besides them
the street contained about 100 men most of them armed and a
great many women and children. The officer in command of the
hussars, M. de Douglas or Jouglas, said that he wished to speak

to the King and to guard him. He was told that he would neither guard him nor even see him. I added that if he thought he was going to snatch the King away from us, all he would get was death at our hands. I ran into the street and exhorted the women to go back to their houses, but to take with them stones to throw at the hussars, if they started any trouble. All this lasted for less than half an hour. Meantime the Commander of the National Guard had two small pieces of artillery placed at the top of the street and two others at the bottom, leaving a space between them about the length of the Pont-Neuf, so that the hussars would be between two fires. He ordered the officer commanding the detachment to make his men dismount and withdraw from the town. Instead of that they showed signs of slipping behind the cannons and seizing them. I seized the bridle of M. de Jouglas' horse and pushing my pistol into his chest, I cried: "Gunners, stand to. Fire if anyone moves." They took up their positions and held up the fuses, on which the hussars retreated. Then after conferring together they came and threw themselves into the arms of the National Guards. Since then they have behaved very well. Their commanding officer escaped. They made a great mistake in giving in so easily, for the guns were not loaded.

Meanwhile in Paris, La Fayette had issued a warrant for the arrest of Louis XVI. The Assembly, presided over by an Aristocrat of the Extreme left, Beauharnais (the husband of a beautiful Creole, Joséphine) was in session when two couriers covered with dust brought them the news on the evening of the 24th that the King had been found at Varennes. The deputies delegated three of their number to go to Varennes and take charge of the situation—these were Pétion, Barnave and La Tour-Maubourg.

Pétion tells the story of his journey. Here is a thumbnail sketch of the narrator, as seen by the Swiss, Etienne Dumont.

He had the comfortable corpulence of a lazy man and looked reasonably good natured. But he was vain and regarded himself as a great orator, because he always improvised like Barnave. He lacked wit and there was nothing striking about him—no power of expression or of thought.

PÉTION:

We discussed at length what would be our attitude towards the King. Each of us said, "The fat pig has become a serious embarrassment." "Will they shut him up?" said one. "Will he go on reigning?" asked another. "Will they give him a Privy Council?"

La Fayette made jokes and sneered. Duport could not understand the situation. At a moment when everyone seemed to be letting himself go, I clearly noticed a strong undercurrent of constraint. I refrained from joining those people, who were obviously playing their cards with care and had doubtless already worked out a line of conduct.

Barnave kept us waiting a long time and we did not get away until four in the morning.

At the city gate we were held up for a while, as no one was allowed to pass and I foresaw that we might have to go back... but all was well. We left in very fine weather and the postilions, who were aware of the object of our journey, drove with great speed.

During the whole of our journey we only stopped for long enough to swallow a scrap of food. At Ferté-sous-Jouarre a procession delayed us for a moment. We got down and went to an inn for luncheon. The municipal officers joined us there, and a great throng of citizens surrounded us: we did not lie down.

When we reached Dormans, where we were intending to drive, some couriers came to say that the King had left Châlons that morning and that he could not be far from Epernay. Others told us that he had been followed by Bouillé's troops and that he might be snatched away from us at any moment. Several persons said, in confirmation of this, that they had seen the cavalry riding through the woods.

Nothing seemed more probable, or more in keeping with this character than a new attempt at rescue by M. Bouillé. We said to one another, "He would sooner perish than abandon the King."

We stayed just long enough to eat a mouthful standing up and to drink a glass and then resumed our journey.

My companions had throughout treated me with the greatest

circumspection and reserve and our talk had been on general subjects. There was only one moment when my suspicions had been roused. Someone had brought up the question of what to do with the King. Maubourg said, "He's a beast that has let itself be driven. Poor devil! one can't help being sorry for him." Barnave remarked that one could fairly regard him as an imbecile. "What do you think about it, Pétion?" he said to me. At the same moment he made a sign to Maubourg—one of those signals meant to put the person to whom it is made on his guard against a third person, who is not meant to see it. However, it is possible that knowing how austere and inflexible my principles were he merely meant to say, "Pétion will condemn him with all the vigour of the law just as if he were an ordinary citizen."

Nevertheless, I replied that I did not dismiss the idea of treating the King as mentally defective, incapable of occupying the throne and in need of a guardian, which might be a national advisory council. On this there were objections, replies and rejoinders. We also spoke of a Regency and the difficulty of choosing a Regent.

M. Dumas was not in the same carriage with us. On leaving Dormans, M. Dumas examined the terrain with the eye of a general. "If M. de Bouillé does come," he said, "he can only get through here. He can be stopped on the height here or in the defile down there. There is no room for his cavalry to manœuvre." He even made certain military dispositions ordering the National Guard of a township to occupy such and such positions.

These precautions seemed not only useless but ridiculous. We laughed over them and I must admit that M. Dumas himself found them amusing. However, the country people took him very seriously and genuinely expected to have to fight.

The zeal by which these good people were animated was really admirable. They flocked from all parts, old men, women and children, some armed with spits or scythes, others with sticks, swords or unserviceable guns. They came as gaily as to a wedding. Husbands embraced their wives and said, "Well, if needs be, we'll go to the frontier to kill this beggar this b—— b——. We shall get him all right, whatever they do." They ran beside our carriage, applauding and crying, "Long live the Nation!" I was astonished and touched by this sublime spectacle.

More couriers arrived announcing the arrival of the King. At a distance of about a league and a half from Epernay as we were driving along a splendid road, we saw far away a cloud of dust and soon heard a loud clatter. Several people came up to our carriage and called out: "There's the King." We pulled up our horses and advanced slowly towards an immense crowd, finally leaving our carriage. The King's carriage halted and we walked up to it, preceded by an usher, observing the ceremonial in the most imposing fashion. As soon as we were observed, someone cried out, "Here come the deputies of the National Assembly!" Everyone made way for us. Order and silence were called for. The procession was superb. There were National Guards on horseback and on foot, some wearing uniform and others not, carrying arms of all sorts. The sinking sun illuminated this wonderful assemblage in the midst of the peaceful countryside. I do not know whether the importance of the moment gave birth to incalculable thoughts, but how various and exalted were the feelings of the people! I cannot describe the respect with which we were enveloped. What a tremendous power the Assembly wields! I said to myself: what a mark it has made on all hearts. Is there anything it cannot do? How guilty it would be if it failed to respond by its actions to the limitless confidence and the touching love of the people!

In the midst of the horses, the clank of arms and the applause of the crowd attracted by their own zeal, but anxious not to hustle us, we reached the carriage door. It was immediately thrown open. Confused sounds were heard. The Queen and Madame Elisabeth, deeply moved, and in tones of anguished entreaty and with tears in their eyes, "Gentlemen, Oh, Monsieur Maubourg!" taking his hand to beg for mercy, "Oh, Monsieur!" taking Barnave's hand also, while Madame Elisabeth merely laid her hand on mine. "Do not allow a disaster to befall, do not victimize those who have accompanied us, spare their lives! The King had no intention of leaving France!" "No, gentlemen, I was not going out of the country. I had already declared my intention not to leave and I repeat that is true." This poignant scene lasted for only a minute, but how vividly it impressed me! Maubourg said something in reply and I uttered some soothing

ejaculations and a few insignificant phrases expressing dignity
without harshness and kindness without affectation. Then changing the subject, I explained in a few words to the King the nature
of our mission and read to him the decree which I was carrying.
During these moments perfect silence reigned.

I then walked round to the other side of the carriage and called
for silence. Then I read aloud to the citizens the decree ordering
the return of the King. The crowd applauded. Then M. Dumas
took command of all the Guards who up to then had been accompanying the King. These made their submission in admirable
fashion. They gave joyful recognition to the military chief, who
now placed himself at their head. As the Assembly had chosen
him, he seemed to have become an object of reverence for them.

We told the King that it was appropriate that we should take
our seats in his carriage. Barnave and I got in, but as soon as we
had set foot inside we said, "But, Sire, we shall incommode you,
we shall crowd you. It is impossible to make room for us here."
The King replied, "I do not want any of those who have accompanied me so far to leave the carriage. I beg you to sit down, we
shall sit close and make room for you."

The King, the Queen and the Prince Royal were on the back
seat and Madame Elisabeth, Mme de Tourzel and Madame on the
front. The Queen took the Dauphin on her knees and Barnave
placed himself between the King and the Queen: Mme de Tourzel
took Madame on her lap and I sat between her and Madame
Elisabeth.

We had not driven ten paces before they once more started
protesting that the King had not meant to leave the Kingdom and
expressing the liveliest anxiety regarding the fate of three members of the Bodyguard who were sitting on the box. They all
talked across one another and all seemed to be saying the same
thing as if they were repeating a watchword, but there was no
measure, no dignity in this conversation and I did not remark
on any of their faces a trace of the grandeur, often very impressive,
which misfortune lends to noble souls.

After the first bout of cackling was over, I perceived an air of
simplicity and family feeling which pleased me. There was no
longer any royal show-off—just easy manners and good natured

domesticity. The Queen called Madame Elisabeth her little sister and Madame Elisabeth responded in the same terms. Madame Elisabeth called the King, my brother. The Queen danced the prince upon her knees and Madame, though more reserved, played with her brother. The King watched his family with a satisfied air, though he seemed unemotional and insensitive.

Raising my eyes to the roof of the carriage I perceived a gold-braided hat in the net. It was obviously part of the King's disguise and I must confess that I was shocked at the thought that they should have allowed to subsist any trace whatever of an action, which it should have been their care to blot out completely from the memory. From time to time I raised my eyes involuntarily to look at the hat, but I do not know if they saw me doing so.

I also examined the garments of the travellers. They could not have been more shabby. The King was wearing a brown plush costume and his linen was very dirty. The women wore very common day dresses.

The King talked of an accident that had happened to a nobleman, who had had his throat cut, and he seemed much affected by the circumstance. The Queen repeated that it was abominable, saying that he had done much good in his district and that it was his own people who had murdered him.

. Another incident had affected her deeply. She complained bitterly of the suspicious attitude of the people towards her during the journey. "Would you believe it?" she said, "I was going to give the leg of a chicken to one of the National Guards, who seemed to be following us very faithfully, when they started calling to the man, 'be careful, don't eat it!' giving him to understand it might be poisoned. Oh! I tell you their suspicion made me indignant, so I immediately shared the chicken among my children and ate some of it myself."

As soon as she had ended this story she said, "Gentlemen this morning we went to mass at Châlons, but it was a constitutional mass." Madame Elisabeth confirmed this, but the King said nothing. I could not help replying that this was as it should be for it was only such masses that the King should listen to. But I greatly disliked this sort of banter especially in the circumstances in which the King found himself.

The Queen and Madame Elisabeth kept on reverting to the men of the Bodyguard, who were on the driving-seat of the coach, and displaying the utmost anxiety.

"As far as I am concerned," said Mme de Tourzel, in dry and determined tones (up to then she had kept silence), "I have done my duty in remaining with the children who have been entrusted to me. They can do what they like with me. I have no cause to reproach myself. If I had to do it again I should do just what I have done."

The King spoke very little and the conversation ceased to be general. The Queen talked to Barnave and Madame Elisabeth to me just as if each of them had said, "You look after your neighbour and I'll look after mine."

Madame Elisabeth gazed at me with soft eyes and with that languid air which unhappiness engenders and which inspires one with lively interest. Our eyes met now and then with a kind of understanding and mutual attraction: night had come and the moon began to shed its gentle light. Madame Elisabeth took Madame on her knee, half on mine. Her head was supported by my hand and she fell asleep. I stretched out my arm and Madame Elisabeth stretched out hers over mine. Our arms were interlaced and mine touched her armpit. I felt a hurried movement of her heart and a warmth passing out through her clothes. Madame Elisabeth's glance seemed to grow ever more touching. I noticed a certain abandonment in her attitude, her eyes were moist and her melancholy appeared to be mingled with a sort of pleasure. Perhaps I was wrong, because it is easy to confuse the sensibility caused by sorrow with that deriving from pleasure. All the same I believe that if we had been alone, if by some enchantment all the others had disappeared, she would have fallen into my arms and abandoned herself to the promptings of nature.

I was so struck by this thought that I said to myself. What! Can this be a trick to buy my loyalty? Had Madame Elisabeth agreed to sacrifice her honour in order to make me lose mine? Why yes, at the Court, they stick at nothing, there is nothing they will not do. The Queen may have devised the plan. But then, thinking how natural she looked, and prompted by my own self-esteem to believe that she might find me attractive and realizing as well that she was of an age when passions are powerful, I persuaded myself—and it gave me pleasure to do so—that she was the prey of lively emotions and that she herself would have liked us to be together without witnesses and would have welcomed those gentle approaches and caresses so delicate that her modesty would surrender without being offended and that her defeat would be accomplished with no shock to her sensibility, with passion and nature alone to blame.

We drove slowly, accompanied by a large escort. Madame Elisabeth talked about the men of the Bodyguard, who were attached to them. She spoke of them with a tender interest and her voice had a strange, flattering tone. Sometimes she interrupted her speech in a troubling manner. I replied with a gentleness equal to her own, but without showing weakness and with a certain austerity devoid of harshness. I took good care not to compromise my character. I was as forthcoming as I thought I ought to be in view of her position, without saying anything which could lead her to believe or even suspect that my integrity could be undermined. I think she realized this perfectly and understood that her most seductive allurements would be powerless to affect me, for I remarked in her a certain cooling-off and a certain distance often observable in women, whose vanity is wounded.

We gradually approached Dormans. I looked at Barnave several times and, though the half-light made it impossible to distinguish things very clearly, his attitude towards the Queen seemed honest and reserved, and there was nothing mysterious about their conversation.

We came into Dormans between midnight and one o'clock. Here we went to the inn and had a meal. Considering the smallness of the place the inn was very clean but it was hardly suitable to receive the Royal Family.

All the same it did not upset me that the court should learn what an ordinary inn was like. The King got down from the carriage and we followed him. There were no cries of *Vive le Roi!* They all cried *Vive la Nation* and *Vive l'Assemblée Nationale*— and there were also shouts of *Vive Barnave* and *Vive Pétion*. This had been our experience throughout the journey.

We went up to the upper floor and sentinels were at once

D

posted at the door of every room. The King, the Queen, Madame Elisabeth, the Prince, Madame and Mme de Tourzel had supper together, while Maubourg, Barnave, Dumas and I supped in another room. We wrote our despatches for the National Assembly. I went to bed at three in the morning and Barnave came later and slept in the same bed. I was already asleep when he came. We rose at five.

The King was alone in a room, where there was a rickety iron bed. He spent the night in an armchair.

It was difficult to sleep in the inn, because the National Guards and all the inhabitants from round about had collected to drink, sing and dance round dances.

Before leaving Messrs. Dumas, Maubourg, Barnave and I inspected the National Guards. We were very well received.

We took our seats in the coach between five and six and this time I sat between the King and the Queen. We were very uncomfortable. The young Prince came and sat on my knees and played with me: he was in high spirits, but he could not keep still.

The King wanted to talk. He began by asking insignificant questions as a preliminary to more important things. He wanted to know if I was married. I said I was. Had I any children? Yes, a boy older than his son. From time to time I drew his attention to the beauty of the landscape. We were then traversing a range of hills, from which we had a fine and varied prospect. The Marne flowed by below us. "What a beautiful country France is!" I said. "There is no Kingdom in the world that can be compared to it." I uttered these words on purpose to see what impression they made on the King. But his face remained painfully expressionless and impassive and I came to the conclusion that this mass of flesh was devoid of feeling. He wanted to talk to me about the English, their industry and their genius for commerce. He uttered a few sentences and then became embarrassed and blushed. I noticed on several occasions that his difficulty in expressing himself made him shy. Those who did not know him would mistake this shyness for stupidity, but they would be wrong. He very seldom speaks away from the point and I have never heard him say anything downright stupid.

He kept studying the regional maps which he had with him

and saying, "Now we are here in such and such a department, district or locality." The Queen talked with me aptly and familiarly. She spoke about the education of her children. She talked as the mother of a family and a well-educated woman. She expressed some very just views on the subject of education. She said that no flattery should be permitted to approach the ears of princes and that they should never be told anything but the truth. However, I have since learnt that this was the fashionable jargon in all the courts of Europe. A very enlightened woman told me that she was fairly well acquainted with five or six princesses all of whom had used the same language, without, however, occupying themselves for a minute with the education of their children.

Moreover, it did not take me long to perceive that everything she said to me was completely superficial and that she never gave expression to a striking thought or an original idea. She possessed in no sense either the demeanour or the mental attitude consonant with her position.

I saw, however, that she wanted to be taken for a woman of character. She frequently repeated that one ought to have character and an incident occurred which made me realize that what she defined as character was something so insignificant, that I was sure she did not possess the real thing.

The windows of the carriage were still down and we were being roasted by the sun and stifled by the dust, but as the country people and the National Guards were keeping pace with us, we could not arrange things otherwise because everyone wanted to see the King.

However, the Queen took an opportunity to draw down the blind. At the time she was eating the leg of a pigeon. The people began to grumble and Madame Elisabeth was for pulling it up again, but the Queen objected and said, "No: one must have character." She then waited for the precise moment when the people stopped grumbling, to pull up the blind herself, wishing to convey the impression that she had not done so because the people had demanded it. Then she threw the pigeon's leg out of the window and repeated the expression she had used. "One must have character at all costs."

This was a trifling episode, but it impressed me more than I can say.

As she entered la Ferté-sous-Jouarre we found a great gathering of citizens crying *"Vive la Nation! Vive l'Assemblée Nationale! Vive Barnave! Vive Pétion!"* I noticed that these cries made a disagreeable impression on the Queen and especially on Madame Elisabeth. The King appeared indifferent, but the embarrassed expressions on the faces of the ladies made me feel embarrassed too.

The Mayor of la Ferté-sous-Jouarre had sent us a message to say that we would receive the King and the King had accepted this invitation. The Mayor's house is extremely pretty and its walls are bathed by the Marne. The garden is well laid out and well looked after, and there is a very pleasant terrace running along the river.

I strolled with Madame Elisabeth along the terrace before dinner and there I talked to her with all the frankness and force I possess. I explained to her that the King was surrounded with bad friends and evil counsellors. I spoke of all the intrigues and manœuvres of the people about the court with the dignity of a free man and the disdain of a wise one. I put force and persuasion into the expression of my sentiments and my righteous indignation gave to the language of reason an element of attraction. She seemed to be listening to what I said and to be touched by my words. I know she enjoyed my talk and I enjoyed talking to her. I should be surprised if she had not a fine and honest soul, although deeply imbued with the prejudices of birth and spoilt by the shortcomings of a court education. Barnave talked for a short time with the Queen but their conversation, as far as I could guess, was of no great interest.

The King came on to the terrace to invite us to dine with him. We conferred—Maubourg, Barnave and I—and discussed whether we should accept. "Familiarity of this kind," said one of us, "might appear suspicious. As it is not etiquette for him to invite us, people might believe that he has done so because he finds himself in an unfortunate situation." We agreed to refuse and went to tell the King that we had to attend to our correspondence which precluded us from accepting the honour which he offered us.

The King and his family were served in a separate room, and

we dined in another. The dinner was splendid. At five o'clock we resumed our journey. As we left la Ferté there was a commotion and some noise around the carriage. The citizens broke the ranks of the National Guards, who wished to prevent them from approaching the carriage. I saw one of our deputies, Kervelegan, fighting his way through the crowd and quarrelling with the National Guards, who were trying to push him back. However, he reached the carriage door swearing and saying, "Here's a lot of fuss for a brute like that!" I put my head out of the window to speak to him. He seemed in a great rage and said: "Are they all there? Take care, they are still talking of rescuing them. You are sitting with some very stuck-up people in there."

Then he withdrew and the Queen said to me with an air of annoyance mixed with fright, "What a rude man!" I replied that he was cross with the Guards, who had been rough with him. She still seemed afraid and the young Prince let out one or two cries of fear.

Meanwhile we proceeded quietly on our way. The Queen, next to whom I was sitting, frequently addressed me and I had the opportunity to tell her with perfect frankness what people thought of the court and what was said about all the intriguers who frequented the Palace.

We talked of the National Assembly, of the right-wing and the left-wing parties, with the informality of friends. I did not stand on ceremony in the least and mentioned to her several topics which were current at the court and which set the people against them. I referred to the newspapers which the King read. The King, who was listening attentively to all this conversation, said to me, "I assure you that I don't read 'L'Ami du Roi' any more than Marat does."

The Queen appeared to take the keenest interest in this discussion. She kept it alive, egging me on, and interpolating subtle and critical observations.

"That is all very well," she said "they blame the King greatly, but they don't really appreciate his situation. He is constantly hearing contradictory reports and does not know what to believe. And all the time he has to listen to advisers who disagree with one another and whose counsels are mutually destructive. He does not know what to do. His position is unhappy, indeed untenable. People only talk to him about private misfortunes and murders. It was all this that prompted him to leave Paris, his capital. His crown," she added, "is trembling on his head. You must know that there is a party, which wants no King and which is daily growing larger."

I thought I clearly perceived the Queen's intention in letting these last words escape her: in other words I could not mistake the meaning she sought to convey.

"Well, Madame," I said, "I will speak to you with all sincerity and I believe you will not suspect my good faith. I am one of those persons described as republicans and, if you wish to know, one of the leaders of the party. It would take too long fully to develop my ideas and, I may say, there are some republics to which I should prefer the despotism of a monarch. But it is none the less true, and I do not ask you to agree with me, that almost everywhere Kings have brought misfortune on mankind, that they have treated their fellow men as their chattels and that surrounded as they are by courtiers and sycophants they have seldom been able to free themselves from the vices implanted by their education. But, Madame, is it true to say that there exists at present a republican party which wishes to overthrow the Constitution to erect another on its ruins? It suits some people to spread this rumour in order to give themselves a pretext for forming another party outside the Constitution, a non-constitutional royalist party with the object of fermenting civil strife. The trap is too obvious. One cannot in good faith persuade oneself that the party styled republican is a menace. It is composed of sensible, honourable men, with the power of foreseeing events, who would never risk a general upheaval which might more easily lead to despotism than to liberty.

"Ah, Madame, the King would indeed have been well-advised, if he had sincerely favoured the Revolution. The troubles, which now agitate the state, would not exist, the Constitution would be functioning and our foreign enemies would respect us. The people are only too prone to cherish and idolize their kings."

I cannot describe with what energy and eloquence I spoke. I was inspired by the circumstances and especially by the idea that the seeds of truth which I was casting before her might fructify and that the Queen might bear this conversation in mind.

On reaching Meaux the King, his family and our party put up at the Bishop's Palace. The Bishop was a "constitutional" prelate, a fact which could not be very pleasing to the King, but he showed no sign of disapproval. Sentries were posted at all the gates.

The King supped very lightly and retired early to his apartment. As he had no underlinen, he borrowed a nightshirt from the usher who accompanied us.

We had food brought to us in our rooms. After a light and hurried supper we wrote our despatches. We left Meaux at six in the morning.

I resumed my original place between Madame Elisabeth and Mme de Tourzel, while Barnave sat between the King and Queen. I do not remember a longer or more tiring day. The heat was extreme and we were enveloped in a swirl of dust. On several occasions the King offered me something to drink and poured it out for me. We stayed for twelve whole hours in the carriage without getting out for a moment. What surprised me particularly was that the Queen, Madame Elisabeth and Mme de Tourzel showed no desire to get out.

The young Prince made water two or three times. The King himself unbuttoned his breeches and made him piss into a large silver cup. Once Barnave held the cup. It has been claimed that the coach contained an English convenience. It may have been so, but I saw no sign of it. One thing I did notice was that Mademoiselle remained sitting on my knees without getting down, while before she had been sitting either in Mme de Tourzel's lap or in Madame Elisabeth's.

I think that this was prearranged and that it was felt that while she was on my knees she was in a safe and sacred place and that the people, if there was trouble, would respect her there. We proceeded quietly as far as Pantin. The Cavalry who had accompanied us from Meaux and a detachment from Paris acted as our escort and surrounded the carriage.

When the National footguards had joined us a little before Pantin there was a row which looked as if it might have serious consequences.

The Grenadiers tried to push the horses back and the cavalry resisted and the chasseurs joined the Grenadiers in their efforts to drive the cavalry back. A brawl developed attended by insulting language; fighting was imminent. Men carrying bayonets kept running round the carriage, whose windows were open. It was quite possible that in the midst of this tumult, ill-disposed persons might have struck the Queen. I saw some soldiers looking very angrily at her. Soon they began to swear at her: "Look at the bitch," they cried in their rage, "it's no good her showing us her child. Everyone knows it isn't his." The King heard these words very clearly and the young Prince, frightened by the noise and the clank of arms screamed a few times. The Queen soothed him, with tears rolling down her cheeks.

Barnave and I seeing that things might become serious went to the windows and harangued the soldiers, who showed confidence in us. The Grenadiers said, "Don't be afraid. No harm will be done to anyone: we answer for that, but the post of honour belongs to us." It was, as it turned out a quarrel for precedence, but it might have become embittered and have led to violence.

When the post of honour had finally been allocated to the Grenadiers, there was no more friction. We progressed very slowly, but no obstacles detained us. Instead of entering Paris by the Porte Saint-Denis, we went round the walls and entered the city by the Porte de la Conférence.

The crowds were immense and it seemed as though the whole population of Paris and its suburbs had gathered in the Champs Elysées. Human eyes have never beheld a grander spectacle. The roofs of the houses were covered with men, women and children. They climbed on to the city gates and up the trees. Everyone had a hat on his head: a majestic silence reigned: the National Guards held their muskets, butt upwards. This forceful stillness was occasionally broken by cries of "*Vive la Nation!*" The names of Barnave and myself could sometimes be heard amidst these cries, which made a painful impression on our fellow-travellers, especially on Madame Elisabeth. A remarkable thing was that not once did I hear a hostile word against the King: They contented themselves with crying "*Vive la Nation!*"

We crossed the river by the swivel-bridge which was

immediately closed and denied to traffic. All the same there were many people in the Tuileries, mostly National Guards. A group of deputies came out of the chamber to witness the spectacle. Among these was Monsieur d'Orléans, which seemed inconsiderate, to say the least. As we arrived in front of the iron gateway leading into the Palace, at the foot of the first terrace, I thought there was going to be bloodshed. The National Guards thronged closely round the carriage in a disorderly mob and refused to listen to reason. The men of the Bodyguard on the box seat excited their indignation and the rage of the spectators. The Guards threatened them with their bayonets and showered terrible curses on them. I foresaw the moment when they would be massacred in front of our eyes. I leaned out of the carriage window and addressed the Guards in the name of the law, adjuring them to abstain from a terrible crime which would dishonour the citizens of Paris. Then I told the men of the Bodyguard that they could come down—I ordered them to do so with an authority they could not disobey. They were seized somewhat roughly but were protected from the crowd and no harm came to them.

Some deputies forcing their way through the people joined us and lent their support, exhorting the crowd to good behaviour in the name of the law.

At this moment M. de La Fayette appeared on horseback in the midst of the bayonets and spoke with warm feeling. He did not succeed in restoring calm but it was easy to see that the crowd had no ill intentions.

The carriage doors were opened. The King got out, greeted with silence. The Queen's appearance was received with violent expressions of disapproval, but the children with good humour and even with endearments. I allowed everybody, including the deputies, to pass in front of me and brought up the rear. By the time I reached the gate, it had been closed and I had a humiliating experience before being admitted. A guard seized me by the collar and was going to reprimand me, not knowing who I was, when they stopped him. My identity was disclosed to him and he made voluble excuses. Then I went up to the Royal apartments. The King and the Queen were in the room before you came to the King's bedchamber, looking like ordinary travellers, tired, untidy and leaning against the furniture.

An original and piquant scene was enacted when Corollaire, a deputy, approached the King and speaking in the style of a schoolmaster, mitigated by a streak of good-humour, reprimanded him as one would a naughty schoolboy. "That was a nice way to behave!" he said. "That comes of having bad advisers. You are a good man and you are liked, but see what a mess you have got into!" And then he burst into tears. Without being present at the scene, one can hardly picture to oneself this fantastic dressing-down.

After a few minutes Maubourg, Barnave and I passed through into the King's apartments. The Queen and Madame Elisabeth went in at the same time. Already all the men servants were assembled there wearing their usual livery. It seemed as though the King was returning from a day's sport. His valets attended to his toilet. If one looked at him observantly, one would never have guessed that he had gone through so much. He was as phlegmatic and impassive as though nothing had happened to him. He immediately began to play his part as King and the persons surrounding him acted as if unaware of the events that had removed the Sovereign for several days and had now brought him back again. I was confounded by what I saw.

We told the King to give us the names of the three members of his Bodyguard, which he did.

As I was absolutely exhausted and panting with thirst I begged Madame Elisabeth to be good enough to order us some refreshments. This she did at once and we had just time to drink two or three glasses of beer. We then went to the men of the Bodyguard and put them under arrest. We also instructed M. de la Fayette to place Mme de Tourzel under supervision, and entrusted him with the custody of the King. He told us that he could not be responsible for anything, unless he could place sentinels even in the King's bedroom and he made us realize that the Assembly should give a positive ruling on this subject. We expressed our agreement and left him, going at once to the Assembly to give a succinct account of our mission.

⚜

Madame de Tourzel remained throughout loyal to the Royal Family. When they were imprisoned at the Conciergérie, she asked to be allowed to share their imprisonment. This was refused, and when Madame Royale remained the sole survivor, she begged to be allowed to be imprisoned with her in the Temple. This favour was also denied her, but the young princess received frequent visits from her former governess. Mme de Tourzel built in the park of her house at Abondant, near Dreux, a small expiatory monument. She died at the age of eighty-two in 1832.

Axel de Fersen was removed from France after the arrest of the Royal Family. He lost his life in 1810, massacred by insurgents in Sweden. He was accused of having plotted the murder of the King's brother, a very popular prince.

Pétion, a lawyer from Chartres, who was elected a deputy in the States General, became Mayor of Paris after the resignation of Bailly in November 1791 (see the tenth of August). During Robespierre's dictatorship he was arrested, but managed to escape and wandered from one hiding place to another. His body was found half-eaten by wolves in a field near Saint Emilion. It is believed that he had poisoned himself.

Jean-Baptiste Drouet refused the reward of 30,000 francs granted to him by the Assembly after Varennes. He got himself elected deputy a year later and joined the leftists. He voted for the death of the King. Later while he was on a mission to the army, he was captured by the Austrians, tortured and kept chained in an iron cage at Brussels. In 1795 he was included in a group of prisoners exchanged against Madame Royale. He was appointed a Sub-Prefect by Napoleon and afterwards banished at the Restoration. Later he returned secretly to France and lived for the rest of his life at Macon under the name of Meyer. Napoleon, when conferring a decoration on him, had said: "You have changed the face of the world."

THE ÉMIGRÉS

❊❊

AT THIS time emigration had become positively fashionable. The hackney-cab, the hired carriages and the vehicles used by the court commonly known as chamber-pots arrived daily at Coblentz. The prostitutes of Paris also took part in the movement. They openly insulted the gentlemen and officers, who showed no disposition to emigrate, by offering them spindles.

The foregoing words were uttered by an émigré, the Marquis de Bouthillier. Here is a contribution from an émigrée, Mme de Gontaut (see the Fourteenth of July), who tells the story of her own departure for Coblentz, one of the rallying points of the Aristocrats on their way to join the united armies of Prussia and Austria, under the leadership of the Duke of Brunswick, the most illustrious general in Europe:

Towards the end of this year my mother was obliged to return to Paris to settle my father's estate. She had difficulty in returning. I had received some friendly letters from Mlle d'Orléans, pressing me to return. I was touched and wanted to see her again. My mother had a distaste for Bellechasse which my young heart could not understand. They had received me so kindly there that I wanted to go back but had not been allowed to do so. However, soon after my return to Paris, Mademoiselle wrote to invite me to a very small dance. It was difficult to be always refusing and eventually my mother consented to take me but so unwillingly that she forbade me to dress up so that I should be able to cut short my visit, if it was desirable.

As we entered the pavilion at Bellechasse, my mother saw at

the top of the stairs the Duke of Orleans talking with a personage, whose name I have forgotten but who made a very painful impression on my poor mother. We entered the drawing room. Mme de Genlis was there, unpowdered (at that time powder was still in fashion). Her strange costume consisted of a tri-colour dress and her face seemed to me to have changed and to have lost its customary charm. They were dancing and it pains me to add that the orchestra was playing the air *"Ah! ça ira, etc."* They had turned that horrible refrain into a quadrille and the tune was sung and hummed all over Paris. The Duc de Chartres asked me to dance, but my mother would not let me. Her refusal caused quite a sensation round us. My mother, noticing this, said, "Oh! Josephine, you wanted to come. Why was I so weak as to allow you to?"

The little princes noticed the distress which my mother's grief was causing me, and lowered their voices. My mother suffered agonies. I perceived this and urged her to leave, making the excuse that she was unwell. We left Bellechasse and never went back there.

As soon as she reached home my mother went to see relatives and friends and consulted them about what had just happened.

It was then that I realized in what danger these incidents might involve my mother. She had not been able to conceal her indignation since the fatal episode of the quadrille and the offensive comments she had heard about the prudishness of the aristocrats —comments which had caused her to hurry away from the ball. My kindhearted and timid grandmother trembled for her daughter. My mother determined to leave Paris as soon as possible. She entrusted her fortune to M. Durvet, banker to the Court, who was devoted to our family. She took with her a comparatively modest sum of money, in the hope of a speedy return, and we left for Switzerland. From there we went on to Aix-la-Chapelle, where we met a crowd of people we knew, including the Comtesse Diane, sister-in-law of the Duchesse de Polignac. We learnt that le Comte d'Artois was at Coblentz, where the Elector of Trèves had housed him in the Palace of Schönbornslust and that Monsieur (the Comte de Provence) was also expected there. We were told that it was hoped that the French *émigrés* would join them there and that they all would come to an agreement with the Prince de Condé, who was endeavouring to raise an army of volunteers to be commanded by himself.

About this time my mother received a letter from the Comte de Provence (brother of the King and the Comte d'Artois) which decided her to go to Coblentz.

I greatly enjoyed our stay there. Young and old, all were filled with hope and illusions. The visits of princes from all countries and among others the Duke of Brunswick and the Prussian princes, enlivened things and gave a fillip to social life. We all gathered once a week at the Elector's palace.

It is easy to give you an idea of the confidence with which the armies inspired us. Here is an extract from a letter which the Comte de Provence received from Paris: "Everything is going according to your wishes: the declaration of war will be your salvation: one more effort and the great work will be done. Within two months the Coalition will be in a position to enable you to finish the season at Brunoy, etc."

The Duke of Brunswick himself talked of the approaching campaign in an astonishingly irresponsible fashion. "Monseigneur," he said, "I perceive with regret that we shall have no obstacles to get over. I would have preferred, for the general good, that the Allies should encounter some resistance, for the French need a lesson which they will never forget." Monsieur was hurt by these words and alluding to the defeats of Brunswick under Louis XV, he replied: "Take care, Prince, not to get held up by some unforeseen obstacle. I presume that the French will defend their country. They have not always been beaten."

❊

The Comte d'Artois makes a triumphal entry into Coblentz. The émigrés, seeking for support all over Europe, receive a warm welcome from the ruler of the district, the Elector of Trèves. His domain, the Rhineland, was then a fashionable resort. Spa—the Cannes or Deauville of the day—was not far away. Listen to Mme Lage de Volude.

All those who had horses rode ahead, the pedestrians simply crossed the floating bridge and waited. The Auvergnats were the first to greet him. He dismounted, walked through their ranks and said to the officer commanding them: "I would like you to name each of these gentlemen: I know many of them but most of them have arrived since my departure." He got into a carriage and drove off surrounded by an escort of brave fellows. At one o'clock they encountered the remainder of the mounted noblemen, the gentlemen of the Bodyguard and the other companies. M. le Comte d'Artois left his carriage again and remained for a quarter of an hour talking to all and expressing his gratitude for their welcome. He said he was not displeased with the outcome of his journey, that at last the prospects of success seemed certain, though not so near at hand as he had hoped: but still he was full of hope.

The spectacle was superb. People were saying, "Here he is, our prince, our hope, the scion of Henri Quatre." They crowded round him and everyone wanted to touch him. He possessed the charm, which delights the French, and he had a way of looking at you like Louis XV, according to what elderly people said. Every one of his words was received with delight. He seemed to be their King. Bad news vanished in his presence and everybody took heart again on seeing him. The Prince de Condé and Monsieur went ahead of him on the other side. We dined at the Elector's with them. After they had left, as well as all the men who were present, we went to the house of Mme de Calonne, who lives in front of the bridge. When the ferryboat with Monsieur on board arrived and before the hooks were fixed le Comte d'Artois jumped on to the deck into his brother's arms. Then cries of Long live the King! Long live the Princes! echoed from both banks of the Rhine. Monsieur threw his hat into the air crying "Long live the King!" The floating bridge crosses the Rhine very slowly and during this time the Princes talked to those standing round them. The Comte d'Artois said, "Gentlemen, I hope that we shall soon find ourselves together to celebrate a more important occasion: *Vive le Roi!*" The vivats were renewed, sweeping from one bank of the river to the other. They all passed in front of our windows and saluted us and we returned their greetings with cries of "*Vive le Roi!*" Then they walked to the palace of the Elector. This Prince went down the steps to

meet them in company with Princess Cunégonde and the
Comtesse de Provence. When the Princes and nobles had reached
the courtyard and caught sight of the Elector, there was a general
cry of "Long live the Elector." This good and worthy Prince was
moved to tears. He embraced his nephews. We, too, had followed
them on foot, but at a distance, and arrived just as the Princes
entered the Elector's study. The two great drawing-rooms were
crammed. We waited for the Princes to come out. When the
doors were opened, there was dead silence, as it was thought that
the Comte d'Artois was going to speak. It was an embarrassing
moment for him, especially as he had nothing very positive to say.
Moreover, now that his brother had come, it was really for the
latter to speak. But neither of them said anything. In the evening
we went to the Château to have supper with Monsieur (le Comte
de Provence). Although it was by way of being an intimate
party, there were a lot of people present, but it was possible to
talk privately. The news was not as bad as it had at first been
thought.   There is of course some delay and uncertainty for
the moment, because of the difficulty of making all these accursed
Powers pull together. They have sent M. d'Esterhazy to Russia
and Baron d'Escars to Sweden. Baron de Roll is following the
King of Prussia, M. de Flasklande is remaining, I believe, in
Vienna, and the Duc d'Havré in Spain. The Emperor failed to
interpret correctly England's reply, which was, indeed, am-
biguous. M. de Calonne used all his eloquence to talk him round,
but the Emperor was unmoved and fresh explanations have to be
obtained. The King of Prussia seems a perfect ally, provided he is
playing straight. I only heard the details today. His journey was
more necessary than ever, for we had been somewhat neglected.
The Emperor for his part has a plan, which the obligation to
come to our aid will interfere with. Anyhow his mind is occupied
with parties and women. More than anything else he likes to
enjoy himself and the last thing one can call him is a statesman.
They say that the Comte d'Artois has spoken at the conference
with heartfelt force and eloquence: he has described the misfortunes of France, the position of the King and Queen, the
plight of the nobles and clergy, as well as the general state of
Europe, with a truthfulness that carries conviction.

. . . It seems incredible, but I haven't yet been to Spa. Perhaps I am the only person here to have been so remiss. Spa has been more brilliant this year than ever before. There have been seventeen princes and princesses, whom you might call brothers, sons or nephews of Kings—as for the German princelings we don't count them, the streets are swarming with them—and one king who is worth a thousand, the King of Sweden. They claim that Spa is the one place in the world where the Revolution is forgotten. I want to go there, if only for a short visit, so that when I come back people may stop making fun of me and saying, "What! you haven't been to Spa!"

The Marquise de Falaiseau, whose husband is in the Army:

We were absolutely delighted on arriving in Coblentz to see crowds of French people walking and riding in the streets, just as if they were in the Bois de Boulogne or the Champs-Elysées.

On the 20th I was presented to the Elector and Princess Cunégonde by the Grand Chamberlain and Baroness Naindorf. The persons to be presented gathered in a very beautiful gallery. Then the Elector arrived with his sister, his brother, Monsieur and the Comte d'Artois. They walked round the circle for about a quarter of an hour talking to all the women and then started to play. Usually there are three games. The Comte d'Artois is in that arranged by Princess Cunégonde (the Elector's sister) which is a game of ombre; the Elector, Prince Xavier de Saxe and Monsieur make up the other games (they usually play *tressept médiateurs*) with the Ministers, Ambassadors and their ladies. Very soon the servants bring glasses of lemonade and barley-water, which is served to the players and the ladies, sitting in a ring round the Princes. The practice is for one to move from table to table. After watching for, perhaps, half an hour at one table, one gets up, curtsies to the Prince or Princess and passes on to another till finally one retires to a part of the gallery where there is no play or goes to visit the lady-in-waiting, who is at a table at the other end of the room.

Behind the women's circle are gathered numerous Frenchmen, who throng forward to see the Princes. Their interest and curiosity are touching. The Princes and all their courtiers are in uniform, which gives a martial and imposing air to the scene. The Princes display the utmost politeness and affability and the same can be said of the Elector and the Princess.

On Tuesday the 22nd, I was presented to the Princes. Tuesday is the day on which they give a dinner with a reception immediately afterwards. The ceremonial is almost the same as at the Residency, except that the guests wait until the play is over and do not move from table to table, while the Princes circulate among the women before and after the play. The first time that Monsieur spoke to me he asked me if it was long since I had emigrated and where I came from. The Comte d'Artois said it must have been very tiring to travel in my present condition. The Elector and Princess Cunégonde asked me if I expected to stay a long time in Coblentz and recommended me to do so.

On Sunday the 27th I dined at the Residency. The company assembled at two o'clock, the Princes arrived and went their round. Then we passed into the dining-room. The custom here, as at Bonn, is not to help yourself but to take what is brought to you. It is true that you are offered something fresh every minute or two. There is a footman to look after every two guests. After dinner the guests go into another room for coffee.

On that day the Archduke Charles, brother of the Emperor, was expected and the company waited a long time for him. The Elector proposed that we should be shown over the Palace. We agreed and Baron Dumesnil, his Prime Minister, took us round. It is really very well furnished.

At five o'clock the Archduke Charles arrived. The Princes hastened to meet him with a joyful air. They came back into the room holding him by the hand. He saluted with an air of surprise and seemed somewhat confused at appearing in travelling clothes in the midst of such a great gathering. The Princes and the Archduke retired to discuss things for about three-quarters of an hour, after which they parted, the Archduke saying that he was in a great hurry because on Tuesday he had to be in Brussels and on Wednesday in the Camp.

On the 29th I dined with the Princes. This is a less formal occasion than at the Elector's. There is more talk and people feel more at home. It is true that the house makes no impression of grandeur or majesty. After dinner and coffee, there is card-playing. The crowd arrives, presentations are made, the Princes finish their rounds, and after the play is over we go home.

On Sundays and Thursdays the Elector gives a dinner for the Princes at which he holds court, while on Tuesdays it is the Princes who receive. They all look very friendly and affectionate towards one another. The Elector is very good to them and practically pays all their expenses, while the French here are privileged in being exempted from the taxes and tolls which the people of the country have to pay.

The Comte d'Artois is adored. His frank, open face and friendly air attract everyone. On the following Sunday I saw at the Residency the Prince de Condé. He looked pleased. He was surrounded by people, who stared at him adoringly. Meanwhile M. de Bouvillé brought to the Residency the news of the arrival of the Prussians and the King of Prussia's decision to take Frenchmen into his service.

. . . My husband was in cantonments with the musketeers, otherwise styled gentlemen of the Ordnance, at Falendorf, a pretty village beside the Rhine, beyond Coblentz. I went down there in a boat to dine.

All the banks of the Rhine are covered with rich and populous villages, occupied at present by French troops. The Bodyguard are at Lindorf, the French guards, under the name of Men-at-Arms, are at Falendorf with two red companies, formerly musketeers. The other two red companies comprising Gendarmes of the Guard and light cavalry are at Neuwictz. These four companies are combined in a single corps—that of the Gentlemen of the Ordnance. They are commanded by the Comte de Montboissier, who formerly commanded the Black Musketeers, and who is eighty years old. This corps is very well equipped. For the last month it has been carrying out manœuvres on foot and on horseback. It numbers 1,200 men of whom 250 are from the Auvergne. It may be considered the best of the provincial forces, especially as it costs the Princes nothing. Its members have raised funds among themselves, which serve to equip those who cannot afford to pay for their own equipment.

The French forces here consist of the King's Bodyguard and those of Monsieur and the Comte d'Artois, Mirabeau's and Polignac's legions, a very fine legion composed of the Royal Dragoons, provincial companies and regiments of all sorts most of whom wear the uniform of the French *émigré* soldiers: royal blue tunic, gold buttons with the fleur-de-lys, blue collar and facings. My son has a complete uniform which my sister had made for him at Tournay.

It is believed that the army of the *émigrés* numbers at present 25,000 men.

After the salons, the cantonments. Here is a picture of life in uniform by an émigré. *A son writes to his father.*

Oppenau.
January 1792.

My dear Papa,

You will certainly be curious to know how we pass our time in this double exile.

In the daytime we scour the surrounding country in an attempt to reconnoitre all the positions which the genius of Turenne with his small army succeeded in defending against the attacks of Montecuculli, who in spite of his superior numbers and his military skill was driven back. Passing through Salsbach we all wanted to kiss the ground where an infernal bullet cut short the life of this illustrious warrior.

There's not a single ruined castle, not a mound, not a rock, which we did not visit map in hand to study the many battlefields of which history has left such glorious records throughout this district. Our mouths have watered with the hope that the age of glorious deeds is not yet over.

On our return from these military exercises, we always find the soup excellent and our food-ration too small. After our dinner, as we cannot frequent the splendid salons of the Prince at Worms, we pass some of our time in the spacious rooms of the inns which they call "stubs" and which are splendidly warmed by enormous stoves that spread their heat into the farthest corners.

A good many officers, whose finances are still in good condition have taken lodgings in these great houses. Here they either have a table d'hôte meal or choose their food according to taste. Those, who are less well-off, merely spend a few hours in the inn. One only has to ask for a half-pint of wine or a mug of beer to secure the good graces of the host or hostess. This small measure of very moderate liquid, added to a roll of bread, is all that three-quarters of us have for supper. In this way we spend our evenings all together. Some of us play cards, others read the old news-papers and discuss politics or the latest news from Headquarters, where the courtiers and others go in search of information every day and pass it on to us. We often are taken in, and in any case the news from France is so depressing, that one prefers not to hear it. Besides when these subjects are exhausted, there are always a few old soldiers, a few men of learning or a few jokers round whom we gather to hear anecdotes of battles, talks about literature or side-splitting or tedious tales. Several of our generals and other senior officers often prefer to play cards in their rooms, where they can enjoy peace.

When the night-watchman calls out that ten o'clock has struck we all retire to our billets: some of us to sleep in a bed, but the greater number to lie on straw laid out on the floor of a small sitting-room. There we lie down, five or six of us side by side with quilts stuffed with feathers to cover us, when there are enough of these in the house, and when there are not, we use our overcoats. When all are ready to turn in, the hostess does not fail to place a bucket in the middle of the room, which each of us is at pains to locate before the youngest man blows out the candle. Anyone feeling an urge to get up at night gropes his way to it. Others prefer to open a casement above their heads and make water through the window. I hope you will forgive this last sentence. It would, perhaps, have been in better taste to leave it out. It escaped me unwittingly. All the same, if one seeks to describe the habits of a set of men like me and my conrades, I don't think one ought to leave anything out.

We pay a very modest price for our beds as well as for our fuel and other supplies. Generally speaking we like our hosts and they like us. Their daughters are chaste and virtuous, though the pretty ones are not above making eyes at us. But failure to understand one another greatly handicaps our advances. Once in a way, however, attention is paid to them. *Honni soit qui mal y pense.*

The quarters in which we live have an inestimable advantage in this cold country. Every inhabitant has his ration of wood, which he gathers in the communal forests or else purchases for a very low price. The whole country is covered with pinewoods, so no one goes short. There is not a single peasant or artisan whose house does not contain a sort of small sitting-room warmed by a stove. These rooms are all panelled with wood and are generally kept very clean. The family lives in them throughout the day, taking their meals at a round table. The table is usually placed in one of the corners sometimes in a turret with so many windows that it looks like a lantern. Each of these has a transom big enough for one to put one's head through the opening. If anything happens in the street or in the country everyone lifts one of these bars and puts his head through the open panes, which produces an amusing effect from the outside. Every time we pass through a village the same thing repeats itself. Imagine five or six hundred heads, projecting as far as their necks through apertures in the windows, in order to see what is going on outside. This happens on every storey and produces an effect of faces in relief, cold and inanimate as they are, which fits in well with the architecture of these houses, most of which are painted in fresco. The effect is rendered all the more odd by the variety of the faces and the diversity of their *coiffure.*

The curiosity of these good Germans is easy to explain in a country where for three-quarters of the winter no one puts his nose out of doors. They never put beds in the best rooms, which consequently are used by all from morning till night. That is an excellent idea. Thus the people of this country have all sorts of conveniences unknown even to our most prosperous peasants. Even the poor people have their *"stube"* and their little separate kitchen. This suits us very well for without these things I don't know how we should have managed to resist the onset of such a rigorous winter.

If the royalists in France ever think of us, which I do not

doubt, they must wonder how most of the people who are here without money are able to carry on. As time goes on we all become the victims of this lack of funds, for, unfortunately, none of us had foreseen a prolonged absence from France. Consequently as it is difficult and, for many, impossible to procure fresh funds, we are obliged to restrict our spending.

We all must try to put aside something for a rainy day, most of us in order to buy a horse next spring, some to provide for their wives and children and others to pay for the keep of the faithful servant whom they have brought from France or who has followed them of his own accord, achieving his greatest happiness in remaining with his master. How many of these men have we seen, the equals, or nearly, of their masters in generosity and fine feeling, who have begged them to accept their small savings accumulated in twenty years of service, their only insurance against starvation when age and infirmity compel them to retire! They ask their masters, who command their deepest affection, to do them this favour, without troubling to reflect if they will ever be able to repay the sum, which, though small, represents their entire assets. It gives them genuine happiness to have this unexpected opportunity of contributing to the well-being of their former benefactors. It makes them groan to see men of such high standing deprived of the necessities of life —a glass of wine or a cup of coffee, which habit has made indispensable to their health.

These fine fellows content themselves with a glass of water and the remains of the boiled beef left by their masters on the table. Royalists, like their employers, their ambition is to go with them to the war and figure among the auxiliary ranks. They want to be there to groom their horses, even if they have to follow their masters on foot, and, more than anything, to be able to look after them if they have the ill-luck to be wounded. Some of them have offered to buy horses for themselves in order to be nearer to these gentlemen-soldiers and to be able to procure them provisions and forage, when there is a shortage. In fact, these plans are a favourite subject of conversation among them and of approach to their former protectors, whose delicacy in refusing their generous offers they hope to overcome.

I see daily two of these men, with whose behaviour and conduct I am familiar and whom I admire unreservedly. But, my dear Papa, how glad I am that I did not follow your advice and that I left my servant behind! You see I am still young and adaptable and able to put up with inconvenience. But I am only sorry that I did not make up my mind sooner. I should have saved the fifty louis I wasted in comparatively luxurious travel and during my stay at Marseilles. In those days I never realized that it was possible for a man of my sort to live for ten or twelve sous per day, without even running the risk of losing much weight.

The active and frugal life I lead is very healthy and perfectly tolerable in the case of young people like me, but one cannot help being very sorry for some, one's fellow-exiles, for whom it must be very painful. Yes, indeed, it gives one a shock to observe the plight of magistrates, even court-presidents, rich country-gentlemen, old knights of Saint-Louis, long since retired from the service, prosperous business-men and men of wealth, who lived for the most part in their warm and beautiful mansions, with parquet floors or splendid carpets to walk on and succulent food on their tables, who never travelled for any considerable distance except in their well-sprung carriages drawn by fine horses. Now it is pitiful to see them marching in column in rain or snow through the mud, often leading a wounded horse or one loaded with forage and to know that they have nothing better to hope for in the way of rest and refreshment, than one or two nasty beds for which twenty men will be drawing lots, a short, unappetizing meal, and if they are ill, a small, open cart to move them from one place to another. Fortunately for them we, who can never lose the qualities implanted by our up-bringing, are always on the look-out to satisfy the needs of these new and unlikely brothers-in-arms. There is nothing we would not do for such men, whose profession was never that of war, or, if it was, who left it so long ago. But nothing could keep them acquiescent among their rebellious countrymen. They had to leave their motherland and all that they held most dear to embark on this new crusade and to fight the perjured, ungrateful felons, who have issued from hell to thwart the fulfilment of good King Louis's promises to France.

Some of these *émigrés* of the better class have not yet come to join us either because they are too old and only left France in order to escape certain death for speaking respectfully of the King or sheltering the worthy curé of their parish or—and these are more readily available—are living with their families in the frontier towns. We meet them every day. Those who live in the neighbourhood of Trèves all come to pay court to the Princes and ask to be registered for eventual service with the Army. Their idea is to join up with us at the first shot they hear fired against the rebels.

There, my dear Papa, I have given you a brief description of our situation. I am sure you will read it with interest, if it ever reaches you.

❧

The Marquis de Falaiseau to his wife.

Bavet 1792.

Since Monday evening, dearest, we have been in France. We had a long and tiring march and are now about two and a half leagues from Thionville. The village in which we are now is fairly large. The inhabitants are very "patriotic" and although quite amenable for the moment, they do not seem intimidated. We pay for everything we take from them. All the same, some of our people have treated them roughly and this displeases me as it is no way to recover their loyalty.

Up to now Thionville has not surrendered and it appears that the citizens mean to defend it. We are bringing up guns for the siege.

In the first village through which we passed, the people cried "Long live the King", to which we replied with a lusty cheer.

The former parish-priests have been reinstated. Just now some gendarmes brought along a "constitutional" curé, bound and gagged—a great rascal, they say. I spoke to the man, who claimed to have taken the oath conscientiously, because the King had sanctioned the civil constitution. He refused to retract.

❧

Livry sur Meuse.

Just when we were least expecting it, we left yesterday at noon, We have passed Verdun and yesterday evening at nine we arrived in this village, in which most of us are bivouacked without rations.

We made a counter-march and are now on the road to Sedan after which we shall be wheeling to the left in the direction of Champagne. Our army numbers more than 100,000 men.

The army of the "patriots" is invested. The day before yesterday they attacked the Austrians with the object of extricating themselves from their unfavourable position. There was very serious fighting. The "patriots" were repulsed three times with heavy losses, failing to attain their objectives. They may be forced to surrender before long. During all this time all the French were in villages many miles away from the field of battle and it certainly looks as if we shall merely be used as a rearguard throughout the campaign.

If we are successful, as appears likely, nothing can stop us marching on Paris and arriving there soon.

For the moment we are forming part of an immense column of cavalry.

The King of Prussia has issued a communication to the inhabitants of France containing a warning to the city of Paris to the effect that the Town can still escape destruction, if the good citizens will liberate the King and refrain from taking extreme measures against his sacred person, but that if the King loses his life the innocent will suffer with the guilty, when the town is sacked.

It upsets me to think that our parents are in Paris. For heaven's sake, send them a message telling them to get away.

Adieu. The trumpet sounds and we must get ready to resume our march.

LA MARSEILLAISE

✤✤✤

LETTER FROM Madame Dietrich, wife of the Mayor of Strasbourg.

My dear Brother,

I want to tell you that for the last few days I have been doing nothing but copying and transcribing music, an occupation which provides me with pleasure and distraction especially at the present moment, when no one talks of anything but politics. You know that we receive a lot of people and that one always has to invent something new in order to vary the topics of conversation and to provide our guests with distractions. Well, my husband had the idea of getting someone to compose a topical song and Rouget de l'Isle, a captain of engineers and an agreeable poet and composer has very quickly written the music for a war song. My husband, who has a good tenor voice has sung the song which has a rousing tune and is rather original. It's like Gluck only better—more lively and more spirited. I, for my part, have made use of my talent for orchestration and have arranged the piece for the harpsichord and other instruments. This has given me plenty to do. The piece has been played in our house and much applauded by the audience. I send you a copy of the music. Your little *virtuosi* will play it for you at sight and I'm sure you will be delighted with it.

Your sister Louise, née Ochs.

Strassburg
May 1792.

✤

Extract from the Journal "Chronique de Paris".

Liberty, Verity, Impartiality
Wednesday 20th August 1792
A War Song

In all our houses of entertainment the public always call for the song: *Allons enfans de la Patrie*. The words are by M. Rougez, a captain of engineers now in garrison at Huningue. The tune is both moving and martial. The *Fédérés* first brought it from Marseilles, where it had become very fashionable. They sing it with the greatest fervour and the passage where, waving their hats and brandishing their swords, they all sing together *Aux armes, citoyens* is truly thrilling. They have sung this martial air in all the villages through which they have passed on their way to Paris and these new bards have animated the countryside with sentiments of citizenship and patriotism. They often sing it at the Palais Royal—sometimes in the theatre between two plays.

✳

Thiébault hears the Marseilles sung in Paris for the first time.

It was on July 30th that these beastly *Fédérés*, spewed up by Marseilles, first arrived in Paris. This invasion of brigands completed the emancipation of the criminal scum of the city. One cannot imagine anything more horrifying than these five hundred fanatics, three-quarters of them drunk, almost all wearing red bonnets, marching bare-armed and dishevelled. They were followed by the dregs of the people and reinforced continually by the overflow from the Faubourgs Saint-Antoine and Saint-Marceau, and they fraternized at all the drinking shops with groups as dangerous as themselves. It was thus that they promenaded dancing through the main streets and some of the boulevards, where my friend Vigearde and I saw them pass. We even thought of tagging on to the loafers that followed them, but indignation and disgust soon caused us to break away and we left them moving towards the Champs-Elysées, where they indulged in satanic dances before taking part in the orgy to which Santerre, a battalion commander in the National Guard, had invited them.

That was how these men from Marseilles made their début in the capital, and if Paris had been growing gloomier since the twentieth of June, it was positively lugubrious since the arrival of this infernal gang of assassins, who as they pursued their bloodthirsty work, howled the airs of *Ça ira* and the *Marseillaise*, songs originally composed, the first to animate the dance and the second with a still worthier object.

THE TENTH OF AUGUST

✢✢✢

PLACE VENDÔME was filled with a mob, who followed the wretches carrying human heads fixed on pikes. I noticed with horror young people, in fact children throwing the heads in the air and catching them on their sticks. This happened a short while before we heard the crash of guns accompanying the attack on the Tuileries. At the first discharge, the multitude, who covered the Place Vendôme and filled the whole of Rue Saint-Honoré, scattered and fled in all directions. Soon afterwards we heard shouts of victory and the crowds flowed back as precipitately as they had dispersed, clustering round the precincts of the Chamber. Soon we saw in the midst of the tumult the famous Téroigne appearing on horseback in a scarlet riding-habit, followed by a large number of workmen carrying ropes and all sorts of tools. She rode round the statue of Louis XIV insulting the great King and crying, "Fall, tyrant!" In a moment the fencing that encircled the pedestal was torn away. Men climbed on to the statue and passed cords round the head, the torso and the neck of the figure and the horse's hind-quarters. Then they made prolonged but useless efforts to pull down the statue. It was not until the next day that after demolishing the pedestal and filing through the supports and the braces, they could overturn the massive figure. It fell and broke in several pieces on the pavement. There was also much disorder in Place Louis XV, where the bodies of the unfortunate Swiss Guards, who had been pursued thither and massacred were stripped, insulted and mishandled by the women. My pen refuses to describe such outrages.

The account of this bloody scene was given by one of the deputies of the right, Mathieu Dumas; it was enacted on the tenth of August 1792 in the morning. By the evening France was to have no king.

It was the threat from outside that caused the Tenth of August. At Coblentz, Monsieur the Comte de Provence proclaimed himself Regent and formed a Ministry. The Duke of Brunswick had just addressed a Manifesto to the French ordering them to submit to Louis XVI and threatening the deputies, National Guards, members of the Commune and the magistrates with judgment by court martial without hope of pardon and finally, in the event of violence being shown against the Tuileries, promising to overwhelm the city and execute all disloyal citizens.

On a day of tropical heat, that strewed dead leaves over the ground, all Paris was out in the streets. The great act of the Revolution was ready to be played. Scene—the Tuilieries. The Rue de Rivoli did not yet exist. Its present site was occupied by gardens. Facing the present Rue de Castiglione stood the Riding School, the meeting place of the Assembly. Where the Palais Royal stands today, a labyrinth of little streets converged on the courtyard of the Louvre. On the site of the Arc de Triomphe du Carrousel were the iron gates of the Tuileries, a building which occupied the whole of the area between the Place des Pyramides (Pavillon de Marsan) and the Seine (Pavillon de Flore). The King's quarters were between the Assembly and the rioters.

Dramatis Personae. 1. The Royal Family whose throne and lives were at stake. They had, to defend them, 900 loyal Swiss guards and an unknown number of gendarmes and National Guards, no longer commanded by La Fayette and already veering towards the rioters.

2. The Assembly, half of whose members foreseeing trouble were absent. Only 300 out of 750 were in their places. The majority, that is to say the Girondins, the Party of the Centre were playing for power, and soon would be playing for their lives.

3. The Commune de Paris sitting at the Hôtel de Ville and led by the deputies of the extreme left, Danton and Robespierre. This party controlled the streets and sounded the tocsin at will.

Roederer, the Attorney-General with administrative powers (something like a prefect) who tells what happens on this day was neither a royalist, a Girondin nor a member of the Commune. He was a man of frigid temperament.

On the 9th at 10.15 p.m. the Minister of Justice came to the Department office. He warned me that the King would send for me, if necessary.

At 10.45 a letter arrived from the Minister ordering me on behalf of the King to go to the Palace. I went and was there at 11. Drummers were beating the call to arms in all the neighbouring quarters. I walked through the rooms. There was a good number of people present, but nothing extraordinary. I went to the Council Chamber or King's cabinet office. He was there with the Queen, Madame Elisabeth and the Ministers. I reported to the King the latest news that we had received in the department. Everyone seemed extremely agitated. I asked one of the Ministers if the mayor had come. "No." So I took a piece of paper and wrote a line telling him to come.

As I was sealing the letter, the mayor, Pétion, came in. He gave the King an account of the state of Paris and then came up to me. We talked for a while about nothing in particular, when Mandat, the Commandant-General of Public Security, and Boubé, Secretary-General to the Headquarters Staff came in. They came over to us. The Commandant-General complained to the mayor that the municipal police officers had refused to supply him with gunpowder. The mayor replied, "You had no right to have any more." There was an argument and the mayor asked if he had not a stock of gunpowder left over from the last issue. M. Mandat replied: "I have only three rounds and many of my men have none at all, and they are beginning to grumble." This closed the conversation. Then the mayor said, "It's stiflingly hot here. I am going down to take the air." For my part I was awaiting news from the department as they had promised to send on all information as it reached them. I remained in the room and sat down in a corner.

About 11.30 a letter came from the department, but it contained nothing concrete. The time to sound the tocsin had not arrived. Then I went downstairs alone to get some fresh air. I went into the courtyard, where I was stopped by some Grenadiers of the National Guard who took me for a deputy on account of my tricoloured collar and talked to me about different decrees which had been or would be issued. I did not reply but merely said that I was not a deputy and added a few conciliatory words.

After that I left them for I wished to be alone, but as others came up every few paces and stopped me, I decided to go into the garden. Not wishing to go too far, I first walked along the terrace which skirts the Palace, until I approached the gate which opens on the Pont-Royal. The sentinels stopped me there and told me that it was forbidden to walk in that part of the grounds, so I returned at once.

When I reached the middle of the terrace, I turned towards the great avenue meaning to walk as far as the Sinvel-Bridge. Then a group came from the direction of the National Assembly, so I stopped. It was Pétion with the municipal officers and some members of the Commune accompanied by some young National Guards, unarmed, who were singing and larking round the mayor and the magistrates. They stopped when they reached me and Pétion proposed that I should take a stroll with him. I agreed.

We went along the terrace, parallel with the quay, still followed by fifteen or twenty youngsters of the National Guard, walking arm in arm and conversing cheerfully among themselves. When we had reached the end of the terrace, we heard a signal from the Palace recalling us which caused us to return.

During our walk the mayor and I talked despondently about the general agitation and the disastrous consequences which I anticipated. The mayor was less disturbed than I was. He said, "I hope that nothing will happen. Commissioners have already gone to the meeting places. Thomas told me there would be no trouble. He ought to know how things are." I do not know who Thomas is.

We went back to the Palace and had come to the foot of the great staircase, when someone came to Pétion and told him he was wanted in the Assembly, so he went off and I went up to the royal apartments.

I walked through the different rooms without stopping and finally came to the King's cabinet office, as my place was neither in the antechamber nor in the *œil-de-bœuf* (the room of the gentlemen-in-waiting).

It was then half an hour after midnight. Shortly afterwards I received a letter from the department reporting on the situation. It stated that there was a great deal of movement in the

E

Faubourg Saint-Antoine but no regular concentration of people.

I informed the Ministers and then the King, the Queen and Madame Elisabeth came one after the other to me and asked me to read them my letter.

Soon after that a verbal report was made directly to the King confirming the department's letter. I do not know from whom the report came, as whenever there was any news or the King made a movement, twenty or thirty persons instantly crowded round him and I remained where I was.

A quarter of an hour later the tocsin could be heard from several directions. The windows of the Palace were open and everyone rushed to them to listen and tried to identify the churches by the sound of their bells.

A fresh letter from the department informed me that the Faubourg Saint-Antoine was in a commotion, but that not more than 1,500 to 2,000 men had collected. However, the Gunners were all ready with their cannons and the citizens were standing in front of their houses armed and ready to march. I read this letter to the ministers and, I think, to the King or the Queen who asked to see it.

One of the ministers, I forget which, asked me if it would not be appropriate to proclaim martial law. I replied that since the law of August 3rd 1791, martial law could be proclaimed when public order was consistently disturbed (last article of the law of August 3rd): "but," I added, "here we have something quite different from a simple disturbance of public order: here we have an insurrection, which is more powerful than martial law or the authorities who could proclaim it. It is absolutely useless to think of applying it in present circumstances, and anyhow it is for the municipality and not the department to judge when the moment is opportune to proclaim it." The minister said he thought that the department had the power to order the municipality to do so. I insisted that this was not so and went to the lamp standing under the clock to study the law. As I was reading it, Madame Elisabeth came up to me. Her curiosity was attracted by the fact that the law which I was reading was bound in the three national colours. "What have you got there?" she said. "Madame, it is the law governing the employment of the forces of law and order."

"And what are you trying to find out?" "I am trying to find out if it is true that the Department has the power to proclaim martial law." "Well, has it?" "I don't think so, Madame."

I went and sat down on a stool near the door of the bed-chamber. There was no formality. Soon the Queen, Madame Elisabeth and one or two other women, one of whom was tall and slim, came and sat on the other stools placed in a line with mine. Then I rose. The Queen asked me when the people from Marseilles expected to leave.

At half-past two I received reassuring news to the effect that it had been difficult to get the crowds to assemble, that the citizens of the faubourgs were growing tired and that it looked as if they would not march. A verbal report made to the King by a tall man in grey confirmed this news. Some wit caused amusement by saying, "The tocsin doesn't pay."

Soon afterwards (between three and four) it was reported to the ministers that M. Manuel, the Attorney of the Commune had given orders to withdraw the guns which were on the Pont-Neuf. They had been placed there by order of the Commandant-General in order to prevent the junction of the Faubourgs Saint-Antoine and Saint-Marceau. The report added that M. Manuel had said to the Commune, "These cannon interfere with communications: the citizens of the two faubourgs have between them an important task to perform." The ministers discussed whether in spite of the orders given by Manuel, the guns should be replaced on the bridge.

At the same time it was reported that a deputation from the Commune had just informed the National Assembly that the mayor was a prisoner in the Palace and demanded that he should be brought back to the Commune. However, we learnt at the same time that the mayor, who had, doubtless, been waiting within reach of the Assembly in the garden, had gone before the Assembly and declared that no pressure had been put upon him to remain in the Palace. Meantime, he stated that he was going back to the Commune. This in fact he did, returning on foot with the deputation, as we realized when at 4 a.m. the mayor's carriage, which had been waiting in the Royal Courtyard, drove away empty.

On hearing the mayor's carriage leave the courtyard, someone opened a shutter in the King's cabinet to see what carriage it was. Dawn was breaking. Madame Elisabeth went to the window and, looking at the crimson sky, said to the Queen, "Come here, my sister, and see the sunrise." The Queen joined her. On that day she saw the sun for the last time.

At about the same time the King, who had retired into his bedroom, reappeared in the cabinet office. He had probably been lying down because when he came back, he had lost half of his powder and his curls were flattened on one side of his head, which contrasted strongly with the powder and curls on the other.

Just then, after the shutters had been opened in the apartment, M. Mandat came to say that the Commune had sent for him for the second time. He was not for going. M. Dejoly (a minister) thought that he was needed at the Palace. My opinion was that as the Commandant-General was officially under the orders of the mayor, it was possible that the latter wanted to go to meet the demonstrators and needed the head of the police with him. On my advice Mandat went, but reluctantly. I argued that it was necessary to clear up the matter of the alleged counter-orders given by Manuel regarding the guns on the Pont-Neuf and to explain to the Commune the measures he thought necessary to maintain public order. Mandat had made himself very unpopular with most of the guards on account of his fanatical devotion to the Court. He was always ready to stake his life on the good intentions of the King and to declare that the Court harboured no evil designs against the people. I was not aware of the odium he had incurred. He should have taken some precautions for his own safety on his visit to the Commune. It appears that he took none and I was distressed to learn that he was killed on the way.

At about four o'clock I was summoned, I do not know by whom or how, to a room where the Queen was seated near the fire-place with her back to the window. I believe the room was that of Thierry, the King's valet-de-chambre. The King was not there. As far as I remember I went in by the door of the small room where the ministers, the commissioners of the department and I had held our meeting, and I assume that it was after the results of our conference had been communicated to the Queen, that she sent for me. She asked me what should be done in the present circumstances. I replied that in my opinion it was necessary for the King and the Royal Family to go to the National Assembly. M. Dubouchage (a minister) said, "What, you propose to deliver the King to his enemies?" "Not so much his enemies," I said. "You forget that they were 400 to 200 in favour of M. de La Fayette. In any case I propose this action as being less dangerous than anything else." The Queen then said in a very downright manner, "Monsieur, this is a conflict of forces. We have come to the point where we must know which is going to prevail—the King and the constitution or the rebels." "In that case, Madame, let us see what measures have been taken for the defence." I proposed that we should send for M. Lachesnaye, the officer commanding in the absence of Mandat. When he had come I asked him for details of the measures he was taking to defend his positions from the outside and if he had made any plans for preventing the demonstrators from reaching the Palace. He said he had and stated that the Carrousel was guarded.

Then he turned to the Queen and said rather crossly, "Madame, I cannot conceal from you that the royal apartments are full of persons of all sorts who interfere greatly with the service and who prevent people from having free access to the King, thus giving much offence to the National Guards." "You are quite mistaken," said the Queen. "I will answer for all the men in the apartments. You can dispose of them as you wish. They are prepared to render any kind of service. You can rely on them fully."

The Queen's remarks made me think that there was within the Palace a strong determination to fight and a faction who had promised the Queen a victory. I guessed that such a victory was needed to impress the National Assembly. All this filled me with confused fears of a bloody but useless resistance and attacks on the legislative body after the troops had withdrawn or been defeated, and these anticipations added an unbearable burden to my responsibility. I insisted that the King should at least write to the National Assembly and ask for help. M. Dubouchage made certain objections, so I said, "If my idea is not acceptable, let two ministers at least go to the Assembly to report on our situation and to ask for commissioners." This was agreed to and it was decided to send MM. Dejoly and Champion to the Assembly.

After they had gone we were discussing the situation with the Queen, when we heard shouts and booings in the garden. The ministers put their heads out of the window. M. Dubouchage, much excited, said, "Good God, it's the King they are booing. What the devil is he doing down there? Come quickly and let us go to him." Immediately he and M. de Sainte Croix went down into the garden. The Queen said nothing, but began to weep, wiping her eyes several times. Then she went into the King's bedroom to await his return. I followed her. Half her face was reddened by her tears. Soon afterwards, the ministers brought back the King, who was quite out of breath and very hot from the effort of running. He sat down at once, but seemed hardly upset by his experience.

The ministers and I withdrew into the little room, where I had previously had a conference with them. The members of the general council of my department arrived at last, nine in number, I think. They confirmed the report, based on good documentary evidence, that the Municipality had delivered five thousand ball-cartridges to the men from Marseilles. The time was about six o'clock. A moment afterwards a citizen, I think a police officer, came into the room with the two municipal officers who had remained in the Palace. He told us that the Commune was dis-organized and that the districts had sent them new representatives. The mayor, he said, was confined to his office and Mandat arrested or killed, the whole of Paris was up in arms, the people of the faubourgs were concentrating and preparing to march with their cannon and the battalion of the Cordeliers and the men of Marseilles were already on the march. I once more urged the ministers to take the King and his family to the National Assembly but M. Dubouchage, deeply agitated by having seen or imagined the King in peril in the garden, said "No, he must not go to the Assembly. It is not safe for him to go. He must stay here."

In these circumstances, seeing that they seemed resolved to await events in the Palace, I proposed that the Council of the department should go with me to the Assembly, communicate the most recent reports and entrust the decision to their wisdom.

This proposal commended itself to those present and we started to walk to the Assembly. When we had come to a point opposite the café on the terrace of the Feuillants, we met the two ministers coming back. "Where are you going, gentlemen?" they said. "To the Assembly." "To do what?" "Ask for help, beg them to send a deputation or summon the King and his family to the Chamber." "That is just what we have been doing—quite unsuccessfully. The Assembly scarcely listened to us. They are not in sufficient numbers to issue a decree: there are only sixty or eighty members in the house." These considerations caused us to stop. Moreover, we saw a crowd of unarmed persons running along the terrace who would reach the Gate of the Feuillants at the same time as we did and several members feared that we should find our way barred when we wanted to return. So we turned about and walked back to the Tuileries.

The ministers went up to the apartments. In the entrance my colleagues and I were stopped by some artillery-men, who were posted with their guns at the gate opening on the garden from the entrance-hall. A gunner said to us in distressed tones, "Gentlemen, will we be obliged to fire on our brothers?" I replied, "You are here to guard this gate and prevent anyone from breaking in. You will not have to fire, if no one fires on you. But if you are fired on, those who fire will not be your brothers." Then my colleagues said to me, "You ought to go into the courtyard and tell that to the National Guards who are there. They all think they are going to be forced to attack and are tormented by the idea." As I was tormented by the same thought, after all that I had seen, I was very glad to do what they proposed. We walked through the hall and out into the courtyard. Immediately in front of the gate of the Palace there were four or five pieces of artillery, as there were on the garden side. On the right there was a battalion of National Guards extending from the Palace as far as the wall which closed the courtyard near the Carrousel— Grenadiers, I believe. Parallel to them on the left was a battalion of Swiss Guards and in the middle at an equal distance from the Palace and the Royal Gate, five or six guns turned towards the Carrousel.

The Royal Gate was shut. I went with the members of the

Council to speak to the National Guards. I made them a speech, which I afterwards reported to the Assembly. As they were strung out at great length, they asked me to repeat at the end of the column the words I had spoken about a third of the way down. After that I went to the gunners in the middle of the court and said more or less the same things in the same words. No attacking, but show a bold front and be strong in defence. A tall, good-looking gunner said to me: "And if they fire on us, will you be there?" "Yes," I answered, "and not behind your guns but in front of them. We shall be the first to go, if anyone has to die today." "We shall all be with you," added my colleagues. At these words the gunner, without replying unloaded his cannon, threw the ball on the ground and put his foot on the match which was lit. At that moment the battalions of the Cordeliers and the Marseillais arrived in Place du Carrousel. A deputy spoke on their behalf to the Swiss, urging them not to offer any resistance to the patriots. The municipal officers were also standing near the Swiss Guards and must have heard what the deputy said.

. . . "We must hesitate no longer," I said to my colleagues. "If you agree, I shall go up now and explain to the King the necessity for him and the Royal Family to go and submit themselves to the National Assembly." They said, "Let us all go." I ran to the Palace followed by the others. We went up the great staircase and went through the rooms which seemed to me fuller than during the night. I found a crowd collected round the door of the King's room, so I said in a loud voice, "Gentlemen, please make way for the members of the department who must speak with the King." They made way and we entered. The King was sitting at a table by the door leading into his cabinet. His hands were resting on his knees. The Queen, Madame Elisabeth and the ministers were between the window and the King. Probably also Mme de Lamballe (first lady-in-waiting)and Mme de Tourzel were there also. "Sire," I said, "the department wish to speak to Your Majesty without other witnesses than the members of your family." The King made a gesture of dismissal and the others moved away but M. Dejoly said: "The King's ministers should remain with His Majesty." I said, "If the King so wishes, I see no objection. Sire," I continued in tones of urgency, "Your Majesty has not five minutes to lose. There is no safety for you except in the National Assembly. The opinion of the department is that you should proceed there without delay. You have not in the courtyards of the Palace enough men to defend the building and, moreover, they are not well-disposed. The gunners, as soon as they were advised to remain on the defensive, unloaded their pieces." "But," said the King, "I did not see many people at the Carrousel." "Sire, there are twelve guns, and a huge multitude is streaming in from the faubourgs."

M. Gerdret, the administrator of the department, a zealous patriot, who was at the same time interested in saving the King's life (he was the Queen's lace-merchant) began to speak in support of what I said. "Be quiet, Monsieur Gerdret," said the Queen. "It is not for you to raise your voice here . . . let M. le Procureur General Syndic speak." Then turning to me she said, "But, you know, we have a defence force here." I said, "Madame, all Paris is on the march", and then, resuming my address to the King with great emphasis I said, "Time presses, Sire. We are no longer begging you to do us a favour or taking the liberty to give you some good advice. There is only one thing for us to do at present and that is to ask your leave to take you with us to the Assembly." The King raised his head, looked at me fixedly for some seconds and then, turning towards the Queen, said, "Let us be going", and rose to his feet. Madame Elisabeth came behind the King and, thrusting her head over the corbel, said, "Monsieur Roederer, will you answer for the life of the King?" "Yes, Madame, with my own. I will walk immediately in front of him." The King looked at me, as if he trusted me. I said to him, "Sire, I ask that Your Majesty be accompanied by no one from the Court and have no other escort than the representatives of the department, who will surround the Royal Family and the men of the National Guard who will march in line on both flanks as far as the National Assembly." "Very well," said the King. "Will you give the orders." Then M. Dejoly called out, "Monsieur Roederer, the ministers will follow." "Yes," I said, "their place is in the National Assembly." The Queen said, "What about Mme de Tourzel, my son's governess?" "Yes," I replied "she may come too." I went out of the King's room and in the threshold of the open door I said in a very loud voice to the persons who filled the cabinet office: "The King and his family are going to the Assembly, alone, with no other escort than the representatives of the department and the ministers and a guard of soldiers. Be good enough to allow us to pass." Then I said: "Is the officer commanding the guard here?" An officer came up and I said to him, "You must bring up some men of the National Guard to march on either side of the King's party. This is the King's wish." The officer replied: "This will be done." The King left his room with the family and my people. He waited for a few minutes in the cabinet office until the guard arrived. He then walked round the circle formed by the members of the Court, to the number of forty or fifty. I did not notice him speaking to anyone in particular but merely heard him say, "I am going to the National Assembly." Two files of Guards arrived and we proceeded in the order proposed by me and confirmed by the King. We filed through all the apartments.

The King, when we were coming into the *œil-de-bœuf* took the headdress of the National Guardsman who was marching on his right and placed his own hat, which carried a white feather, on the Guardsman's head. The man looked surprised and then took the King's hat off his head and put it under his arm.

When we had reached the colonnade at the bottom of the great staircase the King, who was immediately behind me said: "What is going to happen to all the people remaining up there?" I said, "Sire, but the faubourgs are nearly here: all the districts are armed and they are meeting at the Municipality. Besides our numbers here are not sufficient and there is no one with sufficient authority to resist even the crowds in the Place du Carrousel, who dispose of twelve pieces of artillery."

When we were under the trees opposite the café situated on the terrace of the Feuillants, we walked over the leaves which had fallen in the night and which the gardeners had piled up in heaps across the path followed by the King. We sank up to our knees in them. "What a lot of leaves!" said the King. "They have begun to fall very early this year." Several days before Manuel had written in a newspaper that the King would not last beyond the fall of the leaves. One of my colleagues told me that the Dauphin was amusing himself by kicking the leaves into the legs of the persons walking in front of him.

As we progressed very slowly, a deputation from the National Assembly met us in the garden, some twenty-five paces from the terrace. The President said, as far as I can remember: "The Assembly is anxious to contribute to your safety and offers to you and your family a refuge in its precincts."

After that I ceased to walk in front of the King, who, with his family, reached the Assembly without hindrance. When they arrived at the gate of the passage leading into the building there were several guards standing there and among them a National Guardsman from Provence, who placed himself on the King's left and said to him in his native accent: "Sire, don't be afeard. We are decent people, but we don't want to be betrayed any longer. Be a good citizen, Sire, and don't forget to sack those sky-pilots you keep in the Palace. Don't forget. It's high time to take note of this." The King replied good-temperedly. He then walked first into the Assembly, followed by me. There was a block in the passage which prevented the Queen and her son, whom she would not leave, from going forward and following the King. I went into the chamber and asked the Assembly for permission for the National Guards who obstructed the entry to come up into the hall for a moment as they could not go back owing to the crowd in the passage. They almost all were men of the Assembly Guard. This caused a sharp hostile reaction in the party called "the Mountain".

I gather that they suspected a plot against the Assembly and supposed that I had proposed the introduction of some men of the King's guard with the object of carrying out some sinister design. Among the most excited members of the party I noticed M. Thuriot and M. Cambon.

They spoke of bringing an accusation against me and Cambon said he would hold me responsible for any attempt that might be made against the National Assembly. Instead of replying I made half a dozen of the National Guards come up into the Chamber without their arms in order to unblock the passage and then a Grenadier entered with the Dauphin in his arms and placed the child on the table of the secretaries thereby eliciting applause. The Queen followed with the rest of the family and advanced to the bureau of the secretaries after which the King and the Royal Family with the ministers sat down in the seats reserved for the latter.

The King said to the Assembly: "I have come here to prevent a great crime from being committed and I am convinced that I could not be in a safer place than in your midst, gentlemen."

The President replied, "Sire, you can count on the firmness of the National Assembly, whose members have sworn to defend with their lives the rights of the people and the constituted authorities."

The King then sat down by the President. One of the members pointed out that the Constitution laid down that no debates should proceed in the presence of the sovereign.

Accordingly the King and his family were invited to take their places in the minute-writer's office. This they did.

My colleagues and I crossed the chamber. When I reached the benches where we were supposed to sit, I had a feeling that I would be an object of hostility to the deputies who had wished to accuse me, so I made for the exit. However, voices from the Mountain called me back and they insisted that I should remain in the House. So I joined my colleagues and sat down.

At that moment a municipal officer with an adjutant of the National Guard came to the bar of the House. They reported that the mob in the Place du Carrousel had entered the courtyards and were aiming their guns at the Palace. It seemed as though they intended to storm the building. The Assembly immediately sent twenty commissioners with orders to harangue the people and to employ all their powers of persuasion to restore order and safeguard life and property. At the same time they sent twelve other commissioners to the Commune to confer with them about the best ways of maintaining security.

Up to that time the atmosphere had seemed favourable to constitutional methods and they would certainly have continued to be employed, had it not been for the incidents which occurred suddenly.

The boom of guns was heard and the twenty deputies returned saying that the people had prevented them from going to the

Palace in order, as they said, to avoid the murderous fire that was being directed from it. The reports of the cannon redoubled and the garden of the Tuileries was filled with terrible cries. An officer of the National Guard ran up saying: "They have broken through." The members who were looking through the windows into the garden, shouted, "Here come the Swiss Guards." Then we heard a fusillade from near the terrace of the Feuillants. Petitioners flocked to the bar of the House declaring that the Swiss had attacked the citizens after having lured them on. They demanded that the King should be dethroned, that he should be tried, that he should be condemned to death. The fury of the people was extreme. "We demand the dethronement of the King," cried their leaders (meaning that they did not insist on more than that), "but have you the courage to swear that you will save the Empire?" "We swear it," declared the Assembly in chorus. And from that moment it was no longer either free or master of the King's fate.

THE SEPTEMBER MASSACRES

❧❧❧❧❧❧❧❧❧❧❧❧❧❧❧❧❧❧❧❧❧❧❧❧❧❧❧❧❧❧❧❧❧❧❧❧❧

*O*N SEPTEMBER *the second Paris learnt that Verdun had capitulated to the Duke of Brunswick. The Parisians saw the invaders at their gates. As the elections for the new Assembly were imminent, the "Convention" (a term not borrowed from the Americans), meaning the politicians of the extreme left wished to profit by the popular emotion to create an atmosphere favourable to itself. Accordingly the Commune had the tocsin sounded and salvoes fired, and posted up notices saying: "The people must themselves execute justice. Before we hasten to the frontier, let us put bad citizens to death." These bad citizens—aristocrats, the relatives of émigrés, refractory priests— filled the prisons of Paris. So it was that in three days something between 1,100 and 1,400 prisoners were massacred.*

The Lawyer Maton de la Varenne (who had been denounced by a certain Rossignol after a private quarrel between the two men) has just been imprisoned. Here is what he says:

After having my name entered in the same register as that containing the name of Rossignol, accused of murder, and after paying to the different warders what they said was their due, I asked to be confined in a section called the debtors' prison, it being the most healthy and the most comfortable. They hastened to oblige me, as I was known to the Keeper as having rendered important services to several prisoners and a camp-bed was prepared for me in the "victory" room.

As I entered the ward, I was very civilly received by the six prisoners, who occupied it, among whom was Constant. This man had formerly been a hairdresser but had left his profession to play the wild man of the woods and swallow pebbles, which he did both at the Palais—then called Royal—and at the fair of Saint-Germain. He had been brought before the police magistrates on the charge of public indecency committed in company with an almost naked woman whom he had tried to pass off as another savage, and sentenced, with her, to two years' imprisonment. Their sentence had still six months to run. He was much liked by the Keeper on account of his gentleness and had been placed in the debtors' prison, where he earned a lot of money by hairdressing and shaving.

I also recognized one of my clients, one Durand, who was moved to tears by my misfortunes. He forced me to change beds with him, his being far more comfortable, and showed the utmost consideration for me until we parted, as will be seen.

Having to some extent recovered my tranquillity, by thinking things over and trusting to the zeal of my friends and more than all by eating a good dinner, I went down into the garden to take the air until closing-time. There I saw a great throng of persons of distinction and in particular the following Chevaliers de Saint Louis—de la Chenaye, the Treasurer of the Paris Museum, with whom as a member of the Museum, I have had dealings for the past ten years—de Rulhière and de Saint-Brice. I also saw the Abbé Bertrand, formerly a member of the Privy Council and brother of the ex-minister, and Lebarbier-de-Blinière, the episcopal vicar. Then there was Flost, the ex-vicar of Conflans-l'archevèque, a deputy from the Constituent-Assembly, de Chantilly, Louis XVI's gentleman of the bed-chamber and the elder Guillaume, a notary, all of whom had been arrested either in connection with August 10th or denounced for their opinions. We all tried to console one another and each of us promised that the first of us to recover his liberty would use all his credit to help the others to regain their freedom.

After returning to my room, where we were confined behind enormous bolts and locks, I went to bed and reflected until the next morning on all I had to do to hasten my liberation. When dawn came I wrote to several of my friends, who had at all times, shown willingness to help me. Among these were Panis and Danton, now Minister of Justice, and Charpentier, Danton's father-in-law, who had a bar on the Quai de l'École. I also wrote to Camille Desmoulins, secretary to the Keeper of the Seals and now a deputy. My friends, including one with whom I had dined on the day of my arrest, replied that the stormy times in which we were living made them fearful of compromising themselves. Danton promised to take an interest in my case, but did nothing. His father-in-law either did or did not speak to him about me, though he had often promised to recommend me. Desmoulins against whom I had pleaded in 1790 and obtained some judgments, damaging ones too, and whom I might have counted as an enemy, rose superior to all resentment. He saw in me a good man victimized and made every effort to induce Panis to have me interrogated or released. As for Panis, he told the person who delivered my letters that he was not going to receive any more petitions. May the tears which he has caused so many unhappy men and their families to shed fall in burning drops on his heart! May remorse tear his soul to shreds!

I spent the whole of my days in prison writing letters. One of the things I resented most strongly was not being allowed to close the letters I sent nor to receive sealed missives nor to see anyone from outside. Although we were unable to hold any communication with the outside world in regard to what was going on, it transpired, nevertheless, that the prisoners in the Capital were threatened with massacre at an early date. The Abbés Bertrand and Flost refused to believe this rumour and Flost, in particular, said in speaking of the numerous non-juring ecclesiastics, who had been arrested, "If God has permitted us to be banished to this place, He cannot have intended to deliver us to death." This reasoning by a pious man, pronounced with heartening unction, soothed our fears and each of us took heart again.

One night I was trying to sleep, when the door of my room opened with a fearful noise. Delange, serving a criminal sentence was led out, shortly to be followed by an old man of sixty-three called Berger who had been in prison for eighteen months under a similar sentence.

The doors of the other rooms in our corridor were also continually being opened. There were still five of us in my ward all of whom, except myself, expected to be released before daybreak.

Then they came to fetch Durand, who was lying fully dressed on his bed, so as not to keep them waiting. He shook my hand and promising to send me his news, whatever happened to him, went out. At the same time we could distinguish the voice of Delange, who after he had been set free wished at all costs to go to his room and take possession of his things and in particular of a little white poodle, which provided him with his principal diversion. His entreaties were in vain, as the authorities did not wish the prisoners to know of the dreadful things that were happening outside.

While they were emptying the wards, we perceived from ours a man named Caraco who, probably on account of the nature of his crime, feared that he would not be released with other offenders who, rumour had it, were being set free. We saw this man climb the pillars of the gallery, uninhabited since the fire, and reach the roof. From there he climbed down into the street, where he was instantly massacred. Duvoy tried to escape in the same way, but happily his lack of ability prevented him from succeeding. I say happily, because he was eventually saved.

Towards midnight a man named Barat who, from his ward was able to hear what was going on outside, called Gérard, my room companion, and said these words, which I shall never forget. "My friend, we are as good as dead. They are murdering the prisoners as soon as they come out. I hear their cries." When he had heard this deadly news, Gérard said to us, "Our last hour has come. There is nothing more we can do." I had left my bed, so as to be able to see and hear and replied to Gérard (forcing myself to believe it was true) that the noise came from the people in the Faubourg Saint-Antoine, who were enrolling volunteers to march to the relief of Verdun and who no doubt had first to march through the streets to the Hôtel de Ville.

At one o'clock in the morning the wicket-gate leading to our section was opened again. Four men in uniform, each carrying a naked sword and a lighted torch in his hand came up to our corridor preceded by a doorkeeper and entered the ward next to ours to examine a casket, which they broke open. On the way down they stopped in the gallery, where they questioned a man called Cuissa, desiring to know the whereabouts of Lamotte who three months before had swindled one of them out of 300 livres after having invited him to dine with him on the pretext of revealing the secret of a hidden treasure. The wretch they were holding, who lost his life that very night replied, trembling with fear, that he remembered the story very well, but could not say what had become of the prisoner. Determined to find Lamotte and to confront him with Cuissa, they went with the latter into other rooms, where their search proved useless to judge from the fact that I heard them say: "Let us go and search among the bodies for we have got to know, G—— d——n it, what has happened to him?"

You can imagine the panic into which these words threw me. There seemed nothing for it but to resign oneself to death. I accordingly made my will, which I concluded with the following words.

"I ask this favour of those who will deprive me of my life and I appeal to them by the respect due to the dead and in the name of the laws which they violate in murdering their fellow men, for which the nation will one day call them to account, I ask them to send on to these addresses my will and the letter attached to it."

I had scarcely put down my pen, when I saw two more men in uniform one of whom had one arm and the sleeve of his coat covered with blood as far as the shoulder—and his sword as well. He was saying, "For the last two hours I have been cutting off limbs right and left and I am wearier than a mason who has been slapping plaster for two days." Then they began to speak of Rulhière and promising to put him through all the degrees of torture before they killed him. They swore fearful oaths to cut off the head of the man who should give him the fatal thrust. The wretched man was found and handed over to them. They took him away crying, "Might is right," stripped him naked and sliced his body with their sabres held almost flat, which soon stripped him to the entrails and bathed him in streams of blood. At last after half an hour of terrible cries and a courageous struggle against his assassins he expired.

Three-quarters of an hour later, that is to say at about four in the morning they came to fetch Baudin de la Chenaye, whom they forced to dress. As his room was directly above ours and the windows were open I heard the door-keeper say, when he wanted to take his hat: "Leave it there, you won't need it any longer." He went out and walked with the firm step of a philosopher between the two men I have just mentioned (the murderers of Rulhière) till he reached the office of the gaolkeeper, where he underwent a kind of interrogatory. The man who had questioned him ordered him to be taken to the Abbey, which was tantamount to saying "Strike him dead." Passing the entrance door of the Abbey he uttered a cry of terror on perceiving a pile of corpses; then, covering his eyes and his face with his hands he fell stabbed to death.

Countless persons confined in the different wards of the prison such as Staude, called "the German", André Roussey, the Abbé de la Gurdette, Simonot, de Louze-de-la-Neufville, Etienne Deroncières and others suffered the same fate as the unfortunate la Chenaye. Every time the door opened I expected to hear my name called and to see Rossignol come into the room. All the same my troubled state of mind did not prevent me from thinking of possible ways of saving myself from the fury of the assassins. I took off my dressing-gown and night-cap and put on a very dirty shirt of coarse material, a shabby frock-coat without a waistcoat and an old round hat, which, anticipating some such situation, I had sent for two days before. I thought that in such a garb I would not be suspected of belonging to the educated classes and therefore deserving of death as a traitor. It will be seen that this precaution was not altogether idle.

At five o'clock they came to fetch the Abbés de Blinières and Bertrand. A man in the garden shouted, "To the Abbey with them", but a *Fédéré* at the door said they were not to be harmed. I do not know what happened to the first of these two Abbés, but I know that the second escaped with his life, as I saw him again more than a year later.

At half-past six they returned to the cell previously occupied by the two abbés to fetch the notary, the elder Guillaume. All the horrors he had witnessed since the doors had been locked the evening before had caused him to believe that he was in the greatest danger, and he hesitated to open the door which he had either barricaded or bolted on the inside. On this the men who were battering at it burst into loud imprecations, called him an enemy of the people and a criminal and went to look for reinforcements. As soon as they had withdrawn in spite of my own agitation I remarked to him, speaking through the window and unseen by him, that he had acted most imprudently in resisting. He replied to me, not knowing to whom he was speaking, "Well, sir, I don't think they murder people without hearing what they have to say." At this moment the others arrived. He opened the door and they seized him. I was worried about him for more than two weeks but I heard at last that he had been released.

After all these incidents which I have related several of the individuals, who in the jargon they used, dealt out justice to traitors, flocked up to our gallery and said that the other prisoners were to be released. "*Vive la nation*", cried Decombe de St.-Géniés, who was the first to be released, and this cry was echoed by the other prisoners one of whom, Benjamin Hurel-la-Vertu, was led off at once, almost in triumph.

All the cells on my corridor with the exception of mine, had been emptied. There were still four of us there. It seemed that we had been forgotten and we joined in addressing prayers to the Almighty to be delivered from peril. While we remained in this situation, a thousand times worse than death, the doorkeeper Baptiste came to visit us alone. He spoke of the countless murders he had seen committed and told us that he had saved us by saying that we had been imprisoned for assault. He added that they had wanted to kill him for defending us, but that now we had nothing more to fear and that he would answer for our safety. I thought that by assuring us that he had saved our lives he was just employing a device to appeal to our generosity, because I had seen him carry out every order he had received without daring to reply. Nevertheless, I took his hands and adjured him to obtain our release, promising him 100 louis if he would take me to my home or the house of one of my kinsmen. At that point he heard a noise and retired precipitately.

Just then we heard sounds and saw from our windows beside

beside which we were lying flat on our faces, so as not to be seen, twelve or fifteen men armed to the teeth and mostly covered with blood, who were conversing together in low voices in the garden. "Let us go through all the rooms," said one of them, "and not leave a soul. No mercy!"

At these words I took out from my pocket a pen-knife and opened it. I asked myself at what point I should plunge it into my body, when I reflected that the blade was too short to give me a wound that would be instantly mortal and that if I did stab myself I should only be anticipating the torments with which I was threatened. Religion came to my aid—I resolved to await events and repeated several times the *In manus tuas*, urging my companions in misfortune, especially Gérard, to place themselves in the hands of Providence.

Between seven and eight four men armed with blocks of wood and swords came in and told us to follow them. One of these, a tall man wearing a uniform looking like a gendarme's, took Gérard aside. They were talking in a very low voice and gesturing in a way that made me suspect bribery. The conversation ended by the prisoner saying, "As you see, comrade, I was arrested for having slapped an aristocrat's face." Unfortunately for him the accusation was of something of much more serious consequence. I do not think I ought to mention what it was.

While this conversation was going on I was looking everywhere for some shoes to exchange for the Court slippers I was wearing. I had to give up the search and to go down with the others dressed as I have already mentioned. Constant, nicknamed the Savage, Gérard and a third man whose name has slipped my memory were allowed to walk without interference but as for me four swords were crossed over my chest. My companions obtained their release without having to present themselves at the gaolkeeper's office. I was taken before a personage wearing a judge's sash. He was a thin man, lame and rather tall. Seven or eight months later he recognized me and we spoke. I have been told by several persons that he was the son of a former prosecuting magistrate and that his name was Chepy. As I crossed I observed that the Wetnurses' Courtyard, as they call it, was full of murderers being harangued by Pierre Manuel, then Procureur of the Commune.[1] When I came before this terrible court the following questions were put to me. What is your name? What is your profession? How long have you been here? To which my answers were: "My name is Maton-de-la-Varenne; I am a lawyer and I have been imprisoned here for the last week without knowing on what grounds. I hoped to be released last Saturday, but public business prevented it."

I refrained from mentioning Rossignol, because I was surrounded by his comrades who would have sacrificed me to his ill-will. One of these, a man who did not know me was behind me and I heard him say, "Ha! you smooth skinned gentleman, I'm going to treat myself to a glass of your blood." The self-styled judge stopped asking questions, to save time, but he opened the prison register and after examining it said: "I find there is nothing whatever against him." At these words frowns vanished from every face and a cry was raised of *"Vive la Nation"* which was the signal for my release.

It was at this moment more than any other that I realized the magnitude of the danger from which I had escaped and pale and swooning I was carried out of the gate by men who held me up under the armpits and assured me that I had nothing to fear and that I was under the protection of the people.

In the company of these persons I walked down the Rue des Ballets, which was flanked on either side by a triple line of persons of both sexes and every age. When I reached the end of the street I recoiled in horror at the sight of an enormous heap of naked corpses piled up in the gutter and foul with blood and dirt. On these I had to swear allegiance to the nation. One of the murderers had climbed on to the bodies and was exhorting the crowd. I was pronouncing the words which they forced me to utter, when I

[1] On the 18th of August Manuel had gone with Pétion to the quarries at Ménil-Montant, where they had had a shaft reopened, which had been closed several months before. They had also reconnoitred some other works where digging was going on and in particular a place called Isoixe outside the gate of St. Jacques. It is well known that it was to these excavations that were transported the bodies of the persons killed on the 2nd and 3rd of September in the massacres for which these persons (Manuel and Pétion) were responsible.

was recognized by one of my former clients who was doubtless passing by chance. He said he would answer for me, embraced me warmly and extracted some sympathy for me even from the murderers. Colange, his name is, and he is a Neapolitan, a maker of fiddle-strings in the Rue de Charonne.

At first they wanted to take me to eat and drink with the Committee of Saint Louis. I refused on the plea that as I had just escaped from death, I ought to go and console various persons, who perhaps had already given me up for lost. My motives were appreciated. I asked them to fetch me a cab as I was too weak to walk. None was forthcoming but after walking for some distance along the Rue Saint-Antoine, where I was embraced by three more acquaintances, a *fiacre* came in sight. My escort made the passengers descend and I got in with my companions, whose numbers increased so much as we proceeded that every part of the vehicle was covered with them.

It may be remembered that on August 27th I nearly lost my head on the guillotine as I crossed the Quai Pelletier under the guidance of a gendarme. It appears that some malignant spirit was resolved to destroy me, by delivering me into the hands of the assassins both on my way to prison and on my return to my own home, for at the corner of this same Quai Pelletier a man, who by reason of my bedraggled appearance and disturbed mien took me for a conspirator or an ordinary criminal, seized the bridle of one of the cab-horses and, wishing to arouse the indignation of the public against me cried out: "He mustn't be allowed to go any farther. Let us do him in here."

He had hardly finished speaking, when a young man, who was seated on one of the doors struck at him with his sword a blow, which would have split him to the waist, if he had not dodged it in time.

The result of this incident was only to lend fresh pride to my triumphal progress during which I kept remembering the words of the psalmist: *Circumdederunt me dolores mortis.* Around me I heard continual words of congratulation—"Citizens," said one, "here is a patriot whom they locked up for speaking too well of the nation." "Look at the poor fellow," said another, "his parents had him put in the cells in order to seize his property." At the same time everyone was crowding round to see me and I was constantly being embraced through the windows of the cab.

In the midst of these greetings, which exhausted both my powers of appreciation and my physical strength, we arrived at Rue Planche-Mibray. My escort told me they were going to take me across the Pont-au-Change to see laid out on the pier the bodies of the criminals on whom justice had been executed at the Châtelet and then to the court of the Palace, where the corpses of the prisoners from the Conciergerie had been stacked. Then I screwed up enough courage to ask to be excused from seeing this hideous spectacle, which I could not endure to behold a second time. My prayer was granted and we drove across the bridge of Notre-Dame, arriving at last at my father's residence. My mother was overwhelmed with emotion at seeing me again and I almost fainted from the intensity of my feelings, until I felt her cheeks pressed against mine and her tears running down my face. This was, as I have said, on the third of September.

After having passed an hour under the parental roof, where my escort had only accepted the lightest refreshment, my fear that my enemies might come for me again decided me to retire to some safer refuge. On my way I learnt that the unfortunate Lamballe had been butchered just as I was set free. An individual called Cressac in whose favour I had prepared a memorandum was also released at this time. Before his release, a man came into his cell and jovially asked him why he had been imprisoned and promised to interest himself in his case when his turn came as he thought he knew him. He added these words to reassure him. "Anyhow, if you are condemned, do not disturb yourself. I shall see that you do not suffer."

It was about two o'clock when the butchers, tired out and no longer able to lift their arms, though they were continually drinking brandy into which Manuel had put gunpowder to stimulate their fury, were sitting in a ring round the corpses lying opposite the prison to take breath. A woman with a basket full of rolls of bread came past. They took them from her and soaked each piece in the blood of their palpitating victims. No cannibals ever behaved more ferociously. The persons in the prison where I had been detained were not the only ones to be massacred. The same fate befell those in other prisons as well as persons in churches and convents. During the butchery the security forces remained in criminal inactivity. Billaud-de-Varennes proclaimed to the murderers: "Honourable citizens, those you have slaughtered were criminals. You have done your duty and you shall each receive 24 livres." Those blood-thirsty ruffians Gorsas and Brissot kept asking if this man or that was still alive, and from their office in the Municipality breathed with relish the smell of torn flesh. Finally the murderous Marat and a host of beasts of prey like him sent all over France under the seal of the Minister of Justice the following circular letter, which caused massacres of prisoners in Lyon, Orleans, Versailles and other places.

"The Commune of Paris hastens to inform its brothers in all the Departments of France, that a number of the dangerous conspirators detained in the prisons have been put to death by the people of Paris. This act of justice was judged indispensable in order to restrain by fear the legions of secret traitors concealed within the walls of the city at a moment, when the people were preparing to march against the enemy. Doubtless after the long series of treasonous acts which have led the country to the brink of the abyss, the Nation will hasten to adopt these methods, so essential to the public safety."

✤

"I did not eat the heart of the Princess de Lamballe": this might be the title of the contribution to these pages of Jacques-Charles Hervelin. His evidence dates from the day after the Terror. As a result of a denunciation accusing him of having "eaten the heart of the former Princess de Lamballe after having had it grilled", this man though he denied the charge and protested that he was a man of honour, was brought before one of the Committees of Surveillance.

"Before us, the undersigned Commissioners of the above mentioned Committee, an individual, brought hither by the armed force of the Section des Arcis appeared today at six o'clock in the evening. We asked him his name, age, occupation and address.

He replied that his name was Jacques-Charles Hervelin, aged forty-one, for the last three months a drummer in the armed force of the Section des Arcis, that he lived in the house of the Citizens' Committee of this section in the Rue Jean-Pain-Mollet and was a native of Paris.

Q. What was he before joining the section?

A. A drummer in the Gunners' Company attached to the 10th Battalion of the Paris division—called the Friends of the Fatherland.

Q. Why did he leave his battalion?

A. On account of illness. The documents in support of what he said were filed with the Health Authorities. He presented a pass from the First-Aid Commission dated the 29th Ventose, initialled by the Committee of Public Safety on the 2nd Germinal. He also presented a certificate of service from the Gunners' Company dated the 10th Frimaire.

Q. What did he do before entering the Army?

A. He was a drummer in the markets, in proof of which he produced a certificate from the Section dated the 29th November 1792 (old style).

Q. Was he married?

A. Yes.

Q. Did he live with his wife?

A. No. She resided in the section of the Observatory, Rue des Foureurs in the house of citizen Dollet, a baker by trade.

Q. Why, if he was living alone was his bread card made out for two?

A. In order to be able to supply his wife with bread, she having no card.

Q. What did he do during the four months previous to the dates of his certificates?

A. All sorts of things.

Q. He could not be telling the truth, since he had just said that he was a drummer since the commencement of the Revolution.

A. He made a mistake.

Q. Had he been in any parts of Paris during the disorders?

A. In September 1792 as he chanced to go along the Rue Saint-Antoine he saw, opposite the prison of la Force, a heap of dead bodies, which made him shudder. He climbed on to a corner post to look at them and then went away. Having heard some one a few paces away cry out, "There's the Princesse de Lamballe", he returned to his corner post and saw coming out of the prison a little woman dressed in white, whom the executioners armed with all sorts of weapons felled to the ground. He observed a drum-major in the Gendarmerie, who afterwards was killed at la Vendée, cut off the said woman's head.

Q. What did he do then?

A. He saw them drag the headless body as far as Sainte-Marie. He then followed the body along several streets and when they had come to the end of Rue Sainte-Marguerite he noticed that there was a little bulge in the garments the body was still wearing. They examined it to see what it was and found a wallet, which the persons who were dragging the body told him to take to the Committee of the Waifs and Strays in order to have the contents verified. While he was there a man came into the room holding the vitals in his hand. This man then tore out the heart and ate it whole. The members of the Committee handed him the wallet together with a statement of its contents and he took it at once to the General Assembly of the Section, where the President whom he did not know, opened it and having compared the contents with the statement, handed it back to him after commending his behaviour. From there he went to the Legislative Assembly. As it was not sitting he applied to an usher who sent him on to the Committee of Surveillance and Public Security, with whom he deposited the wallet and the statement and was given a receipt, which he said he had lost.

Q. What did he do next?

A. He went to his house in Rue Saint-Germain-l'Auxerrois without stopping anywhere on the way and remained there until the next day.

Q. Was he armed?

A. He had his sword according to the regulations.

Q. Did he follow the remains of the body?

A. No.

Q. Did he go into several wine-shops for a drink?

A. He went into one wine-shop with four individuals who, he feared, would assassinate him on account of the wallet.

Q. Did he know the owner of the wine-shop?

A. Having passed through so many streets he could not remember exactly, but he thought the shop was in the Marais.

Q. It was pointed out that he was contradicting himself, as he had just said that he had gone straight to the Section and from there to the Assembly and consequently as he went by way of Rue Saint-Antoine and la Grève, he could not have gone to drink in the Marais.

A. He was taken there by the people who had accompanied him, when he went to deposit the wallet. They paid for the wine.

Q. Did he stop anywhere else?

A. No, but while returning from the Committee of Surveillance where they had received four notes of five francs each as a reward for their honesty they went to a wine-shop in the Rue des Prêtres-Auxerrois, where they spent their money.

Q. It was pointed out that he could not be telling the truth, as he had previously said that he had gone away without calling anywhere.

A. He must have forgotten.

Q. Did he, on his way, pass through Rue Michel-le-Comte?

A. He did not know Paris well enough to remember.

Q. Did he, on his way, encounter a citizen standing on a chair?

A. He did.

Q. Did he gather what the man was saying?

A. No.

Q. Was there in the crowd surrounding this man a person holding up on the point of a pike either the head or some other part of the said woman's body?

A. No, but he recollected that at this moment he had drunk a glass of beer in a drinking shop near this place. The proprietor had come to fetch him, but he had found in the local no one he knew except the four men, who had accompanied him to make sure the wallet was not stolen.

Q. How did it come about that the wine-shop man, who did not know him, invited him to drink in the street?

A. As he had announced himself as the bearer of the wallet found on the dead woman, the owner of the wine-shop paid him many compliments and invited him to drink with his comrades.

Q. How did he come to tell the public that he was bearing the wallet?

A. He had stopped to tell the crowd about the events that had occurred at la Force, adding that he was carrying the wallet of the above-mentioned woman. He added that his four companions had wanted to stop to drink some beer and that one of them, taking a chair from the wine-shop man had stood upon it and told the people that he had the wallet. At that point he, the witness, came forward and showed it.

Q. Did he also climb on to a chair to show it to the public?

A. No.

Q. It was pointed out to the witness that he was once more contradicting himself seeing that he had previously stated that it was the wine-shop man who had invited him for a drink after learning from him that he was the bearer of the wallet, whereas he now states that he went into the wine-shop of his own accord with his four companions and that he did not announce the fact that he was carrying the wallet till one of them had taken out a chair and harangued the people in the street.

A. He did not remember exactly how it all happened.

Q. Did he, or his companions ask the wine-shop man for a cooking stove ready for use?

A. No.

Q. Did he and his companions go into a grocer's shop?

A. He could not remember.

Q. Was not the woman's head laid on the grocer's counter, while they were drinking in his shop?

A. He did not see it.

Q. Did they not force the grocer to lay out round the head the glasses of brandy they were drinking?

A. He did not see it.

Q. Was it not true that he had roasted the heart of the ci-devant Princesse de Lamballe on the cooking stove supplied by the wine-shop man at the request of himself and the other men, and had he not eaten the heart himself?

A. He had neither seen it nor eaten it.

Q. Had he not carried the sexual organs of the deceased on the point of his sabre?

A. No—only a part of the comb she wore in her hair.

Q. How did this piece of comb come to be stuck on the point of his sword?

A. It was part of her toque.

Q. It was pointed out to him that the comb and the toque are quite different things.

A. They were connected together by a piece of wire.

Q. Where had he picked up these objects?

A. In the gutter opposite the prison.

Q. Had he joined in the procession which marched through the streets carrying the head and other parts of the body of the above-named?

A. No.

Q. It was pointed out to him that instead of going straight to the Legislative Assembly, he seemed to have walked about the streets of Paris carrying on his sword-point the alleged comb of the ci-devant princess.

A. No, he had not gone with the others.

Q. Was it a fact that the citizens who had climbed on a chair in the street where they had drunk beer, was carrying a blood-stained stick, which he displayed to the public?

A. No.

Q. Was it he himself who was carrying the said stick?

A. No.

Q. For what reason did he not dare to return to his wife?

A. For motives of interest.

Q. Is not the real motive of his wife in refusing to live with him the fact that he took part in the murder of the ci-devant Princesse de Lamballe, that he went round with her head and her sexual organs and that he ate her heart, after having roasted it on a cooking-stove in a wine-shop?

A. No. All he had carried was the chignon above-mentioned.

Q. Did he know any of the persons who had joined with him in the killings at la Force?

A. No.

Q. Had they not threatened to throw him out of the window of the house where his wife lived?

A. He had no recollection of it.

Q. Was it not true that eight or ten days previously he had tried to hide himself under a camp-bed in the guard-room of the Section des Arcis?

A. Quite untrue.

Q. Was it not the case that he had been reviled by the women-citizens, who had called him a monster, a criminal, and a butcher and had accused him of having eaten the heart of the Princesse de Lamballe and was it not for this reason that he had taken refuge in the guard-room?

A. No.

Q. Could he honestly not disclose to us the names of some of the butchers at la Force?

A. He had seen a man with a mace and there was also present a cabinet-maker, who was one of the persons who had accompanied him when he was carrying the wallet. The Committee of Surveillance have his name.

Q. Seeing that he claimed to regard these massacres with horror, how could he have consented to walk with and even to drink with one of the butchers?

A. He had only drunk with the men who had accompanied him when he was carrying the wallet.

Q. The cabinet-maker was, according to his own statement, one of the butchers.

A. He replied that he did not know.

The text of these questions and answers was read over to the person interrogated, who persisted in saying that his statements were true and signed—

Hervelin

Below follow the signatures of

Leduc—President

and Delaporte and Tournay, Commissioners."

VALMY

❧❧

*O*N SEPTEMBER *20th, in a drizzle of rain, a German writer Wolfgang Goethe, attracted by curiosity to the scene, came to witness the collision between the Royal and Imperial Armies and the Army of the Revolution.*

To meet the 131,000 men of the Coalition under the Duke of Brunswick, whose force included 9,000 émigrés of whom 5,000 were kept in reserve, the French put 82,000 into the field. The battalion commanders of the volunteers were chosen by their men. Among them were Lecourbe, Suchet, Jourdan, Victor, Oudinot and Marceau.

The scene is set at the windmill of Valmy.

Kellermann occupied an exposed position near the windmill at Valmy on which our fire converged. An ammunition waggon exploded and we thought with joy of the damage the explosion must have caused in the ranks of the enemy. We halted on the road to Châlons near a sign-post pointing to Paris. We had the great city behind us and the French Army standing between us and our country. No line of retreat has, perhaps, been better closed and the situation seemed thoroughly alarming to one who, like me, had been for the last month intensively studying a good map of the theatre of operations. On that day each side fired 10,000 rounds of artillery. Nevertheless, only 1,200 men were killed and wounded. This tremendous displacement of air swept away the clouds. The cannonade was so lively that it often sounded like volley-firing, but it was irregular, being sometimes more and sometimes less intense. At one in the afternoon after a short respite, the fire redoubled in violence. The earth trembled, but no change in the position of the combatants was visible. It was impossible to foretell the issue.

I had often heard tell of cannon-fever and wished to study it. Momentary boredom, combined with a temperament which any danger stimulates to bold, nay rash, action caused me to ride forward undisturbed towards the crescent. Our troops were once more in occupation but the scene was terrifying. Everywhere one could see roofs smashed by gunfire, sheaves of corn scattered far and wide and here and there mortally wounded soldiers. Occasional stray cannon-balls shattered the remaining tiles. Alone and lost in thought I rode along the high ground on the left from where I could take in at a glance the whole well-chosen French position. They were drawn up in a semi-circle, calm and imperturbable. But I thought that Kellermann's position on the left wing was somewhat exposed.

Soon I found myself in good company—that of staff and regimental officers whom I knew. They were much astonished to find me there and wanted to take me back with them, but I explained that I had a particular object in remaining there, and knowing that I was a fanciful sort of individual, they did not insist.

I was in the very centre of the region where the cannon-balls were falling. They make a strange noise, something between the humming of a top, the splash of water and the cry of a bird. The damp ground rendered them less dangerous, for where they fell they sank in. During my crazy venture I was at least spared the risk of ricochets.

What was happening all round me impressed me curiously. I analysed my impressions very precisely, but I could not describe them except by imagery. I seemed to have got into a very hot place and felt that being permeated by the same heat I was in perfect harmony with the surrounding element. My eyesight had lost nothing of its keenness, its lucidity, but all the objects within my vision reflected a reddish light, which caused both the general position and the things in my immediate neighbourhood to assume a disquieting aspect. I noted nothing peculiar about my circulation, but I felt as though I was in the middle of a furnace, and in that sense I could claim to be suffering from a fever. But one must take note that this gripping anguish is communicated solely by the hearing. The thunder of the guns, the snoring, whistling and chattering voices of the bullets as they cleave the air are the real cause of it. As soon as I had retraced my steps and was in perfect safety once more I was surprised to notice that this feeling of heat suddenly ceased without leaving the slightest vestige of fever. Incidentally the condition I have described is one of the most painful one can experience and among my gallant brothers-in-arms I have not met a single one who seemed to enjoy it.

Throughout the day the French remained unmoved. Kellermann had improved his position. Meantime our troops had been withdrawn from the zone of fire and it seemed as if nothing at all had been achieved.

The greatest consternation spread through the Army. In the morning we had been talking of spitting and eating the French. I myself had been drawn into this dangerous adventure by a confidence in our splendid Army and in the Duke of Brunswick. Now everyone was thinking again. People avoided each other's eyes and the only words one heard were oaths and imprecations. In the twilight we assembled and were sitting in a circle. We had not even been able to light a fire as we usually did. Almost everyone remained silent. Only a few men spoke and their reflections seemed illogical or frivolous. At last they pressed me to say what I thought of the events of the day, as my terse comments had often interested or amused our little company.

So I simply said:

"From this place and from this day forth commences a new era in the world's history and you can all say that you were present at its birth."

The Next Day
Kellermann commanding the Army of Metz writes to Servan, the Minister of War.

From General Headquarters at Dampierre-sur-Auve, September 21st, at 9 p.m.

I hasten, Sir, to send you an account of yesterday's engagement.

At daybreak the enemy attacked my advance-guard, which was commanded by M. Deprez-Crassier. He fell back, fighting with courage and intelligence. The enemy in great strength advanced against several of our columns. M. de Valence at the head of his Grenadiers and Carbineers contained them for a long time on high ground in front of the position where I had drawn up my troops.

Finding it difficult to break through, the enemy prolonged their line on my right under the protection of intense artillery fire. To meet them I drew up my troops in battle order. My position was not a pleasant one, but I was loth to believe that a large proportion of their forces had passed through the gap at Grandpré and so I prepared for the battle which continued from seven in the morning until seven at night. They never dared to attack us in spite of their very superior numbers, and the day was spent in a short range artillery duel lasting nearly fourteen hours, which cost us the lives of many brave fellows. I hear that the enemy's losses were very heavy, especially in cavalry and artillery.

The troops commanded by M. Hemget sent to me as rein-forcements by M. Dumouriez and Lieut.-General Chazot, behaved splendidly and made about fifty prisoners.

I held my positions until ten at night and then moved to ground on the right of the enemy, who did nothing to interfere with my movement though it was not completed until this morning.

I cannot say enough in praise of the courage and devotion of my officers—generals, commanders of units and subordinates—and of the troops under their command. At one point I saw whole ranks of soldiers destroyed by the explosion of three ammunition waggons caused by a shell, but the men did not flinch or lose their alignment. Some of the cavalry and in particular the carbineers were frequently exposed to a murderous fire, but they showed a fine example of courage and steadiness.

I had hoped that their cavalry would attack for I had every confidence in the disposition of my own mounted forces.

. . . My losses amount to about 250 in killed and wounded.

I shall send you, as soon as may be, some poor widows whom

I shall ask you to recommend to the Legislative Assembly. They need relief.

signed Kellermann
General Commanding the Army of the Centre.

In the Duke of Brunswick's inner circle was a young French nobleman, Count Roger de Damas. He had been a second-lieutenant at twelve and now bore the badges of a superior rank. The Comte d'Artois had made him his aide-de-camp. Here he talks like a strategist.

The day of the 14th during which I saw no preparations being made seemed to me very long and I did not close an eye all night. At two in the morning a despatch addressed to M. le Comte d'Artois obliged me to wake him up. I took advantage of this opportunity to ask for permission to go forward as far as possible into our advance posts to see whether the enemy had moved during the night. I accordingly proceeded as near as possible to the village of Saint-Juvin and waited for the dawn. The first rays of light showed me positively that neither the camp nor the French troops were still on the height. Several hussar officers in the advance posts expressed their astonishment and all the more so as they had throughout the night heard musketry fire on the right of the Prussian army. I returned to inform the Comte d'Artois of this change of position. He at once went to report it to the Duke of Brunswick, not doubting that he was already apprised of it. He was greatly surprised to find that he knew nothing of this withdrawal. The Count told him that he had learnt this important news from me on my return from visiting the position. The Duke replied that I must certainly have made a mistake, that Dumouriez would not have been crazy enough to quit his ground and that he could assure His Royal Highness that he was still there.

It was now six-fifteen and it seemed to me so improbable that the Commander-in-Chief had not yet received a report from the advance posts and my confidence in him was so firm, that I began to doubt my own senses. However, my uncertainty was not prolonged. By eight o'clock the fact that the French had retreated was public property and the regiments detailed to pursue the retreating forces were already on the march.

The men of Dumouriez' army, convinced that they would be closely pursued had said to the villagers of Grand-Pré that they were prepared to submit themselves to the clemency of the King of Prussia, but they had already withdrawn successfully and blown up the bridges on the Aisne, before the first columns of the Prussian vanguard arrived. Only a few detachments could now be sent in pursuit. All they achieved was the capture of a couple of cannons and 260 men, sixty of whom had been left by Dumouriez with orders to fire at the Prussian right wing and to mask his retreat on Saint-Juvin. This was all the advantage the Duke had been able to reap from the most favourable moment of the campaign.

Meantime, the troops sent in pursuit of the French began to withdraw and it was then that I met the Duke surrounded by all his generals. As soon as he caught sight of me—I was some way off—he said he had many apologies to offer me for not believing my message and added that if he had been able to persuade himself that it was true, we should not be in the situation we were then. Shortly afterwards he attempted to cover up the disgrace of the morning, by exclaiming to M. de Pouilly, a French general attached to his person, in a burst of assumed joviality, "That, Monsieur, was a day on which I can congratulate all good Frenchmen: it was better than a victory." M. de Pouilly replied that he couldn't help wishing that Dumouriez had waited forty-eight hours longer. The Duke, seeing that he was not going to save his face as easily as that, changed his tone and said impatiently how shocked he was by M. de Clerfayt's failure to cut off their retreat. No one was deceived and everyone remained convinced the the Duke owed his failure on that day either to guilelessness or to an undeserved reputation. But how can one allow onself to believe that the Duke's complete absence of success in grasping such an obvious opportunity was due to incapacity? Does not everything show that he did not wish to grasp it? I have followed him and observed him too closely to be deceived in the quality of his talents, certainly superior to those of his critics. When he shows any lack of cleverness, foresight or determination one must blame it on his conscience, not on his military genius. I might hesitate to advance such a solution, if I had to comment on a situation comparable even to one of the least troublesome of those which Frederick II dealt with so triumphantly, when he was resisting a coalition of Powers. But the obstacles which the Duke of Brunswick had to overcome were comparatively simple and the problems, which he failed to solve, uncomplicated, so that, in view of the transcendent talents displayed by him on every march he undertook, at every position which he occupied and in his method of moving troops, I find myself forced to accuse him of falseness and treachery. I see in him a man imbued with all the errors which modern philosophy can suggest to an ill-organized brain, but certainly not an ignorant one. If he had been merely that we should be now in France and the King would be still alive. The Duke of Brunswick had always dreamed of playing the part of mediator in the issue, but he had too much respect for the doctrines of the revolution to wish to dominate the movement as a conqueror. He thought to impress the bandits by his manifesto and to influence and pacify the generals without fighting them. He persuaded himself that a show of force at the outset would enable him later to offer clemency and that in a fanatical war, based on principles which he approved, he would succeed in enlightening his foes, without seeking to crush them. The Duke of Brunswick's defeat in this campaign should be regarded as due to the cleverness of his enemies and not to their military superiority. Ambitious for a new kind of glory, he sacrificed everything in his desire to attain it and in the end was reduced to contenting himself with promises, until the protracted and ineffectual negotiations with Dumouriez made it too late to hope for success.

On the morning of the 19th the whole army marched in the direction of an isolated farm known as the Maisons de Champagne and camped in a village not far away. It was noon when the army entered the camp where it was meant to pass the night, but the camp had scarcely been established when the King of Prussia received information about the position of the French. He sent for the Duke of Brunswick and concerted with him a plan for marching against them, but found little inclination to co-operate in the Duke who raised many difficulties. However, the King forced his hand and the Duke pretended to agree. Orders were immediately given to break camp and to leave all the vehicles, tents, provisions, etc., *in situ* under guard. The troops left at three o'clock. If I wished to give an example of the perfect organization of the Prussian Army, I should quote this particular operation. Never have marching orders been framed in more soldierly fashion, better co-ordinated or tactically better devised for an attack on the enemy. Perfect order and complete silence were enjoined, and the instructions for gaining ground explained that the manœuvres and successive reports of the light troops would indicate where an advance was to be made. Where every step forward was clearly provided for, no individual had cause to be disturbed. Not a word of command, not a trumpet call was to be heard, nor the voice of a senior officer. Everyone was in the place indicated by his rank or his employment, with his mind fixed on doing his own particular duty. I had never seen anything like it in my experience of the Prussian Army under Frederick II. All the cavalry was marching in squadrons and the infantry in sections, and the distance between the columns, battalions, squadrons and sections was kept so meticulously that at any moment it would have been possible to adopt any formation which circumstances might dictate. The army arrived in this order at Sommetourbe at ten o'clock at night.

The Prince of Hohenlohe, who commanded the advance guard had received orders to join the main body of the army and after a perfectly timed march reached Sommetourbe at midnight.

The "patriots" were then at Hans, a league away.

The King ordered the troops to bivouac, while waiting for the dawn. The night was clear and calm. The King, the Duke, Messrs. de Nassau, de Lambert and three or four other persons including myself, spent part of the time in a little peasant's house. The King and the Duke employed the time in questioning villagers about the country, the behaviour of the enemy and their exact whereabouts, in studying the map and issuing orders necessitated by the various reports that came in. At two o'clock we left the King to rest until daybreak. Meantime the infantry of the advance-guard moved forward in three columns. The "patriots" had spent the morning in taking up their positions.

Their centre forming the apex of a right angle was situated on the eminence of Valmy, at the windmill of that village. There they had entrenched a formidable force of artillery. Their right wing extended to the plain, and their left formed the re-entrant of the right angle, while at the end of both wings cavalry were posted. Their whole formation seemed to comprise about 50,000 men.

The Prussians began a general move. Their right wing consisting of some of the infantry of the advance guard and some cavalry as well as a formidable array of guns was based on an outpost called la Lune and they directed their fire against the windmill. The centre, formed up in three lines with the *chasseurs forestiers* and the hussars of Wolfradt in front of them, to cover the movement and the installation of the batteries of the centre, faced the windmill of Valmy. The left wing composed of the rest of the infantry and the cavalry stretched out into the plain. The King was in command of this wing. The cavalry of the Princes would have been posted here, if they had arrived in time to come into the line. Six batteries were placed in front of the line along its whole length, but the most effective were those of la Lune and those of the centre by means of which the Duke of Brunswick meant to cripple the ranks of the "patriots" before attacking them. All the artillery of the army moved with the troops into the field, with the object of supporting on the right the left wing of Hohenlohe's troops and thus forming the centre of the left wing. The last to leave Sommetourbe were the cavalry with the King. This was at about eight o'clock. It is said that what delayed the general movement was the non-arrival of M. de Clerfayt's corps, which was expected to join the Prussian Army and for which everyone had been waiting.

The position of the two armies was pretty well as I have described it at 12.30. The two opposing lines were separated by a distance of 800 yards. The ground sloped gently from our side as far as half-way between the two lines and then climbed slowly up to the "patriot" lines. The effect of this was that the whole of the Prussian centre was masked behind the slope. The Duke after the army had been arrayed in battle order galloped up to the crest of the hill and, on seeing the enemy lines exclaimed, "The Devil!

there are plenty of them." He remained looking at them for a short time and then, returning to his post, said to the Prince of Nassau, "What do you think, Prince, of their positions?" The Prince replied that he foresaw a certain victory. The Duke begged him to explain himself whereupon the Prince pointed out that if he placed a battery in position to enfilade the right hand face of the angle which formed their centre, they would not be able to hold out for more than a quarter of an hour. The confidential adjutant of the Duke could not refrain from saying that the Prince of Nassau was right. The Duke rode up once more to the top of the hill to make a further reconnaissance and on his return ordered a general advance which was carried out at a measured pace to the sound of drums and trumpets and the horns of the chasseurs. The scene was indeed calculated to appeal to the imagination. Here were fifty thousand men marching in battle array against fifty thousand, while a formidable artillery fire was released on both sides to cover the advance or to check it. None doubted or could doubt that the attack had been irrevocably decided on and definitely commenced. But after advancing for a hundred paces the line received orders to halt. The Duke was heard to say to a few members of his staff, "Before continuing the attack, I intend to soften them with gunfire." The artillery duel continued to rage with great zeal on both sides.

Although the Prussian centre was masked by the gentle upward slope behind which it lay it was not safe from ricochets and occasionally a cannon-ball would hit one of the centre battalions at full pitch. Kleist's battalion was entirely destroyed in this way.

This deadly but useless cannonade lasted for five hours without interruption. The patriots on the high ground at Valmy though protected by a small breastwork seemed to be suffering heavy losses. Two ammunition waggons which exploded in the centre made a considerable gap in their line. At last Tempelhof, the major commanding the artillery, set to say that the ammunition was nearly exhausted. The cannonade began to slacken and gradually diminished until when the windmill battery, which had been directing its fire at the guns at la Lune, ceased firing, the latter followed suit. The guns in the centre did likewise and the cannonade came to an end. Now it began to be misty, and if at this moment the Duke had still been minded to attack, he would have had at least to change his plans, as a night attack would have to be envisaged. It was to be feared that too much time had already been lost. At this moment the left wing of the French army moved to the left, in the direction of the Vitry road, whereupon the Duke moved his right wing in order to gain ground on that side. The curtain of ground which prevented the French from seeing exactly what the Prussians were doing caused them to believe that their right wing was in retreat, and the whole line started shouting "*Vive la Nation*".

This reciprocal manœuvre did not last for long. The French halted their left wing and the Duke his right. Night fell and advance posts and sentries were put out between the two lines. The soldiers piled their arms and lighted fires. The weather was abominable with wind and cold rain. The soldiers had no bread and no hope of getting any during the whole of the following day. They were now experiencing the harsh rigour of war.

The Prince of Hohenlohe proposed to attack the enemy by night, but the Duke refused. He, for his part, made arrangements to pass the night in one of the rooms in the two farm-houses. The least dirty of the rooms was reserved for the King, who had neither slept nor eaten for two days. At about ten o'clock he installed himself in this room, while the Duke and the Prince of Hohenlohe took the other. They, like the soldiers, had eaten nothing. The Duke threw himself on a heap of straw with Prince Hohenlohe and suggested that I should sleep between the two of them. After the usual polite deprecations, I accepted the invitation as I was both famished and dead-tired and hoped to assuage my hunger by sleeping. The Duke fell into a deep sleep and, listening to his snores, I propped myself on my elbow, to look at him. "How is it possible," I said to myself, "that a man who has thrown away such a fine opportunity of winning a battle and who, besides, might well be thinking of the problems of the morrow, the sufferings of his troops and the groans of wounded men deposited in a neighbouring room, can sleep so peacefully?"

. . . The Duke now embraced the idea of showing himself as great a statesman as he was a general. In reviewing the situation, he noted that his army was rotten with disease, discouraged by delays, and threatened by famine owing to lack of organization and uncontrolled pillage. The artillery horses were worn out; the weather was cold and rainy which, added to the other disasters of the campaign, disheartened officers and soldiers alike. He was aware also that the most unseemly things were being said about the objects of the war and against the brothers of the King of France and were being communicated to the King of Prussia. In a word all the foundations and all the accessories necessary for a successful offensive were lacking. So the Duke had recourse to the last depressing resort of negotiations. Dumouriez at once realized his own superior position and the intentions of the Duke. Four days of delay reduced the Prussian Army to its last resources, as Dumouriez did not fail to perceive. He flattered the hopes of the Duke so skilfully that the latter thought he was the master. One day when the Comte d'Artois had dined with the King at the Hans, the Duke took him into an alcove and said, "Monseigneur, I have something of the greatest importance to confide to you, but first let us make sure that no one can hear us." Then he added, "I am deceiving everyone here, but I do not wish to hide anything from you. Let me tell you that Dumouriez is our man. In two days he will come over to us with all his troops."

The Comte d'Artois's sense of proportion caused him to be alarmed rather than gratified by this flight of fancy. He could not flatly contradict the Duke's statement, but he gave the Duke an outline of the obvious reasons which might cause Dumouriez to deceive him. The Duke brushed away every difficulty by saying that he was sure of his facts and adding that on the following day M. de Manstein would return to the camp with definite answers from Dumouriez and accordingly requested the Comte d'Artois to send him Baron de Roll at four o'clock in the morning. When the Baron arrived, the Duke told him the same story which the Baron refuted by pointing out the too obvious improbabilities it contained and insisting that Dumouriez was fully aware of the critical state of our forces, since during the past five days he had sent as many as six emissaries to the Prussian camp. This conversation lasted until nine o'clock when Manstein arrived with the news that all negotiations had been broken off and that France had been officially declared a republic.

This news was a deadly blow for the Duke, who wished to close his eyes to it by pretending to favour a new attack. He expressed the wish to convene a council of war at which Marshal de Castries and M. d'Autichamp should assist. The council did in fact meet in the King's quarters and everyone present voted for the attack except the Duke, who without revealing his real views, raised every sort of difficulty that his imagination could suggest. Eventually he left the council, whose advice he had never intended to take, as fully determined as before to do nothing. But now the whole sense of the negotiations was altered.

The only question open to discussion between Dumouriez and the Duke was that of the speediest possible withdrawal of the Prussian force, and of practical arrangements to expedite their retreat. Dumouriez was eager to offer all the assistance at his disposal on condition that the enemy forces should evacuate France in the shortest possible time. The Duke sent an order to the Princes to return by the route by which they had come, while he himself immediately began to withdraw his forces in a movement which deserves the name, not of a retreat, but a ghastly rout. The same soldiers whom the Prussians should have and could have beaten twelve days ago were lent by their general to manhandle the Prussian guns along the roads, their horses being unequal to the task. The roads were strewn with dead and dying men, abandoned by their comrades. The Prussian, Austrian and Royalist armies plundered one another. Verdun was delivered rather than surrendered to the "patriots". In the conferences between the French and Prussian generals the latter were shamefully dictated to and treated like the leaders of a vanquished army. All the inhabitants, who had favoured our cause, were pitilessly victimized for their loyalty.

The conditions for the surrender of Longwy were the same and the "patriots" entered the town before the Prussians were through the opposite gate. Thus two months after his arrogant manifesto the Duke decamped, chased out of France with opprobrium, his army in shreds and at the mercy of the rebels. The Duke, for his part, had an unpleasant day at Longwy. While

at dinner with the King, Prince Hohenlohe, who commanded
part of the Austrian forces treated him in the most humiliating
fashion and there was nearly a violent altercation. At the end of
this same dinner M. Valerian Zouboff, a major-general in the
Russian service and a brother of the Empress's favourite, arrived
with a letter from the Empress. This letter was full of flattery and
compliments. In it the Empress spoke of the Duke as the conqueror of the world and the leader of all the nations and he first
cast eyes on it at the moment when he had just caused Louis XVI,
till then brought low but still a king, to lose his crown. What
is there to hope for from a man who cannot die of grief and
shame?

. . . While I was still at Montabaur one day as I was going out
to dine with the King, the Duke of Brunswick asked me if I
could come and see him after dinner. I called on him at the hour
he named and we sat together tête-à-tête. He questioned me and
begged me to tell him frankly what people were saying about
him since the misfortunes which had just befallen. I tried to make
do with conventional phrases, but that did not satisfy him and he
pressed me urgently to tell him everything. At that I reviewed
his conduct since the beginning of the campaign and as I came
to each outstanding episode I retailed to him all the censorious
observations that his critics had permitted themselves to make
and, of course, I did not omit the terrible and inexplicable
catastrophe of Valmy and his retreat.

When I had reviewed in broad detail the progress of the
campaign and the manner in which he had conducted himself, to
which he listened propping up his head with his hand and with
a depressed and contrite air, he said to me: "I give you my word
of honour that if I wrote an explanation of my conduct and could
make it public, no one would reproach me. But duty binds me
to silence and I cannot do so, which makes me all the more
unhappy."

A few moments later I left him after he had protested his
affection and respect for me. He was ever generous with his
compliments, which in no wise altered my opinion of his blunders
and affected me as little as the sort of explanation he had given in
his defence.

THE MISFORTUNES OF THE ROYAL FAMILY

✣✣

THE FOLLOWING lines were written by Madame Royale in the Temple prison. The daughter of Louis XVI and Marie-Antoinette was then aged fifteen.

The King, my father, arrived at the Temple with his family on Monday, 13th August 1792 at seven in the evening.

The gunners wished to take my father alone to the tower and leave us in the castle. But Manuel had received an order from the Commune while on the way, to take us all to the tower. The gunners were angry about this but Péthion calmed them down and we went into the castle. The men from the municipality kept an eye on my father. Péthion went away but Manuel stayed.

My father had supper with us. My brother was dying to go to sleep. At eleven o'clock Mme de Tourzelle took him to the tower, which was definitely going to be our residence.

My father and the rest of us arrived at the tower at one in the morning. Nothing had been prepared for us. My aunt slept in a kitchen and it seems that Manuel was ashamed when he took her there.

On the next day, the 14th, my father came to have breakfast with my mother and afterwards we went to look at the great halls, where they said they would make some more rooms because the little tower, where we were, was too small for so many people.

After dinner when Manuel and Santerre had come we went and walked in the garden.

They had complained very much of the women servants who

had accompanied us and when we arrived we found others chosen by Péthion to serve us. We did not want them.

The next day but one, as we were dining, they brought a paper from the Commune ordering the persons who had come with us to leave.

My father and mother objected and so did the municipality people who were on guard at the Temple. The order was revoked for the time being.

All of us spent the day together. My father did geography with my brother and then my mother did history with him and made him learn some poetry by heart. My aunt gave him an arithmetic lesson.

My father had been happy to find a collection of books, which occupied his time.

My mother had her embroidery. The municipal guards were very familiar and showed little respect for my father. There was always one of them who kept him in sight.

My father asked for a man and a woman to do the heavy work.

On the night of the 19th-20th August they brought an order from the Commune at one in the morning saying that all persons not belonging to the Royal Family were to be taken away from the Temple. My mother took my brother into his room and I went into the other room with my aunt. We were only separated from my mother by a little room in which was a municipal guard and a sentry.

My father remained in his room upstairs and, knowing that they were preparing other quarters for him, he did not mind. As there were fewer people he no longer felt crowded and besides he was nearer to my mother.

He sent for Paloi the foreman and told him not to finish the room they were preparing for him. Paloi replied insolently that he only took orders from the Commune.

Every morning we went up to my father's room for déjeuner. Then we came down to my mother's room and spent the day there.

Every day we went for a walk in the garden as it was good for my brother's health, and my father was almost always insulted by the guard.

On St. Louis' Day, at seven in the morning, they sang "*Ça ira*" outside the Temple.

Péthion also sent as a turnkey Rocher, the horrible man who broke into my father's room on 20th June 1792 during the riot at the Tuileries and wanted to murder him. This man was always in the tower and tried by every means to torment my father. Sometimes he sang the Carmagnole and other horrid songs and sometimes, knowing that my father did not like the smell of a pipe, he would puff smoke at him as he passed.

In the evening he had always gone to bed by the time we went for supper. We had to pass through his room. Sometimes he was in his bed when we went to dinner.

There was no sort of annoyance or insult which this man did not invent. My father bore it all very sweetly and forgave the man with all his heart.

My father was short of everything. He wrote to Péthion asking for the money, which he should have received, but there was no reply.

The garden was full of workmen who often insulted my father. There was one who boasted that he would strike my mother on the head with his tools. Péthion had him arrested.

The insults redoubled on the second of September. We did not know about the massacres on that day.

People threw stones from the windows at my father. Luckily they did not hit him or anyone else.

At another window a woman wrote on a square of cardboard: "Verdun is taken." She put it for a moment in the window and my aunt had time to read it. The municipal guards did not see her.

Hardly had we received this news when there arrived a fresh municipal guard called Mathieu. He was inflamed with anger and told my father to go up to his room.

We went with him as we were afraid they wanted to separate us.

Mathieu then turned on my father and vented his rage upon him. Among other things he said, "The drums have beaten the call to arms, the tocsin has sounded, the alarm gun has been fired, the enemy are at Verdun. If they come here we shall all die, but you will be the first."

My father listened to these insults and countless others like them with the calm inspired by innocence. My brother burst into tears and ran into the other room. I had the greatest difficulty in consoling him. He already imagined his father dead.

The municipal guards all reproached Mathieu for his violence. All the same they were no better disposed than he was. They told my father they were sure that the King of Prussia was marching against France and killing French soldiers under an order signed Louis.

My father was dreadfully upset by this slander and begged the municipal guards to contradict it outside.

My mother heard the drums beating the call to arms all night, but we did not know what was happening.

On 3rd September at ten in the morning, Manuel came to see my father and assured him that Mme de Lamballe and the other persons, who had been taken away from the Temple were all together at la Force and quite safe.

At three o'clock we heard fearful cries. As my father and mother left the dinner table to play backgammon, the municipal guard, who behaved well, shut the door and windows and drew the curtains so that we should not see what was happening. That was right and proper.

The workmen in the Temple and Rocher, the turnkey, joined the murderers and the noise increased.

Several municipal guards and officers of the National Guard arrived. The latter wanted my father to show himself at the window. The municipality men very rightly objected.

When my father asked what was happening a young officer said to him, "Very well, Monsieur, as you wish to know, the people outside want to show you the head of Mme de Lamballe."

My mother was frozen with horror. The men from the municipality scolded the officer but my father with his usual good nature excused him by saying that it was his fault for having asked the officer, who had merely answered his question.

The din continued until five o'clock. We learnt afterwards that the crowd had wanted to break open the doors but the municipal guards had prevented them by putting a three-coloured sash on the gate. They had, however, allowed six of the assassins to walk round the tower carrying the head of Mme de Lamballe. The crowd wanted them to drag the body round too, but they had to leave it at the door. When the deputation entered the Temple, Rocher uttered cries of joy on seeing the head of Mme de Lamballe and scolded a young man who was sick with horror at the spectacle.

Hardly was the rioting over when Péthion who should have been occupied in putting a stop to the massacre coolly sent his secretary to my father to count out some money for him.

The municipal guard who had sacrificed his sash in putting it on the gate got my father to pay him the cost of it.

My aunt and I heard them beating the call to arms all the night. We did not think that the massacre was still going on. My poor mother could not sleep all night. It was only later that we learnt that the massacre had lasted for three days.

One could not credit the extraordinary behaviour of the municipal men and the guards: they seemed to be afraid of everything—a bad conscience no doubt. One day a man with a new gun fired it off outside to try it. They put him on a charge and questioned him closely.

Another evening at supper time the call to arms was heard several times. The guards thought the foreigners had come and that horrible Rocher took his great sabre and said to my father, "If they come here, I shall kill you." It turned out to be nothing but a misunderstanding between patrols.

Another time a hundred workmen tried to force open the iron gates on the side of the Rotunda. The municipality men and the guard hurried up and dispersed them.

All these fears caused discipline to become stricter. Nevertheless, we found two of the municipals who alleviated my father's misery by showing him kindness and encouraging him to hope. I believe they are dead.

There was also a sentinel who had a conversation with my aunt through the keyhole. This poor fellow never ceased weeping all the time he was at the Temple. I don't know what has happened to him. May heaven reward him for his loyalty to the King.

I studied the rules of arithmetic and copied out extracts from books with a municipal always looking over my shoulder, thinking I was planning some sort of a conspiracy.

They took away the newspapers from us, fearing we should learn the news from abroad. But one day, full of glee, they brought one to my father, saying there was something interesting in it. What a horror! It said that they would put his head inside a red-hot cannon-ball.

And one evening a municipal, on arrival, offered us threats and insults that we should all be killed if the enemy approached. He said the only one he was sorry for was my brother, but that as he was born of a tyrant he would have to die too.

This was the usual time-table of my august parents. My father got up at seven and prayed until eight, after which he dressed until nine with my brother to keep him company. Then he went up to breakfast with my mother.

After breakfast my father came down again with my brother to whom he gave lessons until eleven. Then my brother played until noon, after which we all went for a walk in the garden, whatever the weather, because the guard was relieved at this time and the new guard wished to see my father and be sure that he was in the Temple.

Our walk lasted till two o'clock, when we dined. After dinner my father and mother played backgammon or picquet.

At four my mother went up to her room with my brother, because my father generally slept then.

At six my brother came down and my father gave him lessons or played with him until supper.

At nine o'clock, immediately after supper my mother undressed my brother and put him to bed. Then we went upstairs again as my father did not go to bed till eleven.

My mother's life was more or less the same as my father's. She worked a lot at her embroidery.

My aunt often said prayers during the daytime: she always went through the service for the day, read many religious books and spent much time in meditation. Like my father, she fasted on the days ordained by the Church.

. . . On Sunday the 20th we learnt from the street-vendors of my father's death (sentence of death).

At seven in the evening they came to tell us that an order from the Convention authorized us to go down to my father. We ran to his room and found him very much changed. He wept for our grief, but not on account of his own death. He told my mother the story of his trial, making excuses for his murderers. He repeated to my mother that they wanted to have Primary Assemblies but that he was against them as they would upset France. Then he gave my brother some good religious advice and told him in particular to forgive the people who had ordered his death. He gave his blessing to my brother and me.

My mother was very anxious for us to spend the night with my father, but he refused as he needed to be quiet.

My mother asked leave to return to him next morning. He agreed to this, but after he had gone away he asked the guards to see that we did not come down again, because it caused him too much pain.

. . . One night my brother felt very ill, so they sent for Thierri with a surgeon called Soupé and a truss-fitter named Pipelet to bandage him for hernia.

Mme Tison (the wife of the gaoler) went out of her mind. She was very upset by my brother's illness and tormented by remorse. She had been unwell for a long time. After a time she would not go out into the air and then she began to talk to herself. Unfortunately that made me laugh and my poor mother—and my aunt as well—looked at me kindly, as though my laughter did them good. Mme Tison kept talking about her sins and the ruin of her family, as well as about the prison and the scaffold. She thought that the persons she had denounced had been killed. Every evening she waited to see whether the municipal guards she had denounced would come or not. When she did not see them, she went to bed and had terrible dreams which made her worse.

My mother and my aunt could not have been kinder to this woman, though they had no reason to be grateful to her. They nursed her and encouraged her all the time she was in the Temple.

One day they took her from the tower and put her in the castle. Then as her madness got worse they placed her in the Hôtel-Dieu and put a woman spy along with her to question her on behalf of the Government. The municipals asked us to send some linen to this woman, who had looked after our linen when she was with us.

On the 3rd July at ten o'clock at night they read to us a decree issued by the convention saying that my brother would be separated from my mother and placed in the safest room in the tower.

As soon as my brother heard this he started screaming and threw himself into my mother's arms begging not to be parted from her.

My mother too was horrified by this cruel order and would not give him up. She defended his bed against the municipals. But they insisted on taking him and threatened to use violence and to send for the guard to carry him off by force.

An hour was spent in discussion and argument, insults and threats by the municipals and tears and opposition from all of us. At last my mother consented to give up her son. We got him up and when he was dressed my mother handed him over to the municipals after bathing him in tears, as if she foresaw that she would never see him again.

The poor little fellow kissed us all tenderly and departed in tears with the men.

My mother told the municipals before they went to ask the general council urgently to give her leave to see her son, if only at mealtimes. They undertook to do this.

My mother felt she had reached the height of unhappiness in being separated from her son. However, she thought that he was being looked after by an honest and educated man. Her misery increased when she knew that the shoemaker Simon, whom she had known as a municipal, was in charge of her unhappy child.

My mother repeatedly asked for permission to see him, but did not receive it. Meanwhile, my brother cried for two whole days inconsolably and begged to see us.

The municipals no longer remained in my mother's room; we were locked in, day and night. The guards only came three times a day to bring our meals and to examine the bars of the windows to see if they were in order. We often went up into the tower. My brother went up every day and the only pleasure my mother had was to watch him going by through a little window. Sometimes she waited there for hours to get a glimpse of her darling child.

My mother got a little news of him from the municipals and

from Tison, who went down on washing days, saw Simon and heard from him how he was.

Tison tried to make amends for his bad conduct. He behaved better and gave my mother some news of her son, but not much.

Simon treated my brother very badly, when he cried at being separated from us, till at last the child was so frightened that he did not dare to weep.

The convention had heard a false report that my brother had been seen on the boulevards and learning that the guards were grumbling because they never saw him and said that he was no longer in the Temple, they had him sent down to the garden, so that people might see him.

My brother complained of being separated from my mother and asked to see the law ordering this. When the members came up to my mother's room, she complained of the cruelty of taking her son away from her. They replied that this was one of the measures which they thought necessary.

Henriot, a new general, also came to see us. His rough manners astonished us. From the moment he came in to the moment he went out he used bad language.

On 2nd August at two in the morning they came and woke us up to read a decree from the convention ordering that on the demand of the prosecutor of the Commune my mother should be taken to the conciergerie for trial.

My mother heard this order without flinching. My aunt and I immediately asked to be allowed to go with my mother, but as the decree did not say so, they refused.

My mother packed up her clothes in a bundle. The municipals did not leave her and she was obliged to dress in front of them. They asked for her handbags which she gave them. They went through them and took out whatever was inside, though there was nothing of any importance, made a parcel of the contents which they said would be opened by the tribunal in the presence of my mother. They only left her a handkerchief and a bottle of smelling salts in case she felt unwell.

At last my mother went after having embraced me and told me to be brave and to look after my health. I did not reply. I was quite sure that I would never see her again.

My mother had to stop at the bottom of the tower because the municipals had to draw up a paper for her discharge from the Temple.

As she went out she knocked her head against the lintel of the door, which was lower than she thought, but she did not hurt herself very much. After that she got into a carriage with a municipal and two gendarmes.

Several days later my mother sent for her things and among others her knitting, which she was very fond of as she was knitting a pair of stockings for my brother. We sent it to her but heard afterwards that it had not been delivered for fear she should harm herself with the needles.

At first we heard a little news of my brother from the municipals, but that did not last long.

Every day we heard him singing with Simon the Carmagnole, the Marseillaise and many other horrid songs.

Simon made him wear a red bonnet and a carmagnole jacket and he forced him to sing at the windows so as to be heard by the guard and to utter fearful blasphemies against God and to curse his family and the aristocrats. My mother happily did not hear all these horrors for she had already gone.

After her departure they came to look for my brother's coloured clothes. My mother had said she hoped he would continue to wear mourning, but the first thing Simon did was to take off his black suit.

The change in the manner of his life and the ill-treatment he suffered made my brother ill at the end of August. Simon gave him horrible food and made him drink a lot of wine, which he detested. All that made him feverish. They gave him some medicine which did no good and which disturbed his health. He got very fat but did not grow in height. However, Simon made him go for walks and take the air on the roof of the tower.

At the beginning of September I was upset and worried about my mother; every time I heard the drums beat I feared another second of September.

We spent the month of September quietly enough going up on to the tower every day. The municipals visited us punctually three times a day, but their strictness did not prevent us from getting news, in particular of my mother, about whom we were anxious.

We learnt that she was accused of writing to people outside, so we at once threw away our writing materials and our pencils, fearing they would make us undress before Mme Simon and that the things we had might compromise my mother. We had always managed to keep, in spite of the searches, some ink, pens and pencils. I no longer fear to mention this as my parents are no longer alive.

We also learnt that my mother had thought of escaping and that the wife of the jailer was kind and was taking care of my mother. Afterwards we learnt that she had been questioned secretly, but we did not know about what.

The municipals came again to ask for underlinen for my mother, but they would not give us any news of her health. They took away the embroidery we were doing as they feared it consisted of magical and dangerous characters.

We did not know, my aunt and I, if my mother was alive or dead and though we had heard a street-seller cry out that they wanted her trial to take place without any interruption, hope, the natural consoler of the wretched, made us believe that she would be saved.

We could not picture to ourselves the unworthy conduct of the Emperor of Austria who left the Queen, his kinswoman to perish on the scaffold without doing anything to save her. But that is what happened, though we could not believe that the House of Austria could be guilty of such baseness.

There were times when we were full of apprehension for my mother, seeing the rage of the people against her. All this time —a year and a half—I remained in this painful uncertainty, till at last I learnt of the death of my good and august mother.

We also learnt from the hawkers of the death of the Duc d'Orléans: that was the only news we got during the winter.

Then the searchings began again and we were treated harshly. My aunt who had a sore on her arm had great difficulty in getting something to treat it with. They kept her waiting a long time. At last one day one of the municipals protested against the in-humanity of this behaviour and sent for some ointment.

They also took away my herb tea, which I used to drink every morning for my health.

When they no longer gave my aunt fish on fast days, she asked urgently to be given fast-day dishes so that she could do her duty. This was refused on the ground of equality. It was pointed out that there was no difference in the days, that there were no longer weeks but periods of ten days. They brought us a new almanack, but we didn't look at it.

Another day when my aunt asked for lenten fare, they said to her: "But, citizeness, you don't know what is happening. One can't get everything one wants in the market." After that my aunt asked no more.

They kept on searching our room especially in the month of November. Orders were given to search us three times every day. One of the searches lasted four hours and only finished at half-past eight at night. The four municipals who made the search were drunk. I cannot give an idea of their talk, the rudeness and their bad language during all this time.

They took away a lot of silly things like hats, playing cards with kings and books with the royal arms. They left us our religious books, after hurling many insults at our religion.

Simon accused us of making false *assignats* and corresponding with the outside world. He insisted that we had corresponded with my father during his trial. He made a statement to this effect in the name of my brother whom he forced to sign it.

The noise, which he believed was made by us coining money, was the sound of tric-trac, which we used to play in the evenings.

The winter passed quietly enough. There were many visits and searches, but they did give us some wood.

On January 19th we heard a great noise from my brother's room from which we guessed that they were taking him away from the Temple. We felt sure that this was so when, looking through the shutter we saw a lot of parcels being carried away. During the following days we heard his door being opened and believed they had taken him away and had put some German or foreign prisoner in his room. We felt the need to give this unknown prisoner a name, so we called him Melchizedek, but I learnt afterwards that it was only Simon who had gone away.

He had been given the choice of becoming a municipal guard or staying with my brother, so they were cruel enough to leave my poor little brother quite alone.

I think it unheard of savagery to leave an unhappy child of eight alone, locked in a room behind bolts and bars with no one to help him and only an inefficient bell which he never pulled as he preferred to go without things rather then ask his persecutors for them.

His bed was not made for six months as my brother was not strong enough to make it. He was covered with bugs and fleas which swarmed on his body and in his clothes. His stools remained in his room. He never threw them out, nor did anyone else. The window was never opened and the smell of the room was unendurable. By nature my brother was inclined to be dirty and idle and might have taken more care of his person.

Often they gave him no light. The poor boy was frightened to death, but he never asked for anything. He spent the day doing nothing and the wretched existence he led had a bad effect on his moral and physical welfare—not that his health was absolutely undermined, but to have kept well for so long shows that he had a good constitution.

During this winter the people in the Temple generally addressed us as "tu".

❧

After Thermidor Austria managed to secure the exchange of Madame Royale against some members of the Convention who were in their hands. Marie-Thérèse married her first cousin the Duc d'Angoulême, the son of the Comte d'Artois. She did not like to be reminded of what she had gone through. When the daughters or wives of victims of the Terror talked to her of those unhappy times, she listened to them with extreme coldness. She came back to France during the Hundred Days and when Napoleon returned from Elba, she showed herself to the army and the people in a desperate attempt to inflame the zeal of the Royalists. Napoleon impressed by her ardour said, "She's the only man of the family."

On August 10th, 1792 when the Royal Family left the Tuileries for ever, a man escaped from a window. He was the valet-barber of Louis

XVI, Jean-Baptiste Cléry. He went into hiding in the country, but when he heard of the arrest of the King, he went to see Pétion, the Mayor of Paris and asked permission to serve the prisoner. This was granted and Cléry looked after the King for five months in the Temple. After the King's execution Cléry asked to be attached to the Dauphin. His application was refused and he himself was imprisoned first in the Temple and then at la Force. He managed to conceal the notes he had written day by day during the King's captivity, and put them into shape after his own release.

On Thursday January 17th, M. de Malesherbes came in about nine in the morning. I went to meet him. "All is lost," he said, "the King has been sentenced to death." The King seeing he had arrived, got up to greet him. The Minister threw himself at the King's feet. He was stifled by his sobs and for a while could not speak. The King lifted him up and gave him an affectionate hug. M. de Malesherbes then informed him of the decree, sentencing him to death. The King made no movement expressing surprise or emotion. He only appeared moved by the sorrow of this worthy old man and sought to console him.

. . . His Majesty accompanied him to the door and asked him to come early in the evening and not to desert him in his last hours. "I felt very much moved by the grief of this good old man," said the King as he returned to his room where I awaited him.

Since the visit of M. de Malesherbes I had experienced a general feeling of faintness and trembling. However, I was able to prepare everything the King needed for shaving. He lathered himself while I held the basin. As I was obliged to concentrate on what I was doing, I had not yet dared to glance at my unhappy master till by chance my eyes met his and my tears began to flow in spite of myself. I do not know if it was my lamentable condition that reminded the King of his own situation but, in any case, a pallor overspread his face and even his nose and ears turned suddenly white. At the sight of this my knees began to give way under me. The King seeing that I was fainting seized my two hands and gripped them strongly, saying in a low voice, "Come now, don't give way!" He was under observation:

without speaking I was able to convey to him all my misery and he seemed to sympathize. His face recovered its animation and he continued to shave himself quietly. Then I dressed him.

His Majesty remained in his room until it was time for dinner, reading or walking about. Towards evening I saw him going to his office and followed him in case he might need my services. "You have heard," he said "the account of my condemnation." "Oh, Sire," I exclaimed "you must hope for a reprieve. M. de Malesherbes thinks they could not refuse it." "I see no hope of that," said the King, "but it really pains me to see that M. d'Orléans, my kinsman, voted for my death. Read this list." On this he handed to me a list of names, which he was holding. "The public," I said, "are murmuring in no uncertain manner. Dumouriez is in Paris. It is said that he is bearing a message from his army disapproving of Your Majesty's trial. The people are revolted by the infamous conduct of the Duke of Orleans. A rumour is going round that the ambassadors of the Foreign Powers are going to meet and go all together to the Assembly. Indeed there are many who believe that the party of the Convention fear a popular rising." "I should be sorry indeed if that happened," said the King. "It would only mean fresh victims. I do not fear death," he added, "but it makes me shudder with horror to think of the cruel destiny that awaits my family—the Queen and our poor children. And all the faithful servitors who have not deserted me, those old men who had nothing to live on except the modest pensions I have been paying them. Who will help them now?" He had picked up somewhere an old copy of the *Mercure de France* containing a riddle he wanted me to guess. I sought in vain for the right word. "Why, cannot you guess it? It is particularly applicable to me at this moment. The word is 'sacrifice'." The King ordered me to search in the library for the volume of the History of England which contained the account of the death of Charles I. During the following days he read the volume. I then learnt that His Majesty had read 250 volumes since he came to the Temple.

On Saturday the 19th at nine in the morning a member of the Municipal Guard called Gobeau came in with a paper in his hand. He was accompanied by the doorkeeper Mathey who brought with him writing materials. He had orders to make an inventory of the furniture and other effects. His Majesty left me alone with him and retired to his room in the tower. Then, under the pretence of making an inventory, the municipal began to search the room most meticulously in order to make sure that no weapon or sharp instrument had been hidden there. He waited to go through a little desk containing papers. The King was obliged to open all the drawers and to take out and show the man all the papers one after another.

While this search was being carried out in the tower, His Majesty went into his room wishing to warm himself. Mathey, the doorkeeper, was at that moment standing in front of the fire with his collar turned up and his back to the blaze. The King could only warm himself partially as the insolent doorkeeper did not budge from his place. Finally His Majesty told him sharply to move. This caused him to withdraw and the municipals went out at the same time, having finished their search.

That evening the King told the Commissioners to ask the Commune why his counsellors were prevented from coming to the tower as he wished to consult with M. de Malesherbes at least. One of the Commissioners then stated that they had been forbidden to communicate to the General Council any request from Louis XVI which was not written and signed by his hand. The King said: "Why have they left me for two days in ignorance of this change of procedure?" He then wrote a note and handed it to the municipals, who only took it to the Commune the next day. The King asked to see his counsellors freely and complained of the order that he was to be watched by day and night. "It should be realized," he wrote to the Commune, "that in my present position it is very painful for me never to be alone and to be unable to meditate peacefully as I need to do."

On Sunday January 20th the King, as soon as he had risen enquired of the municipals if they had communicated his request to the Council of the Commune. They assured him that they had done so immediately. At about ten o'clock I went into the King's room. He at once said to me, "I am waiting for M. de Malesherbes to arrive." "Sire," I said, "I have just learnt that he has called several times but has been refused access to the tower." "I am going to find out the reason for this refusal," said the King. "The Commune will doubtless have taken some decision regarding my letter." Then he walked about the room, read, wrote and occupied himself thus throughout the morning.

It had just struck two o'clock, when the door was suddenly opened. It was the Executive Council. From twelve to fifteen persons came in all together. Among them were Garat, the Minister of Justice, Lebrun, the Minister of Foreign Affairs, Grouvelle, secretary of the Council, the President and the Procureur Syndic of the Department, the Mayor and the Procureur of the Commune, the President and the Chief Attorney of the Criminal Court, Santerre, who entering first told me to announce the Executive Council. The King had heard the sound of many footsteps outside and, rising to his feet, walked a few paces towards the entrance but on seeing this large body of people he remained between the door of his room and that of the antechamber, in a noble and imposing attitude. I was near him. Garat, wearing his hat upon his head acted as spokesman and said, "Louis, the National Convention has instructed the Executive Council to signify to you its decrees of the 15th, 16th, 17th, 19th and 20th of January. The secretary of the Council will read them to you." Then Grouvelle, unrolled the decree and read it in a weak and trembling voice.

Decrees of the National Convention
of the 15th, 16th, 17th, 19th, and 20th of January

Article I

The National Convention declares Louis Capet, last King of the French, guilty of conspiracy against the liberty of the nation and of attempting to undermine the safety of the State.

Article II

The National Convention decrees that Louis Capet shall suffer the death penalty.

Article III

The National Convention declares null and void the document presented to the Court by the advisers of Louis Capet and described as an appeal to the Nation against the judgment given against him by the Convention, forbids all persons whatsoever to give effect to it, on pain of being prosecuted and punished on the charge of attempting to undermine the safety of the Republic.

Article IV

The provisional Executive Council shall communicate the present decree to Louis Capet during the day and shall take the necessary police and security measures to ensure that it shall be executed within twenty-four hours, dating from its notification and shall render an account of everything to the National Convention, as soon as it has been put into effect.

During the reading of this document the King's expression remained unchanged. I only noticed that in Article I, when the word conspiracy was uttered a smile showing scornful indignation appeared on his lips. But when it came to the words "shall suffer the death penalty", a heavenly glance directed at all those standing round him proclaimed that death held no terrors for the innocent. The King took a step towards Grouvelle, who handed him the decree. Then he folded it up, took his wallet from his pocket and placed it in it. At the same time he took another paper from his portfolio and said to the minister Garat: "Minister of Justice, I request you to hand this letter forthwith to the National Convention." As the minister appeared to hesitate, the King added, "I shall read it aloud to you", upon which he read the following lines without faltering in the slightest:

"I ask you to grant me three days so that I may be able to prepare myself to appear before God. To assist me in this I ask to be allowed to see freely the person whom I shall indicate to the Commissioners of the Commune, and that this person should be assured that he need have no fear or anxiety resulting from the charitable service to be rendered by him to me.

"I ask to be delivered from the constant supervision which the General Council has recently imposed on me.

"I ask, in the interval, to be able to see my family, whenever I wish and without witnesses. I would further express the wish that the National Convention should immediately interest themselves in the future of my family and should permit them to leave their present quarters and establish themselves wherever they think fit.

"I recommend to the good offices of the nation all the persons formerly in my service. Many of these have spent all their private means in the service, and as they no longer receive salaries, must be in need. And there are others, who only had their pay to live on. Among the pensioners there are many old people and women and children, who lived entirely on their pensions.

"Done at the Tower of the Temple this twentieth day of January seventeen hundred and ninety-three.

Louis."

Garat took the King's letter and assured him that he would deliver it to the Convention. As he was going out the King felt in his pocket and took out his portfolio again saying, "Monsieur, if the Convention grants my request in respect of the person whom I wish to visit me, here is his address." His Majesty then handed it to one of the municipals. The address, not written in the King's handwriting bore the name: Monsieur Edgeworth de Firmont, No. 483, Rue du Bac. The King retired a few paces and the Minister and those with him left the room.

His Majesty paced up and down for a few moments. Meanwhile I was leaning against the door with my arms crossed, emptied of all feeling. The King came up to me and said, "Cléry, ask for my dinner, will you?"

A few moments later two municipals called me into the dining-room and read me an order the substance of which was "that Louis was not allowed to use a knife or fork at his meals. A knife would be given to his valet to cut his bread and meat in presence of two Commissioners, after which it would be taken away." The two municipals told me to give the King this message. I refused.

When he went into the dining-room the King saw the basket containing the Queen's dinner. He asked why the family had been kept waiting for an hour and added that the delay might have caused them anxiety. After sitting down to the table he said,

"I have no knife." The municipal Minier then informed His Majesty of the Commune's orders. "Do they think me such a coward as to attempt my own life?" he said: "they impute crimes to me but I am innocent and shall die without fear. I would that my death might bring happiness to the French and ward off the dangers which I foresee." There was dead silence. The King ate little. He cut his beef with his spoon and broke his bread with his fingers. His dinner only lasted a few minutes.

I was in my room a prey to the deepest misery when, at six in the evening, Garat returned to the tower. I was about to announce to His Majesty that the Minister of Justice had returned when Santerre, who was walking in front of the Minister, approached the King and said in a low voice, but with a laughing air: "Here is the Executive Council." The Minister, coming forward, said that he had delivered the King's letter to the Convention and that they had instructed him to convey to the King the following reply: "Louis was authorized to send for any minister of religion he might choose and to see his family freely and without witnesses. The Nation, invariably generous and just would see to the future of his family. Just payments would be made to his creditors. The National Convention had set aside the question of a respite of three days."

The King listened to the reading of this message without making any remark. Then he went into his room and said to me: "I thought, from Santerre's cheerful manner, that he was going to tell me that the respite had been granted." A young municipal called Botson, seeing the King speaking to me, came up. "You look as if you had some sympathy for my situation," said His Majesty: "receive my thanks." The Commissioner, surprised, did not know what to answer and I was myself astonished at the King's remark seeing that only a few moments before this young municipal, with his gentle and interesting expression had said in my hearing: "I asked leave to come to the Temple to compare his face with the one he'll pull tomorrow." "And I too," said Mercerault the stone-hewer: "No one wanted to come, but I would not have given up the chance for a lot of money." Such were the vile and savage men whom the Convention detailed to guard the King in his last moments.

G

After the reading of the reply from the Convention, the Commissioners took the Minister of Justice aside and asked him how the King was to see his family. "In private," said Garat, "that is the will of the Convention." The municipals then communicated to him the decision of the Commune ordering them to keep the King in view by day and night. It was agreed between the municipals and the Minister that, in order to reconcile the two decisions, the King would receive his family in the dining-room, where they could be seen through the glass partition, but that the door would be closed, so that their conversation should not be heard.

The King called back the Minister of Justice to ask him if he had notified M. de Firmont. Garat replied that he had brought him in his carriage. He was now with the Council, but would soon come up. His Majesty handed to a municipal commissioner called Baudrais, who was talking with the Minister, the sum of three thousand francs in gold and asked him to deliver it to M. de Malesherbes, to whom it belonged. The man promised to do this, but actually took it straight to the Council, and the money never reached M. de Malesherbes. M. de Firmont appeared. The King went with him into the little tower and shut himself up with him. As Garat had left, there were now just the three municipals in His Majesty's apartment.

At eight o'clock the King came out of his study and told the Commissioners to take him to his family. They replied that they could not do this, but that if he wished, they could bring the family down to him. "Very well," said the King "but can I at least see them alone in my room?" "No," said one of the men, "we have arranged with the Minister of Justice for you to see them in the dining-room." The King replied: "You have heard that the decree of the Convention permits me to see them without witnesses." "That is right," said they: "you will be in private. We shall shut the door, but we shall keep an eye on you through the glass." "Bring down my family," said the King.

After this His Majesty went into the dining-room. I followed him and put the table on one side and arranged the chairs at the end to make more room. The King said, "I want you to bring me some water and a glass." There was on the table a carafe of iced water, so I just brought a glass and put it by the carafe. The King said: "Bring me some water that is not iced. If the Queen drank from that carafe, it might upset her. You will tell M. de Firmont," he added, "not to come out of my study. I am afraid that the sight of him would cause too much pain to my family." The Commissioner who had gone to fetch them was absent for a quarter of an hour. During this time the King went back to his study, but came out from time to time to the entrance door, showing signs of deep emotion.

At 8.30 the door opened. The Queen appeared first holding her son by the hand, then came Madame Royale and Madame Elisabeth. All of them rushed into the King's arms. There was a sad silence lasting several minutes only interrupted by the sound of sobbing. The Queen made a movement to lead His Majesty to his room. "No," said the King. "Let us go into the dining-room. I can only see you there." They entered and I shut the door which had glass panels. The King sat down with the Queen on his left, Madame Elisabeth on his right, Madame Royale almost opposite, while the young prince stood upright between his father's knees. They all leaned towards him and often embraced him. This sad scene lasted for an hour and three-quarters, during which it was impossible to hear anything. One could only see that after each sentence spoken by the King, the princesses started to sob once more and after an interval of minutes the King began to speak again. It was easy to judge from their reactions that the King had informed them of the sentence.

At a quarter past ten the King rose and all the others did likewise. I opened the door. The Queen was holding the King's right arm. Their Majesties were each giving a hand to the Dauphin. Madame Royale, on the left, had her arms round her father's waist. Madame Elisabeth, on the same side but more to the rear had hold of the left arm of her august brother. They took a few steps towards the entrance door, groaning and sobbing painfully. "I assure you," said the King "that I shall see you tomorrow morning at eight o'clock." "You promise?" they said all together. "Yes, I promise." "Why not at seven o'clock?" said the Queen. "Very well," replied the King "at seven: adieu." He pronounced this word of farewell in such a touching manner, that they all broke out sobbing afresh. Madame Royale fell in a faint at her father's feet, which she held embraced. I lifted her up and helped Madame Elisabeth to support her. The King, desiring to put an end to this heartrending scene, embraced them all most tenderly and then had the strength of mind to tear himself from their arms. "Adieu . . . adieu," he said and went back into his room.

The Queen and the Princesses went up to their quarters. I wished to go on helping Madame Royale up the stairs, but the municipals stopped me at the second step and forced me to go back. Although the two doors of the King's apartment were closed, one still could hear the cries and lamentations of the Princesses on the staircase. Meantime the King rejoined his confessor in his study in the little tower.

Half an hour later he came out and I served his supper. The King ate sparingly but with appetite.

(I had been at pains to order for the King's supper chicken fried in bread crumbs, a few small pasties, a dish of boiled beef, which he liked very much, some mashed turnips—all of them things which he could eat without the help of a knife or fork. The King ate with appetite two wings of chicken and a small portion of vegetables and drank two glasses of wine and water. For dessert he had a sponge-finger and a little Malaga.)

After supper His Majesty went into his study. His confessor came out a moment later and asked the Commissioners to take him to the Council Chamber. His object was to demand certain vestments and all the objects necessary for him to celebrate Mass next morning. M. de Firmont only obtained his requirements with difficulty. They went to the church of the Capucins in the Marais, near the Hôtel de Soubise, which had been made into a parish, to fetch the articles necessary for the service. On his return from the Council Chamber M. de Firmont went into the King's apartment and both of them disappeared in the tower and remained there till half-past twelve. Then I undressed the King and as I was going to dress his hair, he said, "It's not worth while." Then when I had put him to bed and was drawing the curtains he said: "Cléry, you are to awake me at five o'clock."

He had hardly lain down, when he fell into a deep sleep and

slept until five o'clock without waking up. M. de Firmont whom the King had ordered to rest for a while, threw himself on my bed and I passed the night on a chair in the King's room, praying God to give him strength and courage. I heard five o'clock strike and lit the fire. The noise I made awakened the King and he drew the curtain of his bed and said: "Has it struck five?" "Yes, Sire, several church clocks have struck the hour, but not the clock in this room." The fire now being alight, I approached his bed. "I have slept well," said the King, "and I needed to. I was tired out by yesterday. Where is M. de Firmont?" "On my bed." "And you, where have you passed the night?" "On this chair." "I'm sorry" said the King. "Ah, Sire, how can I think of myself in such a moment?" He took my hand and clasped it affectionately.

I dressed the King and did his hair. While I was doing this he took a seal from his watch and put it in his waistcoat pocket. Then he laid the watch on the chimney-piece. Afterwards he took a ring from his finger and looked at it several times. Then he put it in the same pocket where he had placed the seal. He changed his shirt and put on the white waistcoat he had worn the day before and I helped him on with his coat. Then he took from his pockets his portfolio, his quizzing glass, his snuff-box and several other objects, and he also put his purse on the chimney-piece—all this in silence and under the eyes of the municipals. When he had finished dressing the King told me to warn M. de Firmont. I went to do so, but found him already up. He followed His Majesty into his study.

In the meantime I placed a chest of drawers in the middle of the room to act as an altar for the celebration of the Mass. At two in the morning they had brought all the things necessary for this purpose. I now took the priest's vestments into my room and when they were laid out in order, I went to tell the King. He asked if I was able to serve the Mass. I said "yes" but that I did not know the responses by heart. He was holding a book in his hand; he opened it and turned up the part about the Mass, which he handed to me. Then he took another book. During this time the priest was robing himself. I had placed before the altar an armchair and laid a big cushion on the floor for His Majesty to kneel on. The King made me take it away and went himself into his study to fetch a smaller one stuffed with horsehair which he generally used for his prayers. As soon as the priest came in, the municipals retired into the anteroom and I shut one of the sides of the door. The Mass began at six o'clock. Silence reigned during this holy ceremony. The King, kneeling throughout, heard the Mass with saintly composure. His attitude was most noble. His Majesty received the Communion. After the Mass the King went into his study and the priest retired to my room to disrobe.

I took this opportunity to go into His Majesty's study. The King took both my hands and said to me in a voice full of emotion, "Cléry, you have served me well." "Ah, Sire," I said, throwing myself at his feet, "I wish I could disarm your executioners by my own death and so preserve a life so precious to all good Frenchmen! Let us hope, Sire, that they will not dare to strike you." He answered: "Death does not frighten me. I am quite prepared for it. But you—you must not expose yourself. I am going to ask that you be allowed to remain in attendance on my son. Give him all your care in this wretched existence. Tell him, remind him how much I feel for him in his sufferings: perhaps one day he will be able to reward your loyalty." "Oh, my master, my King, if my absolute devotion, if my zeal and my care for you have won your satisfaction, all I ask of Your Majesty is to receive your blessing: do not refuse it to the last Frenchman who stands by your side." All this time I was on my knees, holding one of his hands and as I knelt there he granted my prayer and gave me his blessing. Then he raised me up and embraced me. "Remember me to all the persons who are attached to me, and tell Turgi, too, that I am grateful to him. Go back now, and be careful to arouse no suspicion against yourself." Then recalling me, he took up a paper which he had laid on the table and said, "Here is a letter which Pétion wrote to me when you came to me in the Temple. It might help to enable you to remain here." I took his hand again and kissed it, then I went out. "Adieu," he said once more "adieu!"

When I went into my room I found M. de Firmont kneeling in prayer beside my bed. He rose and said, "What a prince! With what resignation, what courage he goes to his death! He is as calm and undisturbed as if he had just heard Mass in his palace in the midst of his courtiers." "He bade me the most touching farewell," I said. "He deigned to promise to ask them to let me stay here in the Tower in attendance on his son. When he goes out, Monsieur, I beg you to remind him of his promise, because I shall not again have the happiness to see him alone." "Do not fear: I shall do so," replied M. de Firmont as he went to join His Majesty.

At seven o'clock the King left his study. He called me and drawing me into a corner by the window said: "I desire you to hand this seal to my son . . . and this ring to the Queen. Tell the Dauphin that it grieves me to leave him. This little packet contains locks of hair of all my family. Give it to him too. Tell the Queen, my dear children and my sister that though I had promised to see them this morning, I decided to spare them the pain of such a cruel parting. But it was a hard sacrifice to me to leave them without receiving their last embraces." He wiped away a few tears and then added in an agonized voice, "I charge you to bid them farewell for me." Then he went back into his study.

The municipals, who had drawn near, had heard what His Majesty said and had seen him hand me the different objects which I still held in my hands. They told me to give them to them, but one of them suggested that I should be left in charge of them until the Council had decided what was to be done and this view prevailed.

A quarter of an hour later the King came out of his study and said to me, "Ask them if I can have a pair of scissors." Then he went back. I asked them and one of them said: "Do you know what he wants them for?" I said I did not. They said we must know. So I knocked at the door of the study and the King came out. A municipal who had followed me said: "You have asked for some scissors, but before we ask the Council, we must know what you want to do with them." His Majesty said, "I want Cléry to cut my hair." The municipals withdrew and one of them went down to the Council Chamber, where after half an hour's debate the scissors were refused. On his return he announced this decision to the King, who said, "I would not have touched the scissors: I would have asked Cléry to cut my hair in your presence. Try again, monsieur. I beg you to convey my request to the Council." The municipal returned to the Council but they persisted in their refusal. At this point they told me to prepare to accompany the King in order to undress him on the scaffold. This news terrified me but, gathering all my force, I was steeling myself to perform this last service for my master to whom the idea that it should be left to the executioner was repugnant, when one of the municipals said that I should not go after all adding: "The executioner is good enough for him."

Paris was under arms since five in the morning: one heard the drums beating the call to arms. The clank of arms, the movement of horses and the rumbling of guns being transported—the Tower was filled with all these sounds.

At nine o'clock the din increased. The doors were flung open noisily. Santerre, accompanied by seven or eight municipals and followed by ten gendarmes entered the room and dressed them in two lines. At this moment the King came out of his study and said, "Have you come for me?" "Yes," said Santerre. "A minute, please," said the King and returned to his study, only to come out a moment later with his confessor. The King was carrying his will in his hand and, addressing a municipal named Jacques Rous, a constitutional priest, who was prominent in the line said: "I beg you to deliver this paper to the Queen, my wife." "None of my business," said the priest as he refused to take the paper. "I am here to take you to the scaffold."

His Majesty then turned to Gobeau, another municipal, and said to him: "Please deliver this paper to my wife. You can read it, if you like. There are certain dispositions which I desire the Commune to know."

I was behind the King near the fireplace, when he turned to me and I offered to put on his overcoat. "I do not need it," he said, "just give me my hat." I gave it to him, our hands touched and he shook my hand for the last time. Then turning to the municipals he said, "Gentlemen, I would like Cléry to remain with my son who is accustomed to his ministrations. I trust that the Commune will grant this request. Let us go now," he said, looking at Santerre.

These were the last words he uttered in his apartment. As he came to the staircase he met Mathey, the guardian of the Tower and said to him: "I was a little sharp with you yesterday. Don't bear me ill will." Mathey made no reply and made as if to withdraw when the King spoke to him.

I remained alone in the room, numbed with grief. The drums and trumpets announced that His Majesty had left the Tower. An hour later salvoes of artillery and cries of *Vive la Nation, Vive la République* filled the air. The best of Kings was no more.

⚜

A great doctor, Philippe Pinel, attended the execution of Louis XVI. He it was who had freed the mentally afflicted from their chains and separated them from the criminals and it was owing to the gratitude of his patients that he escaped the guillotine. The persons who owed their liberty to him drove away the sans-culottes who had come to arrest him.

I doubt not that the King's death will be described in different ways, as the partisan spirit dictates, and that garbled versions of this great event will appear in the newspapers and be noised abroad in such a manner as to distort the truth. As an eyewitness, who has always been far removed from the prejudice of parties, and who is but too well acquainted with the worthlessness of the *aura popularis*, I am going to give you a faithful account of what happened. I greatly regret that I was obliged to attend the execution bearing arms with the other citizens of the section and I write to you now with my heart filled with grief and my whole being stunned by the shock of this dreadful experience.

Louis, who, fortified by the principles of religion, seemed completely resigned to meet death, left his prison in the Temple about nine in the morning and was taken to the place of execution in the mayor's carriage with his confessor and two gendarmes, the curtains being drawn.

When he arrived at his destination he looked at the scaffold without flinching. The executioner at once proceeded to perform the customary rite by cutting off the King's hair which he put in his pocket. Louis then walked up on to the scaffold. The air was filled with the roll of numerous drums, seemingly intended to prevent the people from demanding grace. The drum-beats were hushed for a moment by a gesture from Louis himself, but at a signal from the adjutant of the General of the National Guard, they recommenced with such force that Louis's voice was drowned and it was only possible to catch a few stray words like "I forgive my enemies." At the same time he took a few steps round the fatal plank to which he was drawn by a feeling of horror natural to any man on the brink of death or, maybe, he conceived that the people might appeal for grace, for what man does not cling to hope even in his last moments?

The adjutant ordered the executioner to do his duty and in a trice Louis was fastened on to the deadly plank of the machine they call the guillotine and his head was cut off so quickly that he could hardly have suffered. This at least is a merit belonging to the murderous instrument which bears the name of the doctor who invented it. The executioner immediately lifted the head from the sack into which it fell automatically and displayed it to the people.

As soon as the execution had taken place, the expression on the faces of many spectators changed and, from having worn an air of sombre consternation, they shifted to another mood and fell to crying "*Vive la Nation!*" At least one can say this of the cavalry who witnessed the execution and who waved their helmets on the point of their sabres.

Some of the citizens followed suit, but a great number withdrew, their spirits racked with pain, to shed tears in the bosom of their families.

As decapitation could not be performed without spilling blood on the scaffold many persons hurried to the spot to dip the end of their handkerchief or a piece of paper in it, to have a reminder of this memorable event, for one need not have recourse to odious interpretations of such actions.

The body was carried to the cemetery of Ste. Marguerite, after the Commissioners of the Municipality, the Security Department and the Criminal Court had drawn up the minutes.

His son, the former Dauphin, in an access of childish simplicity, which attracted much sympathy, had in his last conversation with his father urgently begged to be allowed to go with him to the scaffold to ask the people to pardon him.

❖

The revolutionary tribunal charged the advocate Chauveau-Lagarde with the defence of Marie-Antoinette. Later on the same lawyer was commissioned to defend Charlotte Corday (see following chapter) and then himself imprisoned. He was released at Thermidor. This is what he says:

On October 14th 1793 I happened to be in the country when I received the news that I had been named with M. Tronson-Ducoudray to defend the Queen before the revolutionary tribunal, and that the trial was to start on the following morning at eight o'clock.

I immediately set out for the prison filled with a sense of the sacred duty which had been imposed on me, mingled with an intense feeling of bitterness.

The Conciergerie, as is well known, is the prison in which are confined persons due to be judged or those due to be executed after sentence.

After passing through two gates one enters a dark corridor which one could not locate without the aid of a lamp that lights up the entrance. On the right are the cells, and on the left there is a chamber into which the light enters by two small barred windows looking on to the little courtyard reserved for women.

It was in this chamber that the Queen was confined. It was divided into two parts by a screen. On the left, as one entered, was an armed gendarme, and on the right the part of the room occupied by the Queen containing a bed, a table and two chairs. Her Majesty was attired in a white dress of extreme simplicity.

No one capable of sympathetic imagination could fail to realize my feelings on finding in this place the wife of one of the worthiest successors of St. Louis and the august descendant of the Emperors of Germany, a Queen who by her grace and goodness had been the glory of the most brilliant court in Europe and the idol of the French nation.

In presenting myself to the Queen with respectful devotion, I felt my knees trembling under me and my eyes wet with tears. I could not hide my emotion and my embarrassment was much greater than any I might have felt at being presented to Her Majesty in the midst of her court, seated on a throne and surrounded with the brilliant trappings of royalty.

Her reception of me, at once majestic and kind put me at my ease and caused me to feel, as I spoke and she listened, that she was honouring me with her confidence.

I read over with her the bill of indictment, which later became known to all Europe. I will not recall the horrible details.

As I read this satanic document, I was absolutely overwhelmed, but I alone, for the Queen, without showing emotion, gave me her views on it. She perceived, and I had come to the same conclusion, that the gendarme could hear something of what she said. But she showed no sign of anxiety on this score and continued to express herself with the same confidence.

I made my initial notes for her defence and then went up to the registry to examine what they called the relevant documents. There I found a pile of papers so confused and so voluminous that I should have needed whole weeks to examine them.

When I observed to the Queen that it would not be possible for us to take cognizance of all these documents in such a short time and that it was indispensable to ask for an adjournment to give us time to examine them, the Queen said, "To whom must we apply for that?"

I dreaded the effect of my reply, and as I replied in a low voice: "The National Convention", the Queen, turning her head to one side said: "No, never!"

I insisted, explaining to the Queen, that as we were charged to defend her, our duty was to neglect no steps to refute these falsehoods, that we were determined to fulfil our mission to the best of our ability, and that without examining the alleged documentary evidence we should be powerless, in part at least, to do so. I further made it clear to Her Majesty that I did not propose to formulate in her name a request to this Assembly, but to address to it a petition in the name of the counsel for the defence deprecating any precipitate action, which under the terms of the law constituted a clear denial of justice.

I saw that my words were undermining the Queen's resistance, but she could not yet make up her mind to countenance an action she found repugnant. However, I persisted, begging her to forgive me for returning to a subject, which I knew she regarded with aversion.

I added that we had to defend in the person of Her Majesty not only the Queen of France, but also the widow of Louis XVI, the mother of his children and the sister-in-law of our Princess, who were accused with her in the bill of indictment.

This final consideration overcame her scruples. At the words sister, wife and mother natural feelings rose superior to a sovereign's pride. Without uttering a single word, though she let a sigh escape her, the Queen took up her pen and wrote to the Assembly in our names, a few lines full of noble dignity in which she complained that they had not allowed us time enough to examine the evidence and claimed on our behalf the necessary respite.

The Queen's application was transmitted to Fouquier-Tinville, who promised to submit it to the Assembly, But, in fact, he did nothing with it or, at least, nothing useful for the next day, the fifteenth of October, the hearing began at eight in the morning.

※

Rosalie Lamorlière, a chambermaid.

I was a chambermaid in the house of Madame Beaulieu, mother of the famous comedian, when King Louis XVI was condemned to perish on a scaffold. Madame Beaulieu already old and in bad health, nearly died of grief, when she heard the news of this judgment. She kept crying out things like this: "Unjust and barbarous nation, one day thou wilt shed tears of despair on the tomb of so good a King."

Madame Beaulieu died soon after the massacres of September after which her son passed me on, as a favour, to Madame Richard, the concierge of the Palace.

It was very repugnant to me to take service with a jailer, but

M. Beaulieu, who, as is known, was a good Royalist and who used to plead without a fee on behalf of the unfortunate victims of the revolutionary tribunal, begged me to accept this post where, he said, I should have the chance of making myself useful to a crowd of honest folk confined in the Conciergerie. He promised to come and see me as often as he could as his theatre in the city was only a short step from the prison.

Madame Richard, my new mistress was not so well brought up as Madame Beaulieu, but she was a kind-hearted woman and having once been in the dressmaking business, she maintained in her house and her person a high standard of cleanliness.

At this time it needed much presence of mind to manage a huge prison like the Conciergerie, but I never saw my mistress embarrassed. She said what she had to say in few words; she gave her orders clearly; she slept only for brief spells and nothing happened within the prison or outside of which she was not speedily informed. Her husband, less capable than his wife, was hardworking and conscientious. I gradually grew attached to this family because I saw they did not disapprove of the sympathy I felt for the poor prisoners of those times.

On the first of August 1793 after dinner Mme Richard said to me in a low voice: "Rosalie, tonight we shall not go to bed. You will sleep on a chair. The Queen is going to be transferred from the Temple to this prison." And I immediately heard her giving orders to move General Custine from the council-chamber in order to put the Queen there. A turnkey was sent to the prison upholsterer (Bertaud, whose place was in the courtyard of the Sainte Chapelle,) to ask for a trestle bed, two mattresses, a bolster, a light blanket and a wash-basin. This little collection of furniture was brought into the damp room vacated by M. de Custine, and to it were added an ordinary table and two prison chairs. Such was the furniture destined for the use of the Queen of France.

At about three in the morning I was asleep in an armchair when Mme Richard took me by the arm and awakened me brusquely with these words: "Come now, Rosalie, wake up. Take this torch. Here they are."

I got down from my chair and went with Mme Richard to M. de Custine's cell, which was situated at the end of a long dark corridor. The Queen was already there. A number of gendarmes were standing in the passage in front of the door. Inside the room there were several officers and people belonging to the administration talking in low tones to one another. The day was beginning to dawn.

Instead of confining the Queen in the registry with a glass partition situated on the left of the first lobby, she was locked up in de Custine's cell. The formalities having been completed, everyone withdrew and only Madame Richard and I remained with the Queen. It was very hot. I noticed the drops of sweat on her face, which she wiped two or three times with her handkerchief. Her eyes took in with astonishment the horrible bareness of the room. They also paid some slight attention to Mme Richard and me. After which the Queen standing on an upholstered stool which I had brought her from my room, hung her watch on a nail she had noticed in the wall and began to undress to go to bed. I approached her respectfully and offered to help her. "Thank you, my girl," she replied without a touch of pride or ill-humour. "Since I have had no one to look after me, I look after myself."

It was now broad daylight. We took away our torches and the Queen lay down in a bed, doubtless quite unworthy of her, but which we had at least provided with very fine linen and a pillow.

In the morning they put two gendarmes in her room and appointed to serve her an old woman of nearly eighty, who, as I since have learnt, was the former concierge of the Admiralty which was situated within the precincts of the Palais de Justice. Her son, aged about twenty-five, was one of the turnkeys of our prison. Her name was Larivière.

During the first forty days of her imprisonment, I had no business with the Queen. I only went with Madame Richard or her husband to bring her breakfast at nine o'clock and her dinner at two or half-past. Mme Richard laid the table and I, out of respect, remained by the door. But Her Majesty condescended to notice me and honoured me by saying: "Come nearer, Rosalie; don't be afraid."

Old Mme Larivière after having patched and repaired the Queen's black dress very neatly, was judged unsuitable for this service. She went back to her own home in the former Admiralty building and was at once replaced by a young woman called Harel whose husband was employed in the secret police. The Queen had treated the old woman with trust and consideration, but she did not form such a favourable judgment of this new person, to whom she hardly ever spoke.

The two gendarmes, who were never changed, were called Dufrêne and Gilbert. The latter seemed rougher than his comrade, who was a sergeant. Sometimes Her Majesty, to relieve her boredom, watched them playing cards for a little, while Mme Richard and I were laying the table.

One day Mme Richard brought to the Queen's cell her youngest child, a fair-haired boy with pretty blue eyes and a charming face, considering his station. They called him Fanfan.

The Queen on seeing this beautiful little boy trembled visibly. Then she took him in her arms and, as she covered him with kisses and caresses, fell to weeping. She then spoke to us of the Dauphin who was about the same age, and said she never stopped thinking about him. This meeting had caused her bitter grief and Mme Richard, when we went back told me she would take care never to bring her son to the Queen again.

Towards the middle of September, a terrible thing happened, which must have done the Queen a lot of harm.

A disguised officer, named M. de Rougeville, was introduced into the Queen's cell by a municipal officer called Michonis. The officer, who was known to the Queen dropped a carnation near the skirt of her dress and I heard it said that this flower contained a paper with plans for a plot. The woman Harel observed the whole incident and made a report to Fouquier-Tinville, who used to come and visit the prison every evening before midnight. The two gendarmes were also questioned. The Government believed that there was a great plot in Paris to rescue the Queen and at once orders were given, far more strict and fearful than those in force before. M. and Mme Richard and their eldest son were put in prison, the former at Sainte-Pélagie and the other at the Madelonnettes. The woman Harel no longer appeared. The two gendarmes were removed from the Queen's cell and we saw the head-jailer of la Force, a man called Lebeau, come to take the place of Richard.

Lebeau appeared harsh and severe at first sight but at bottom he was not an ill-natured man. The administration said I was to remain as cook in his service, as no one had any ground to distrust me and because, in the house, I did my job and nothing else. They added, however, that I was no longer to go marketing as I had done in the time of Mme Richard and that I was to remain inside the Conciergerie by order of the Government as were the jailer and his young daughter Victoire, today Madame Colson of Montfort-l'Amaury.

It was decided that Lebeau should be responsible with his life for the person of the Queen and that he alone should have the key of her cell. He was ordered not to enter it except for essential purposes and when he did so he must be accompanied by the gendarmerie officer or his sergeant.

A sentinel was posted in the women's courtyard from which the Queen's cell drew its light and as the two small windows were almost on a level with the pavement, the sentry outside could see without difficulty all that went on in the cell.

Although Her Majesty had no communication with the Conciergerie, she knew what had happened to the poor concierges. People from the public security department, came to interrogate her on the subject of Michonis and the carnation and I heard that she answered all questions with the greatest prudence.

When Lebeau appeared in the Queen's cell for the first time, I accompanied him and brought her the soup she usually had at breakfast. She looked at Lebeau, who, in order to be in line with the fashion of those days was wearing a combined jacket and trousers called a carmagnole. The collar of his shirt was open and turned back, but he was not wearing a hat. With his keys in his hand he stood against the wall near the door.

The Queen taking off her night-cap took a chair and said to me in a friendly voice: "Rosalie, I want you to do my hair today." Hearing these words the jailer ran up, seized the comb, and pushed me away saying: "No, no: that is my business." Upon which the Queen looked at Lebeau with an indescribably majestic air and said: "I thank you." Then rising to her feet she arranged her hair herself and put on her night cap.

Since she came to the Conciergerie her method of doing her

hair had been extremely simple. She parted her hair over her forehead after sprinkling some scented powder on it.

Madame Harel used to tie up the ends of her hair with a piece of white ribbon about an ell in length, and then gave the two ends to the Queen, to arrange a chignon on the top of her head. Her hair, incidentally, was golden, not red.

On the day when, after thanking Lebeau for his offer, Her Majesty decided in future to do her hair herself, she picked up from the table the roll of white ribbon, which was left, and said to me in sad and affectionate tones, which sank deeply into my soul: "Rosalie, take this ribbon and keep it always in memory of me." The tears came to my eyes and I curtsied to Madame and thanked her.

When the jailer and I were in the corridor, he took my ribbon and when we had gone up to his room he said: "I am very sorry to have upset that poor woman, but my position is so difficult that the least thing makes me tremble. I cannot forget that my comrade Richard and his wife are in a dungeon. In God's name, Rosalie, don't do anything imprudent or I am a lost man."

On the second of August during the night when the Queen arrived at the Temple, I noticed that they had not brought with her any dresses or underclothes of any kind. On the next day and on every day afterwards the unfortunate lady asked for fresh linen and Madame Richard, who feared to compromise herself did not dare to lend her any garments or to purchase them for her. At last the Municipal Commissioner Michonis, who was at heart a decent man went over to the Temple and on the tenth day they brought from the dungeon a parcel which the Queen hastened to open. It contained lovely cambric chemises, handkerchiefs, fichus, silk or floss-silk stockings, a white négligé for morning wear, several *bonnets-de-nuit* and a number of lengths of ribbon of different widths. Madame was affected by the sight of these things and, turning to Madame Richard and me said: "From the careful way in which all this has been prepared, I recognize the loving hand of my dear sister Elisabeth."

When she came to the Conciergerie, Her Majesty was wearing her great mourning bonnet (her widow's head-dress). One day in my presence she said to Mme Richard: "Madame, I should like, if possible, to have two bonnets instead of one, to make a change. Would you have the goodness to hand my mourning hat to your dressmaker? I think it contains enough lawn to make two simple bonnets."

Mme Richard carried out this commission for the Queen without difficulty and when we brought her the two new bonnets, quite simple ones, she appeared satisfied and said to me: "Rosalie, I have no longer any possessions I can dispose of, but, my child, I gladly give you this brass frame and this piece of cambric, which the dressmaker has returned."

I bowed humbly to thank Madame and I still keep the piece of lawn, which she did me the honour to give me.

The Queen suffered one great privation. They refused to let her have any kind of needles and she loved to occupy herself with handwork. I noticed that from time to time she would tear out coarse threads from the canvas panels on the walls. With these threads, which she polished with her nails she made a sort of tapestry, very closely knit, using her knee for a cushion and a few pins for needles.

She admitted that her love for flowers had been a passion for her. In the beginning we used from time to time to put a bouquet on her little oak table. M. Lebeau did not dare to permit this attention. He feared me to such an extent that during the first few days after his arrival, he had a screen made, seven feet high to prevent me from seeing our prisoner when I came to serve the meals or do the room. I saw the screen but it was never used, for Lebeau contented himself with the one we gave to the Queen when Mme Richard was there, which was only four feet high. It formed a sort of half curtain along the Queen's bed and shielded her from the view of the gendarmes, when she was obliged to obey the calls of nature. At such times the authorities were barbarous enough to allow her no privacy.

A convict called Barassin had the duty of carrying out the commode and then Madame used to ask me to burn some juniper wood to clear the air.

In the morning when she got up, the Queen used to put on a pair of little slippers with trodden-down heels, and every other day I used to brush her lovely black velvet shoes with St. Huberty heels two inches high.

Sometimes they sent for the jailer to attend to some indispensable business in connection with the prison. Then he left me under the supervision of the gendarmerie officer. One day what was my astonishment to see the officer taking one of the Queen's shoes and scratching off the damp brick-dust with the point of his sword, just as I did with my knife. The clergy and noblemen detained in the courtyard watched us at work through the grating. Seeing that the officer was a good fellow and would not mind they begged me to come to them and show them the Queen's shoe. They took it at once and, passing it from hand to hand, covered it with kisses.

Mme Richard on account of a new law that had come out, had hidden her silver. The Queen had to be served with pewter, which I kept as clean and bright as possible.

Her Majesty had a fair appetite: she cut a fowl in two, to make it last two days. She stripped the bones with unbelievable skill and care. She never left uneaten any of the vegetables which were her second course.

When she had finished, she said her grace in a low voice and then got up and walked about the room. That was the signal for us to depart. Since the carnation I was forbidden to leave even a glass at her disposition. One day M. de Saint-Léger, the American, was coming from the registry to rejoin his comrades in the courtyard, when he saw in my hands a glass half full of water. "Has the Queen been drinking this water?" said this Creole. I said she had. M. de Saint-Léger at once uncovered himself and drank the remainder of the water with respect and satisfaction.

Her Majesty, as I have already said, had neither a chest-of-drawers nor a wardrobe in her room. When her little stock of linen arrived from the Temple she asked for a box to put it in so as to keep the dust out. Madame Richard who did not dare to ask this favour from the Administration, authorized me to lend the Queen a cardboard box, which she received with as much satisfaction as if she had been given the finest piece of furniture in the world.

As the rules of the prison did not permit a prisoner to have a looking-glass and as Madame kept asking for one every day, Mme Richard allowed me to lend my hand-glass to the Queen. I blushed to offer it to her. This little mirror bought on the quays had only cost me 25 sous in assignats. I can still call it to mind. It had a red frame, and pictures showing life in China were painted on both sides of it. The Queen accepted this little mirror, as though it were something important and used it until the last day of her life.

As long as Mme Richard was there, the Queen was fed well and, I venture to say, with distinction. The best food was bought for her and there were three or four women in the market who, recognizing the jailer, gave him the most tender fowls and the finest fruit with tears in their eyes: "For our Queen," they said.

When the Richards were put in prison none of us went to the market any more, but the dealers came themselves to the Conciergerie, and displayed their provisions piece by piece in the registry, in the presence of policemen or the sergeant.

The Queen on seeing the difference in the fare quickly realized that everything had changed since the carnation. But she never let a word of complaint escape her. I now only brought her soup and two other dishes (every day a dish of vegetables and then chicken or veal on alternate days). But I took the greatest care in preparing her food. Madame, who was always spotlessly clean and most particular, looked at my well-washed, white linen and her eyes seemed to thank me for showing her this consideration. Sometimes she held out her glass for me to fill it. She never drank anything but water, even at Versailles, as she sometimes told us. I admired the beauty of her hands, which were indescribably graceful and white.

Without moving the table, she always placed herself at meal-time between the table and the bed. I was thus enabled to admire the elegance of her features, which showed up very clearly in the light from the window. One day I noticed a few very faint traces of small-pox. These were almost imperceptible and invisible from a few steps away.

When Lebeau was in charge, Madame did her hair in front of him and me, while I was making her bed and folding her dress on a chair. I noticed patches of white hair on both her temples. She had practically none on her forehead or on the other parts of her head. Her Majesty said it came from the trouble of the sixth of October.

Madame de Lamarlière, who is still alive and resides in Paris had begged me several times in the days of Mme Richard to procure me some of the Queen's hair to put in a locket. This would have been easy for me as Her Majesty from time to time shampooed her hair.

After the incident of the carnation, Mme de Lamarlière had to wait a long time before being allowed to visit her husband who was a prisoner.

Before the Richards had got into disgrace the Queen used to have her washing done by Mme Saulieu, our regular washerwoman, who lived just by the Archevêché. After the dreadful business of the carnation she did not come back to us. The registrar of the revolutionary tribunal took the Queen's underclothes, but not the bonnets or the fichu and it seems that she only received her chemises back, one by one, and at long intervals. Worry, bad air and lack of exercise undermined the Queen's health. Her blood became heated and she suffered severe hæmorrhages. I became aware of this and she secretly asked me for some linen, so I immediately cut up some of my nightgowns and put the pieces of linen under her bolster.

On the fourth or fifth day after her arrival at the Conciergerie, the Administrators took away her watch which she had brought from Germany when she came to us as Dauphine. I was not with her when they did her this wrong, but Mme Richard talked about it in our room and said that she had wept bitterly when she was forced to give up this gold watch. By good luck the Commissioners did not know that she wore a very precious oval locket hanging on a string of black braid. This locket contained the curls and a portrait of the young King. It was folded in a little yellow bag which the Dauphin used to wear.

When she came from the Temple the Queen had still kept two pretty diamond rings and her wedding ring. The two gem rings had become, though she probably never thought of it, a sort of game for her. As she sat and dreamed, she would take them off and put them on again and quickly pass them from one hand to another.

At the time of the carnation, her room was visited on several occasions. They opened her drawer, searched her person and turned the chairs and the bed upside down. Having seen the glitter of her diamonds these wicked men took the two rings from her and told her that they would be restored to her when all was over.

After that, her cell was visited at all hours of the day and night. The architects and administrators kept coming to see if the iron bars and walls were in good condition. I constantly saw them puzzling over things and heard them asking one another: "Could she escape this way or that?" They never left us alone and seemed never to take time off.

Fearing some treachery from within or a surprise from outside they were the whole time round us in the Conciergerie. They took their meals, uninvited, at the Concierge's table and every day I had to prepare dinner for fifteen or eighteen of these people.

I had heard Madame Richard say: "The Queen does not expect to be tried. She continues to hope that her relations will obtain her release. She told me so with the most charming frankness. If she leaves us, Rosalie, she will take you with her as her maid."

But after the carnation the Queen seemed to me disturbed and much less confident than before. She seemed to be thinking a lot and sighed as she walked up and down in her cell.

One day she noticed in a room with iron bars facing her windows, a prisoner with clasped hands and eyes raised to heaven, who seemed to be praying. "Rosalie," said this great and good princess, "look up there at that poor nun. Do you see how ardently she is praying to God?"

I am sure that the nun was praying for the Queen. That is how most of those ladies spent their days.

My father came from our country home to see me, but as they did not allow anyone to enter the prison since the carnation conspiracy, he had the greatest difficulty in reaching me. Eventually M. Lebeau admitted him and came with him to my room. He said to him: "I am forbidden to receive or permit any visit, not even from my own family. Don't stay with your daughter more than four or five minutes and see that you do not come back, man." I could not even offer my father any refreshment. I showed him a fowl that was on the spit and said in a low voice: "That is for the poor Queen who is in here." My father sighed and we parted from one another.

One day as I was making the Queen's bed, I let drop a morning paper which I had under my shawl and did not miss it till I had got back to my room. Feeling very upset, I told M. Lebeau. He was much more worried, being timid by nature: "Come along quickly," he said, "let us go back to the cell. Take this carafe of fresh water. We'll exchange it for the one she has got there. I see no other way to get out of this mess." We had to warn the gendarmes again. Then we went to the Queen's cell where I found my paper, which she had not noticed.

If the Queen had suffered from the heat in the month of August, she suffered no less from the cold and the damp during the first half of October. She complained in her gentle fashion and as for me I felt terribly unhappy at being unable to relieve her sufferings. Every evening I used to take her nightgown from under her bolster and hurried with it to my room where I heated it till it felt burning hot. Then I replaced it and her night-shawl in her bed.

She noticed these little attentions which, in my respectful loyalty, I was able to pay her and by the kindness of her glance she expressed her thanks just as if I had done her some extra-ordinary service quite outside my duty. They never allowed her a lamp or a torch so I used to prolong as far as I could the business of doing her room for the evening so that my respected mistress did not have to retire into darkness and solitude quite so early. Generally all the light she had to go to bed by was the feeble glimmer which came through her window from the lamp-post in the women's courtyard.

On the 12th of October about two hours after she had gone to bed, the judges of the court came to interrogate her at length. The next morning when I came in to make her bed, I noticed that she was hurriedly pacing up and down in her poor cell. I felt heartbroken and scarcely dared to look at her.

For several days she had not been alone as they had put an officer in her cell to keep watch on her.

At last that awful day the 15th of October arrived. At eight o'clock in the morning she went up into the court-room to receive judgment and as I don't remember having brought her any food that morning, I assume she was fasting when they made her go up.

During the morning I heard several persons talking about the trial. They said, "Marie Antoinette will get off. She gave her answers like an angel. They will merely deport her."

At four in the afternoon, the jailer said to me: "The hearing is suspended for three-quarters of an hour. The accused will not come down. Go up quickly and take a bowl of soup to her."

I immediately took a bowl of excellent soup which I had been keeping in reserve on my own range and I went up to the Queen. When I was just going into the room in which she was, one of the commissioners of police by the name of Labuzière, a short, snub-nosed man, seized the bowl from me and gave it to his mistress, an overdressed young creature, saying: "This young woman has a great desire to see the widow Capet: this is a lucky chance for her", on which the woman went off with the soup, half of which had got spilt. It was in vain that I begged and prayed Labuzière to let me take it to the Queen. I had to obey him. What must the Queen have thought when she received the soup from the hands of a person she did not know.

A little after four o'clock in the morning on October 16th, they came to tell us that the Queen of France had been condemned to death. I felt as though a sword had pierced my heart and I went to my room stifling my cries and sobs. The jailer heard the news of the sentence with sorrow, but he was more accustomed to such things than I, and pretended to be indifferent to it.

Towards seven M. Lebeau ordered me to go down to the Queen's cell and ask if she wanted something to eat. When I came into the cell where two lights were burning I saw an officer of the gendarmerie sitting in a corner on the left while Madame, dressed all in black, was lying on her bed.

Her face was turned towards the window and her head rested on her hand. "Madame," I said in a quavering voice, "you had nothing to eat yesterday evening and practically nothing the whole day. What will you take this morning?" The Queen was shedding tears freely. She said, "My girl, I need nothing more. Everything is finished for me." I took the liberty to say: "Madame, I have kept hot for you a bouillon and some vermicelli. You need to keep your strength up, please let me bring you something."

Her tears flowed afresh and she said, "Rosalie, bring me a bouillon." I went and fetched it and she then sat up but could not swallow more than a few spoonfuls. I declare before God that her body had received no other nourishment and I had reason to believe that she was losing all her blood.

A little before the day had full come an ecclesiastic authorized by the Government introduced himself to the Queen and offered to hear her Confession. Hearing from him that he was one of the regular curates of Paris she gathered that he had sworn allegiance to the revolution and refused his ministrations. They were talking of this in the house.

When it was day, that is to say about eight o'clock, I returned to Madame's cell to help her to dress as she had told me when I brought her the bouillon. Her Majesty then got into the narrow space which I usually left between the camp bed and the wall. There she unfolded a chemise which they had brought her, probably in my absence and having signed to me to stand in front of the bed to prevent the gendarme from seeing her body, she bent and slipped down her dress in order to change her underclothes for the last time. The gendarmerie officer at once walked up to the head of the bed and watched the Queen changing. Her Majesty immediately draped her shawl round her shoulders and said in very gentle tones to the young man: "In the name of decency, Monsieur, allow me to change my linen without a witness."

"I could not consent to that," said the gendarme roughly. "My orders instruct me to keep an eye on all your movements."

The Queen sighed, put on her chemise for the last time, taking every precaution to protect her modesty and put on, not her long mourning dress which she had worn at the trial, but the white négligé which she usually wore in the mornings. Then unfolding her muslin scarf she wrapped it round her neck and doubled it under her chin.

The annoyance which the gendarme's brutality caused me prevented me from noticing if the Queen was still wearing the locket with the portrait of the Dauphin. But I did see her rolling up her poor bloodstained chemise and putting it into one of her sleeves, like a weapon in its sheath, before she crammed it into an open space between the canvas wall-paper and the wall.

On the previous day knowing that she was going to appear before the public and the judges she had thought it seemly to do her hair higher on her head than usual. She had attached to her linen bonnet with its little pleated fringe the two pinners, which she had kept in the cardboard box, and under these streamers she had put a piece of black crape, the whole making a very becoming widow's head-dress.

But to go to her death she had only kept the simple linen bonnet without streamers or other signs of mourning. As she had only a single pair of shoes she kept on her black stockings and shoes of prunella which she had not spoilt or rendered shapeless during the seventy-six days she was with us.

I left her without daring to say farewell nor even to curtsey to her for fear of embarrassing her or causing her pain. I went away to cry in my little room and to pray to God for her.

After she had left that awful house, the chief usher of the court with three or four other colleagues came to the jailer to ask for me and ordered me to follow him to the Queen's cell. He let me take back my hand-glass and the cardboard box. As for the other articles which had belonged to Her Majesty, he told me to wrap them all up in a sheet. They even made me wrap up a wisp of straw which was lying on the floor of the cell. Then they carried away these pitiful relics of the best and unhappiest queen that ever existed.

The Execution of the Queen: Extract from the Moniteur *of 27th October 1793*

During her examination Marie Antoinette preserved almost invariably a calm and assured demeanour. During the first hours it was noticed that she kept running her fingers along the arm of her chair in an absent-minded way and as if she were playing the pianoforte.

When she heard the sentence pronounced, no trace of emotion appeared in her face and she left the court without addressing a word to the judges or the public.

It was then half-past four in the morning on the 25th day of the first month (16th October, old style); she was led back to the condemned cell in the prison of the Conciergerie.

At five o'clock the call to arms was sounded in all the sections and at seven the armed forces were already at their posts. Cannons were placed at the ends of the bridges and in the squares and cross-roads from the Palais as far as the Place de la Révolution and by ten o'clock numerous patrols were circulating in the streets.

At eleven Marie Antoinette, the widow Capet, wearing a white morning dress was led to the scaffold in the same manner as other criminals accompanied by a constitutional priest dressed as a layman, and escorted by numerous detachments of mounted and dismounted gendarmerie.

The following extract is taken from Prudhomme's Les Revolutions de Paris, *a periodical founded by this journalist which bore the following motto: "The great only appear great to us because we are on our knees. Let us stand upright."*

Marie Antoniette of Austria, the widow Capet, after an ex-amination lasting three whole days in succession, was sentenced to death by the revolutionary tribunal and paid the penalty for her political and personal crimes at noon on the 25th day of the first month in the Place de la Révolution at the foot of the statue of Liberty.

Citizen Sanson, the executioner, appeared in her cell at seven in the morning. "You have come very early, Monsieur," she said: "could you not have waited?" "No, Madame, my orders were to come now." She was already fully prepared, that is to say dressed in white, like her husband on the day of his execution. This affectation was noticed by the people and made them smile.

White, the symbol of innocence, was hardly a suitable colour for Marie Antoinette. She wanted to go to the guillotine bareheaded, but this favour was not granted her. She had cut off her hair, herself. They came to her cell in the prison to tell her that a priest of Paris was asking if she wanted to confess. She was heard to reply in a low voice: "A priest of Paris? There isn't such a thing." The confessor came forward and said: "Would you like me to accompany you, Madame?" "As you please, Monsieur," she answered. But she did not make confession and said not a word as she drove to the scaffold.

On leaving the Conciergerie she was seen to make a movement of surprise and indignation when she saw the cart. She had felt sure they would drive her in a carriage, like her husband. Nevertheless, she had to climb on to this vehicle which wounded her proud spirit and one can be sure that her agony began at this moment, though she made a show of resolution. It was easy to see that this appearance of resolution cost her much. From that moment her features were drawn. Her hands were tied behind her back as was usually done (they ought to give up this practice and allow criminals to enjoy their liberty till the last moment). During the whole of the route she observed the same expression, except when passing the former Palais Royal. This house probably recalled memories to her mind which could not fail to touch her now. She cast an animated glance at the building. The people watched her calmly enough as she drove by. At certain places there was applause, but in general the crowd seemed for a moment to forget all the harm done to France by this woman and only to think of her present situation. Justice was being done, that is all that the people demanded.

As she climbed on to the scaffold Antoinette trod by mistake on citizen Sanson's foot causing the public executioner to give a cry of pain. She turned round and said to him, "Monsieur, I beg your pardon. I did not do it on purpose." It may be that she contrived this little scene to add an interest to her memory, for there are some people whose vanity persists as long as life itself.

CHARLOTTE CORDAY

✤✤✤✤✤✤✤✤✤✤✤✤✤✤✤✤✤✤✤✤✤✤✤✤✤✤✤✤✤✤✤✤✤✤✤

*E*XTRACT FROM La Gazette Française *of July 14th 1793:*

Today at eight o'clock in the evening Marat was assassinated by a woman who for several days had been trying to see him in order, it is said, to obtain a pardon for the citizens of Orleans. He was at the time in his bath and the murderess plunged a dagger into his breast, causing instant death. The woman made no attempt to escape. She waited calmly in her carriage, till they came to take her. "*Je m'en fous,*" she cried, "the deed is done, the monster is dead!" This incident has made a great sensation and untoward consequences are feared.

✤

L'Ami du Peuple, *a journal of the extreme left, was widely read, and its director and editor, Marat, a doctor by profession who had been elected to the Assembly, was hated or revered. The woman, who killed him, aroused the same passions. Here is a picture of her as seen by an* employé, *Laurent Bas, who was folding numbers of* L'Ami du Peuple *in Marat's office when the crime was committed. Laurent Bas refers to himself in the third person:*

At half-past seven on Saturday, July 13th 1793, the second year of the one and indivisible Republic, a person of the female sex, dressed in a spotted négligé costume and wearing a high hat with a black cockade and three lines of black braid, descended from a hackney cab and asked to speak to citizen Marat. She was carrying a fan in her hand. The janitress replied that he was not visible for the moment, on which the visitor said that this was the third time she had called and that it was disagreeable and odious not to be admitted. She asked if the letter she had sent him in the morning by the district post had been delivered to him. Citizeness Marat, sister of the deceased, replied that if the letter had been written it had probably reached her brother. She then went to ask her brother if the person was to be admitted and citizen Marat answered in the affirmative.

He was in the bath working and writing. The woman, having been shown in, sat on a chair beside the bath-tub which was placed in a very small room having space for two persons at most. She closed the door.

Seven or eight minutes after the entry of this person into the bathroom, citizen Bas and the three women in the office heard citizen Marat cry out in a strained and stifled voice: "Help me, my dear! Help!" (He was calling his sister.)

Citizen Bas and the three women then got up: the doors of the two intervening rooms were open and the caller was in the room next to the bathroom. Citizen Bas noticed some blood which had spurted from the bathroom into this room. The three citizenesses ran out to call for the guard. Citizeness Marat ran to her brother and placed one of her hands over his wound, but the unhappy man was no longer breathing. A large new table-knife was lying on the ledge of the bath-tub. It was the weapon with which the murderess had deprived the Nation of one of its Representatives.

Citizen Bas seeing the assassin coming towards him took up a chair in order to stop her. The monster, by a great effort had succeeded in reaching the anteroom, when Bas gave her a blow with the chair which stretched her on the ground. She got up at once and looked significantly at the window of the anteroom, which opened on to the court-yard. Bas seized her by the breasts, threw her down and struck her. As he was holding the murderess down, he saw coming into the room a citizen unknown to him whom he subsequently learnt was the principal tenant of the house. After him came citizen Cuisinier, a public-house keeper from Place du Pont Saint-Michel, who was on guard duty in the section of the Théâtre-Français, now called de Marseille, in the Rue des Cordeliers. Bas cried out, "Help! citizen Cuisinier, help!" Citizen Cuisinier and the other citizens from the same post arrived, one after the other and seized the criminal.

Soon afterwards citizens Hébert, deputy prosecutor of the Commune, appeared followed by several other citizens wearing civic decorations, whom Bas took for Commissioners of the Section of the Théâtre-Français and of the Municipality and some others who Bas was told were members of the National Convention.

The description of the scene of the murder was officially recorded and the murderess was taken towards midnight to the prison of l'Abbaye.

✤

Who was Charlotte Corday d'Armont? Mme Loyer de Maromme, a lady of Caen and a friend of her family, describes her as she appeared to her friends.

A short while before our departure from Caen, Mme de Bretteville gave us a parting dinner. The guests interested us for more than one reason. M. d'Armont had just come to Caen with his younger daughter and his young son who was on the point of emigrating with the intention of joining his elder brother at Coblentz. A young relative of Mme de Bretteville, M. de Tournélis, had also come to Caen with the same intention. So it was doubly a farewell dinner since we were on our way to Rouen and the young people to the Rhine. M. de Tournélis had appeared to find Mlle d'Armont very much to his taste and my mother would have been glad to see the respective hopes of the two families realized by a very suitable alliance between this amiable young man and our friend. But the latter appeared by no means inclined to favour this arrangement and by a kind of spirit of contradiction, she expressed more frankly than ever opinions hostile to the ambitions of the emigrants. M. de Tournélis endeavoured, as we did, to lead the lost sheep back to the right path, as he attributed to incorrect thinking the sentiments to which she often gave utterance. He forgave her infatuation for Rome and Sparta, never thinking that she could desire the overthrow of our ancient and glorious monarchy. This opposition gave rise to a good-tempered battle of wits between the two young people.

I shall never forget this farewell dinner. It was St. Michael's day 1791. Mlle d'Armont, wearing a dress made of one of those beautiful materials given to her by an old relative, was a dazzling spectacle. I had helped her to dress and do her hair in the hope of making a complete conquest of her father. I can still see her clad in an over-dress of pink taffeta, with white stripes opening on an underskirt of white silk. Her costume showed off her figure to perfection. She wore a pink ribbon in her hair which harmonized with her complexion. She looked more animated than usual owing to her uncertainty as to how her father would receive her and by reason of the emotion she felt at being once more in the bosom of her family. On that day she was, in truth, an ideal creature.

At first everyone was very gay and full of hope. Our future *émigrés* thought they were just off for a short trip to the banks of the Rhine with the prospect of returning to winter quarters in Paris when all was over. Mlle d'Armont chaffed them about the speed of their march and their early return. She compared them to Don Quixote and said that they hoped to find Dulcineas and would only find sluts. We all laughed and chaffed and till that moment all went well. Then someone proposed the King's health. We all rose to our feet simultaneously except Mlle d'Armont, who remained seated and left her glass on the table. "To the health of the King!" said someone, for the second time. She remained unmoved and silent. M. d'Armont looked down with knitted brows and an expression of displeasure. My mother gently touched the young lady's arm to persuade her to rise. Mlle d'Armont looked at her with her usual calm and sweet expression, but she did not move. "How is this, my child!" said my mother in a low voice. "You refuse to drink to the health of our good and virtuous King!" "I believe him to be virtuous," she said in her gentle, harmonious accents, "but a weak king is not a good king: he is not able to save his people from misfortune." Dead silence! I was angry and my mother found it hard

H

to disguise her irritation. This did not prevent us from drinking this cherished toast, but each of us sat down depressed and out of temper.

✣

A deputy of La Plaine (the Centre Party) named Harmand is present at Charlotte's examination; he reports:

After she had dealt Marat his death-blow, she was taken to the Committee of Public Security. At that moment I was not a member and, indeed, was not fit to lace up the shoes of the members composing it. However, I attended the hearing out of curiosity, like several other deputies. I wished to have a near view of this modern Judith.

Her interrogation was finished, but not yet re-read nor signed. The cynical Chabot was sitting near her. He put to her extremely impudent questions, adding some extra ones which were not recorded in the minutes. He only wanted to make her talk.

Perceiving a paper in the front of Mlle Corday's dress, he snatched at it. It appears that Mlle Corday had forgotten she was carrying it, because the movement she made to protect herself against Chabot's gesture and the look she aimed at him seemed to indicate outraged modesty and the fear of an attack. She flung her shoulders back so quickly and with such force, as if wishing to shield her breast with her bodice, that the pins and ribbons which held it together broke loose in such a way as to expose her bosom completely and though she rapidly bent forward with her head and chest over her knees, her nudity was none the less exposed to view.

Mlle Corday's hands were tied. She asked that they should be untied to enable her to arrange her dress. There were no women in the court and she was acutely embarrassed. The person who untied her wrists was so near to her! When she was free she turned her face to the wall and did not take long to repair the painful disorder of her dress. During this time the paper which had given rise to the incident had fallen and was picked up by the man who had wished to snatch it from her. It was the Bulletin du Calvados or that of the meeting which the proscribed and fugitive deputies were holding at Caen. They took advantage of the moments when her hands were untied to ask her to sign the record of her examination. I cannot swear that she signed it, but I think she did because she read it through from the beginning to the end and made certain remarks indicating her intention to do so. However that may be, she gave us a striking example of a fabulous memory and unusual presence of mind. After they had read out to her the whole contents of the interrogatory, they proposed to re-read the record to her article by article. She said there was no point in doing that and then proceeded to remark that during the fifth series of questions, which I quote as an illustration, she had been asked a certain question to which she had replied in a certain manner, but that one or more expressions of which she had made use had been changed. She asked that the text of her replies should be reconstituted to give it authenticity. She also noted that in the twelfth series the sense of one of her answers had been altered by the substitution of another word for the one she had used.

Altogether she made six or seven observations of this nature as she ran through the whole of her examination in her memory without making the slightest error in her references to questions and answers, and there were many of them.

Certainly such a feat of memory would at any time be uncommon and particularly in circumstances such as those in which Mlle Corday found herself and which must certainly have given her much else to think about. Her imperturbable presence of mind was no less worthy of admiration. Here was an instance of it.

The cords with which her wrists had been tied were so tight, that her wrists bore marks of them. When the formalities of the examination were concluded, they began to tie her hands again. At that moment she showed her wrists to her tormentors and said these words which I have retained and which I quote textually. "If you have no objection, gentlemen, to making me suffer less, before you put me to death, I would beg you to allow me to pull down my sleeves or to put on gloves under the bonds you are preparing for me."

She did both of these things.

⚜

The lawyer appointed by the Court to defend her, Chauveau-Lagarde.

As the public prosecutor was speaking, the jurymen sent word to tell me to keep silence, while the President advised me to confine my defence to the statement that the accused was insane. They all wanted me to humiliate her.

As for her, her expression did not change. Only, I judged from the way she looked at me, that she did not wish to have excuses made for her. I could not in any case have found a cause for justification as all the evidence, apart from her own confession, constituted a legal proof of premeditated murder.

When I rose to speak, at first I heard muffled, confused sounds indicating stunned astonishment. Then there was a deathly silence which froze my very entrails.

Nevertheless, I was determined to do my duty, while saying nothing which my own conscience or my client might disavow. And then, suddenly, the idea came to me that I would limit myself to a single observation which in a popular assembly or a legislative one, might have furnished the material for a complete defence. I said:

"The accused cold-bloodedly admits that she committed this horrible crime and as cold-bloodedly confesses to a long premeditation. She discloses the circumstances in all their horror. In a word she admits everything and does not even seek to justify herself. There, citizens, is her whole defence. This imperturbable calm, this complete self-abnegation unsoftened by any remorse and maintained, so to speak, in the presence of death, have a certain sublimity, which is not in the natural order of things. They can only be explained by the exaltation of political fanaticism which placed a dagger in her hand. It is for you, citizens of the jury, to judge what moral weight should be given to this consideration in the scales of justice. I rely upon your wisdom."

As I said these words, an expression of satisfaction lit up her features.

✤

A German, Klause, witnessed the execution.

She looked with an expression of indescribable sweetness at the ebb and flow of the multitude and when the populace, mad with excitement or a group of furies disguised as women hailed her with strident cries, a glance from her beautiful eyes was often sufficient to reduce them to silence. It was by her smile alone that she revealed to the outside world what she was feeling. As she approached the scaffold she seemed to be coming to the end of an exhausting voyage. She was alone. Unaided she climbed the steps of the bloodstained platform preserving to the last the pink and white cheeks of a contented young girl. It was only when her neck was bared before the people that a deeper hue rushed to her virginal cheeks. Her noble head, her bare shoulders and the quiet looks, which she cast around her, deeply impressed those who were there to see. Already half transfigured, she looked like an angel of light. She greeted the persons round the scaffold with a friendly air and wanted to address the people, but this they forbade her to do. Then she approached the deadly machine and, of her own accord, placed her head on the appointed place. The plank descended more slowly than usual. A solemn silence reigned. The fatal blade came down and cut off that most beautiful of all heads.

The executioner's assistant displayed the bleeding head to the people. One could still see on its features the traces of a smile. But the wretch was vile enough to strike the head with his open hand. A general groan of displeasure confirmed the saying "The law punishes but does not avenge itself." Sanson himself was indignant, and the Police Court inflicted on the infamous Legros the penalty that his contemptible action deserved.

Here and there cries of *Vive la Nation! Vive la République!* could be heard. The people had never yet seen a figure so inspiring and they took back to their homes a memory of great courage and great beauty.

✤

A letter addressed by Rousillon, one of the Jury on the Revolutionary Tribunal, addressed to La Chronique de Paris:

Paris, July 20th, 2nd year of the Republic

Citizen,

After the sword of the Law had struck off the head of Marat's assassin, a man named Legros, one of the executioner's assistants, having seized the head to show it to the people, permitted himself to slap the face of this inanimate and now innocent head several times. This barbarous action incurred the censure of the people and citizen Michonis, the police-chief, felt obliged to administer a correction to this savage, or at least cowardly, fellow. The Tribunal, seized of his indecent behaviour, caused citizen Legros to be cast into prison and proposes to administer a public rebuke.

I have thought it my duty to bring this act of justice to the knowledge of the public, who, always generous and always just, will approve of a measure of which the Friend of the People himself would have approved, had he survived his wound. He was too great of soul to countenance so base an action. He knew, and everyone should know, that, when a crime is punished, the law is satisfied.

A few persons made the mistake of believing that it was the executioner himself who was guilty of this misconduct. This is quite wrong. Sanson is an excellent citizen and much too well-educated to deviate thus. Far from it: he was much upset by the incident.

Fraternal greetings—

Roussillon.

The body was taken to the hospital of la Charité. Two doctors, specially appointed, examined the corpse in the presence of an assistant and two members of the National Convention, one of whom was the painter David. When the post-mortem was over, those present declared unanimously that Charlotte Corday died a virgin.

In certain provinces the death of the Friend of the People was felt to be an occasion for national mourning. Here is an account of an

expiatory ceremony at Bourg-Régénéré (Bourg-en-Bresse) recorded in
the proceedings of the Société des Sans-Culottes.

A cannon-shot fired at dawn was the signal for all the Sans-
Culottes to rise. Each one of them went to his post.

A hundred girls, their heads crowned with garlands of oak-
leaves, surrounded a chariot containing five venerable old men
clinging to one another and supported in the arms of fifteen
nubile maidens, at pains to warm them with their pure breath
and appointed to take care of them throughout the ceremony.

A battalion of Patriots, who had not slept all night for fear they
might not awake early enough, led the procession.

The mothers of patriot families, the public authorities and the
members of the Société des Sans-Culottes marched together in an
orderly confusion following the simple dictates of nature.

Some of them carried the bust of our friend Marat, while
others raised aloft all the different emblems of liberty which the
Society had been able to collect.

When they reached the Place Jémappes, the Citizen-President
read a speech in memory of Marat and concluded by causing all
the women to surround the pyramid erected in his honour after
having hung their garlands on the spikes of the iron grille enclosing the tomb.

The procession then proceeded to the church, where tables
had been prepared to which each patriot had brought his dinner
to be shared with the poor as principal guests.

A spirit of fraternal geniality breathed through the gathering.
The President of the Society bestowed, in the name of all, the
Sans-Culotte kiss on a deputy from the neighbouring societies,
an old man, a young girl and one of the defenders of the
country.

The Mayor proposed a toast to the memory of Marat, accompanied by the following words of command.

Attention—prepare the urns—empty the urns—fill the urns—
align the urns in order—let incense be burnt to the memory of
Marat—clasp the urns—raise them towards the great vault of
heaven—lower them to the level of your hearts—draw near to
the tomb—shed tears—cease weeping—fall into line!

Set down the urn on the catafalque all together and in three simultaneous motions.

Step back, Sans-Culottes and declaim together three times: Marat is happy; Marat, our friend, has died for his country.

The repast was enjoyed in cheerful, orderly fashion. There was no drunkenness. Three thousand citizens from the town and from the country gave brilliance to the festival.

Done at Bourg-Régénéré, capital of the Department of the Ain, on the 20th day of Brumaire of the second year of the Republic, one, indivisible and democratic.

THE COLLAPSE OF THE ÉMIGRÉS

✧✧

WHILE THE French armies are winning victories, what is happening to the French émigrés? Here is a report from the future Madame de Gontaut, now in distress.

. . . . A little later the Prussians besieged Thionville commencing on August 24th 1792. They failed completely. Several other disastrous engagements took place, among them that of Valmy. The campaign in Champagne ended with the retreat of the invading armies across the Rhine and into the Low Countries.

Let me recount my personal experiences. I have tried to justify the illusions with which we comforted ourselves at Coblentz. They were based on certain plans for the escape of the Royal Family about which there was too much talk. A confidential messenger, sent to my mother by M. Durvet, brought her a piece of ribbon, which had been sewn into the lining of a garment. On it were written these words: "Will you authorize me to lend a part of your daughter's dowry, which you have placed in my hands? It will be restored to you by the person whom you love, when next you come together which I hope will be soon. Let me have your reply by the same route." "Yes, a hundred times yes," was my mother's reply. Alas! the arrest of the King at Varennes rendered my mother's sacrifice useless. It had helped to make up the sum required to cover the cost of the King's escape and was confiscated at the time of his criminal arrest.

During the previous year when we were at Bagnères and Pau, there had been talk of my marriage with M. de Saint-Blancard. My mother was much attached to his family, and favoured his suit but decided to postpone the marriage until order should be re-established in France.

M. de Saint-Blancard was at Coblentz serving in the army of the Princes. He knew of my mother's devotion to the cause and was generous enough to applaud the sacrifice she had made.

When the army of the Princes started to march into France by way of Thionville, permission was given to women to accompany it.

People availed themselves of this chance with alacrity. Numerous carriages filled the roads and this remnant of Parisian elegance combined with the confidence that everyone felt made the journey a joyful one. As we cheerfully parted from our friends we almost made arrangements to meet again in Paris.

There was a young M. de Quinsonnas, who possessed a little treasure, which he did not wish to expose to the risks of war. He looked around, but the people he saw all seemed young and frivolous, until at last he met an old lady, the wife of the oldest holder of the Cordon Rouge—the Order of the Holy Spirit. "Can't hope for better than that," he said to himself and entrusted his precious nest-egg to this venerable couple. The old lady swore she would give it back to him in Paris. After the rout, he looked for the old lady and eventually found her. She turned pale when she saw him. "What!" said she, "you are not dead!" "What about my treasure?" he asked in a panic. "Here it is," said the old lady, "there ain't much left."

During the disasters that followed I often heard the saying, often with a smile on the speaker's face, "There ain't much left."

We now entered upon a new era of vicissitudes, privations and hardships, which only resignation to the will of God and my love for my mother enabled me to endure.

When our armies began to fall back we were at Luxemburg, where the sound of the guns coming from Thionville buoyed up our hopes. But the chaos of the retreat was horrible. We were overrun by the troops who swarmed over all the roads.

We were obliged to drive at a foot's pace. Worn-out soldiers sought relief in the carriages and huddled together on the box-seats. At the close of each painful day, one looked for a resting-place. We fought for accommodation in barns and were content to sleep on the straw. The sight of a church tower gave us hope of asylum, but our hopes were dashed when we read the words "No admittance to Jews and *émigrés*".

To give an idea of our situation I shall recount here an episode, which in the midst of the miseries of this journey, revived for a spell our French sense of humour.

A roomy barn and a sufficiency of fresh straw gave us the prospect of a good night. The Duchesse de Guiche, Mesdames de Poulpry, Delage and other ladies including my mother and myself had bedded themselves down in the straw along the wall. One of the Duchesse de Guiche's huntsmen, carrying a drawn sword had received orders to watch over us. In the middle of the night we were awakened by repeated knockings on the door and the voice of a woman demanding shelter. "Open," cried the voice, "it is I." The door was opened and in walked Mme de Calonne, the wife of the Minister, in full fig, curled, made up and powdered, wearing a beautiful dress with a hooped skirt and train and high-heeled shoes. "Where are the rooms?" she said. Then, looking round in consternation, "But, what do I see? A hospital? Women on the straw? An armed man? Holà! Where are my lackeys? Bring light, torches!" Her servants ran up and when the barn was lit up, her cries redoubled. "Where am I? What do I see? Men hanging on the wall?" And then we saw for the first time the skinned carcasses of two dozen sheep fastened on the wall in readiness to be taken to market next day. Then we recognized one another and everyone burst out laughing. The poor lady was having her baptism of hardship. She gathered from looking at us to what discomforts she would have to resign herself and, like us, she put a good face on it.

We underwent a thousand inconveniences and all sorts of privations during the retreat of the troops until we finally reached Mayence. There we stopped for a few days. As the Prussians were heading in a different direction, we hoped to reach Coblentz more easily.

On our return to Mayence my mother managed to send letters to my grandmother suggesting persons whom her agents might make use of to send us the funds we needed. But the French advanced with such rapidity that we could not wait for the eagerly awaited replies. We were obliged to sell our diamonds and other jewels as well as our carriage and other possessions to pitiless Jews, who hastened to profit by our situation.

The orders to evacuate the town were peremptory, so we had to embark for Coblentz. We found that town a prey to extreme agitation. The French troops were expected to arrive shortly. The fortress of Ehrenbreitstein had already been attacked. We had to continue our flight, and were exposed to great danger as we sailed down the Rhine. Shells discharged from the fortress fell all around the frail bark in which we sought to escape from this dangerous region. As soon as we could, we continued our journey in carts and in this deplorable manner we finally arrived at Rotterdam where we hoped to find letters from the family. But, in fact, the news we received was terrible. The list of executions contained the name of my grandmother's brother, as well as that of my mother's own brother.

While she was reading the list my poor mother had a seizure, followed by a fit of depression, and I feared for her life. What a ghastly situation we were in! Alone, unfriended, with winter coming on! And what a winter! The waters were rising in an alarming fashion and we had to climb through a window to reach the canal from the little house in which we were staying.

My mother was prostrate and I felt my own strength was failing, but God in His goodness sustained me and I realized that, in order to restore my mother's courage, I must brace up my own. A merchant, to whom an important personage at Coblentz had recommended us, often came to see us. I am sure that he sympathized with our plight. One day I spoke to him of my wish to put to some useful purpose the lessons I had learnt in childhood. He was a man of taste and advised me to make use of my own by learning to paint on stone and ivory. I took lessons and began to hope that I should be able by my own efforts to supply the deficiency when our means were exhausted. I worked hard and put by some money, feeling able to face the future without fear now that I was confident of my ability to support my good and well-loved mother.

After the disaster that befell the army of the Princes, M. de Saint

Blancard succeeded in reaching us. His arrival was an unexpected joy. He had guessed that we were in trouble and had come to bring us solace. He urged us, in view of the precarious condition of Holland, to leave that country and he considered that our most suitable place of refuge would be England. I was very anxious to go there. He won over my mother to this idea and asked her to let him take charge of our future and look for some suitable little place where we could settle down. He asked her to let him know when it would suit her to start.

As soon as the spring came I called on my mother to fulfil her promise and at least we left dreary Holland. When we arrived at Harwich the first word of English which I heard and could understand caused my heart to beat with the hope of a better future. This was a moment of happy presage for from thenceforward the kind and honest hospitality of the English never failed us.

*

The Marquis de Falaiseau tells how he saw an old nobleman marching barefoot through the mud.

An army, says Chateaubriand, is generally composed of soldiers of about the same age, the same size and the same physical strength. Our army was something very different; a confused mass of grown men, greybeards and children fresh from their dove-cotes, all speaking with the accents of Normandy, Brittany, Picardy, Auvergne, Gascony, Provence or Languedoc. A father could be seen serving with his sons, a father-in-law with his son-in-law, an uncle with his nephews, brothers with brothers, cousins with cousins. This rearguard, absurd as it may have seemed, contained an honourable and touching element, because it was animated by sincere convictions. It presented a picture of the old monarchy, the final scenes of a world that was passing away. I have seen in this company stern old gentlemen with grey hair, torn clothes, carrying haversacks and muskets slung over their shoulder, dragging themselves along with the help of a stick or being held up under the arm by one of their sons. I noticed M. de Boishue, the father of my comrade whom I had seen massacred at Rennes, marching, forlorn and barefoot in the mud carrying his shoes on the point of his bayonet so as not to wear them out. I have seen young men lying mortally wounded under a tree and a chaplain in field-dress and wearing a stole, on his knees by them, sending them to join St. Louis, whose heirs they had striven to defend. And all the soldiers in this impoverished host, who did not receive a penny from the Princes, made war at their own expense, while their fortunes were being confiscated under the decrees, and their wives and mothers flung into dungeons.

✤

The Comte d'Artois is in torment. He writes to Vaudreuil, the Creole nobleman, whom the hazards of war (the siege of Gibraltar in 1782) made a friend and the hazards of love a confidant. For Artois and Vaudreil are, in fact, the lovers of two sisters-in-laws, Mme de Polastron and Comtesse Jules de Polignac. They are taken for two brothers-in-law and no one takes offence not even the husbands. Indeed the Comte d'Artois asks Vaudreuil to get Jules to read the first part of his letter.

Liège
19th November, 1792.

One would need the pen of a Jeremiah, my dear Vaudreuil, to give you a true picture of our position since you left us. I had hoped to be able to keep up my spirits, but I must admit that I feel terribly distressed about everything.

You should know even better than I do the reasons which prevent the Court of Vienna from replying to the memorandum which I addressed four weeks ago to M. de Mercy. Comte Jules has a copy of it and I told him to stress the more important articles and doubtless he has done everything he could. But the Emperor's silence places us in a terribly embarrassing situation. Messrs. de Mercy and Metternich have advanced us a sum of 87,000 frs., mainly to guarantee the loans made to the regiments. But since we are not receiving a single écu from anywhere else and as the King of Prussia has not yet given us the 100,000 frs. which he promised me a month ago, we have had to employ a part of this sum in saving the most needy of our companies from death by starvation and in paying our butcher and our baker.

I should add that we were able to do this because the Brussels government handed us the 87,000 frs. without specifying how they should be spent.

We have knocked at so many doors, where we had a right to hope for some relief, but the defeat of the Austrians and their retreat towards the Meuse have ruined our prospects. In the first place the money markets closed down, though this did not do us any harm. But later, we were forced to restrict the number of our cantonments and even to convey the greater part of our forces across the Meuse, thus using up the last of our resources and being forced to consume in eight days supplies on which we could have subsisted until the first of December. For, to put you in the picture, I must tell you that General Schoenfeld left us three days ago with the warning that the King of Prussia would furnish us with no supplies after December the first. He even handed over to our Commissariat the amounts required to pay our victuallers up to the end of the month.

So you see that is all we have to live on. I ought to add that M. le duc de Bourbon having separated his forces from the Austrians by a retrograde movement, which was not to their liking, now receives nothing from them in the shape of supplies for his men and has consequently become a charge on us.

We do not wish to disband the army nor can we do so without learning the intentions of Vienna and receiving the money promised by the King of Prussia. However, everything is falling to pieces insensibly and we are all starving to death. My morning's work is a continual penance. All the time we are awaiting the Emperor's reply. We have also sent two couriers to the King of Prussia and are sustained by a crumb of hope.

I went myself to Louvain to find Duke Albert and Clerfayt, and offered to raise from four to five thousand men, horse and foot, for their army. I begged and insisted, but though they received me very politely, they refused my offer on the ground that they could not afford to maintain such a force and that in any case they must have direct orders from Vienna before accepting it.

Such being my position, you may well ask, my friend, why I am not already on the way to Petersburg and Monsieur is not heading for Madrid. My answer will be short and precise. The reason is that we have not got a sou towards the expenses of our journey, though they calculate that the cost for me and my children will amount to 80,000 frs. I believe that the latter will eventually go to Naples. We are moving heaven and earth to obtain funds, but it is quite impossible to know at what date we shall receive them and if, in the meantime I should hear that I was not welcome in Russia, upon my honour I don't know what would become of us.

I wrote to poor Calonne (the former Finance Minister) asking him to try to procure funds for us but the only reply I received informed me that he had been imprisoned for several hours for underwriting a promissory note of ours. His banker has got him out of trouble for the moment, but he is still in a very embarrassing situation. He hardly dares to leave his house for fear that his enemies may cook up some new charge against him. He has now sent me M. de la Palisse for the purpose of arranging for a fair and profitable disposal of the last monies we are due to receive under the Cohen loan. I wrote at once to M. de Metternich to tell him about this and I hope for his assistance: but all that poor Calonne is likely to gain is the possibility of a sea-passage to Italy to rejoin his wife there. That would mean that we should have to give up the hope of settling Calonne in England. Besides, it distresses me to see a man whom I like and who has sacrificed himself to help me exposed to persecution.

Ah! my dear friend, what a multitude of misfortunes! I assure you that I constantly feel myself on the verge of losing my reason and if I were not attached to life by a bond which every day grows more dear, more precious and more essential to me, I do not know what I might do. Please acquaint Jules with the first part of my letter. I am also sending him a message by Rivière, but I want you to keep him posted regarding details.

Thank God, my friend, at least, is well. She will not leave for Vienna until the date of my own departure has been definitely fixed. But then she will start without delay. For the moment she is waiting for the money and the passport which her sister is to send her.

You and Jules are the only people I write to. I should depress your friend, if I wrote to her, as I never felt more dejected.

However, I am trying to preserve my brains, my strength and my health, and I don't mean to lose heart.

Give my love to all good friends. The life I lead is becoming unbearable as time goes on. Rivière will tell you about it in detail.

I count on your affection more than ever and you know I am your friend in life and death.

❧

Vaudreuil's affection for his illustrious friend suffered, during the Vendée campaign, from the fact that the Comte d'Artois remained in Germany and made no attempt to assist the royalists in the West. Comtesse Jules de Polignac died in 1793, after which Vaudreuil went to live in England, married one of his cousins and became an English gentleman.

THE TERROR

❋❋

*A PARISIAN RETURNS to his native city after ten months'
absence. This Parisian is none other than the patriot who
(see July 14th) narrated to us the story of the storming of the
Bastille. Since then the progress of events has kept him away from the
capital, and he now looks at Paris under the Terror with the eyes of a
provincial.*

So there I was packed into a stage-coach surrounded by sinister
faces, for at that moment, none but revolutionaries and government agents dared to move about. My mind was filled with the
darkest presentiments and every stage on my way to Paris
seemed to bring me nearer to the scaffold. As I thought of my
wife and my children, I reproached myself for having left them
so rashly and for not having embraced them yet once more before
we parted. During the whole journey the sight of a rock, an
agreeable bit of landscape or a tree noticed by the wayside stamped
on my mind a melancholy impress, which I cannot describe.
I cherished a wish to see them again on my way back, saying to
myself: "If I see them again, that will mean that I have got out
of Paris, and if I get out of Paris I shall see my wife and children
once more."

Just before reaching the modern Babylon we changed horses
and I got out to stretch my legs. I tried to banish the painful
thoughts that haunted me, and went into an inn with the object
of eating something, if the burden of worry which oppressed me
allowed me to do so. Sitting down at a table I picked up a newspaper lying there and, glancing over it, was instantly struck by a
news item describing the execution of a man—a good man and

one of my friends. He had been a notary and, in that capacity, had countersigned without reading it, as was the practice, a document whose contents were unknown to him. The Bloody Assize had condemned him to death. His hair had been cut and he was waiting to be beheaded, when he was snatched from the Guillotine to have his case examined afresh. The Convention had ordered this humane intervention, but the court presided over by Fouquier, who did not wish to be thought capable of condemning an innocent man, had the victim dragged back to the scaffold and beheaded. And so Chaudot, a good, honest man, had the misery of drinking twice over the cup of death.

I was overwhelmed by this story. My strength failed me. I wanted to eat but could not get anything down. I raised a glass of wine to my lips, but had not the heart to drink. I hurried back to the diligence, where I remained plunged in a mood of the deepest melancholy from which I was aroused when one of my companions cried: "Here we are at the barrier. We've arrived." These words shook me out of my lethargy but they made me shudder. I put my head out of the window. It was dark, though it was scarcely eight o'clock.

What a change! Formerly—even when I left the city not so long ago—eight o'clock was the hour when Paris was most brilliantly illuminated, especially in the populous quarters. The light of innumerable street lamps blended with the blazing windows of the shops, where art and luxury had accumulated thousands of objects which vied with one another for elegance and value. It was the hour when the cafés were lit up and when the gleam of candles shone from every storey; when luxurious equipages passed one another swiftly in the streets on their way to theatres, concerts and balls in every quarter of the capital. Now, instead of this bustling life, these animated crowds, this impressive brilliance, a sepulchral silence filled all the streets of Paris. All the shops were already shut, and everyone hastened to barricade himself in his own home. One might suppose that the weeds of mourning had overspread all that breathed.

We reached the terminus. I got down, taking under my arm a packet containing a few articles of clothing which I needed and I was leaving the coaching office for the home of a friend from whom I intended to beg for hospitality. At the door of the office there was a sort of sentry who took my packet away from me on the ground that I was not allowed to carry anything at night. He told me I could come and call for it next day at the guard room. I withdrew without making any remark and proceeded to the house of my friend who had heard nothing of me for a year and a half and who, having turned Jacobin in the interval as a form of insurance, thought more about his own safety than about the fate of his former friends.

It was nearly nine o'clock when I knocked at his door. This would not have been thought unduly late in normal times, but as it was, my knocking at the door at such an hour caused a panic among all the people who lived in the house. Domiciliary visits were usually carried out at night and most of the crowd of citizens who thronged the prisons had been arrested after dark. The sound of a hammer caused every hearer to tremble, and my former friend seemed to be particularly alarmed when he saw me come into his house. Without asking after my health or enquiring what had happened to me and why I had come to Paris, he gave me to understand in curt, clear language, that as I had left Paris some time back it would be dangerous for me to stay in the city and for him to offer me shelter. "What? It would be dangerous for me to stay the night?" I asked. "Yes, it would," he replied. "If they came now to search the place, I should be a lost man."

In face of so blunt a statement I could not insist and as it had never entered my head to wish to ruin anyone not even a Jacobin I left him, begging him to tell me of some furnished rooms near by where I could find a lodging. He had the courage to take me to a fruiterer who had some rooms to let in a very skimpy-looking house. However, as the fruiterer refused to take me in at this late hour, my friend went home saying that I should find a lodging elsewhere. He left me in the street without appearing to care what happened to me, though as he closed the door he advised me not to remain too long on the pavement, unless I wished to be picked up by one of the patrols, who were usually reluctant to release persons who fell into their clutches.

If my friend's manner of receiving me was not brilliant, neither was the advice, which he was kind enough to offer me, reassuring,

I began to be afraid and knocked once more at the fruiterer's door. He refused to open. I went on knocking and finally he let me in. As he was lighting the lamp, he told me that the reason why he went to bed so early was because it was impossible to procure candles in Paris. He added: "Of course you have your passport?" I said I would show it to him. Before reading it by the light of the lamp, he eyed me intently. Then after looking at it he said: "But this passport is not signed by the revolutionary committee of this section." "Yes, but I have only just arrived," I said. "The committee is not in session at this hour and I cannot get them to sign it tonight. Give me a bed for tonight and tomorrow when I get up I shall go and get the visa." "Impossible," said the man, "impossible. If they came tonight, and they visit furnished lodgings almost every night, I should be put in prison for having taken you in without your passport being duly visa-ed by a revolutionary committee. So, dear sir, out of my house you go and at once." And suiting the action to the words he slammed the door in my face as civilly as my friend the Jacobin had done not long before.

Once more in the street I began to be seriously alarmed. Walking at random and uncertain whither to direct my steps, I formed the idea of going to a distant quarter, where I hoped for more compassionate treatment from a person to whom I had formerly rendered a service. After crossing several important streets without meeting a soul, I heard a dull sound apparently approaching me and inarticulate cries. I stopped to see what it was and, in order to avoid being seen, I huddled into the corner of an adjacent street where a carriage entrance afforded darkness and security.

I could not have chosen a more suitable refuge from which to witness what happened or one better calculated to get myself arrested. The dull sound which I had heard was nothing else than that caused by two files of pikemen on the march, who were escorting in their midst a carriage with windows closed, doubtless to silence the cries of the persons inside. I was able to satisfy my curiosity more freely than I wished, for the procession stopped in front of a door almost opposite the entrance in which I had taken refuge. I did not dare to move. The armed men surrounded the gate of what must have been a monastery and now served as a prison. They opened the carriage door to let out a person, whom they intended to incarcerate, and whose voice proclaimed her to be a woman. "Inhuman monsters," she cried, "after murdering the father must you tear the mother from her children! No, I will not get out—you may kill me first. My Arsène, my own child, whom I nursed! He will die—No, I won't get out. . . . Oh, very well, I will, but give up my child, my child."

After having pulled the woman out of the carriage and flung her into prison, they moved away rapidly, being unwilling to linger in the cold rain that was falling.

As I did not know where to go and had by now given up the idea of going to any particular place, I remained for nearly two hours in the same place with my arms crossed over my chest and my eyes fixed on the door of the convent to which the unfortunate woman had been dragged. Finally the sound of a clock striking midnight disturbed my reverie. My feet were numb with cold and I felt myself shivering, so I decided to walk in the hope of getting warm. But I had not gone a hundred yards when, at the entrance to a street, I ran into a patrol which, as my charitable friend had foretold, made a prize of me and refused to release me until they had taken me to the coaching-office and checked up on my arrival. The register and my package having proved my story to be true the patrol left me in the office, where I begged the *employé* who was slumbering by a stove to allow me to share his sleeping quarters, in which I went to sleep stretched out on some parcels.

When I awoke there was a fresh *employé* in the room. I welcomed the change. Forgetting that I had come to Paris to procure some funds and desiring nothing more than an opportunity to get away, I asked when the next diligence would start for the place from which I had come. I was told that one left every day at eight o'clock in the morning. I was beside myself with joy and instantly reserved a place for which I paid and was given a receipt. As it was then seven o'clock I ran to get some breakfast in a coffee house near the coaching-office and then to make sure of catching the coach, I took my seat inside. The horses had been put in and the diligence was ready to start when a police officer asked all the passengers if they were in order. I showed my receipt. "Don't want that!" "What *do* you want?" "Your passport." "Here it is." "You must get out, you are not in order." "What do you mean?" "This passport has not been countersigned by the revolutionary committee of the section in which you lodged." "Citizen, I did not take lodgings anywhere. I arrived at seven and finished my business at eight. I spent the night in this office and now I want to go." "Never mind about your business. No one can leave Paris without having his passport visa-ed by a revolutionary committee. The orders of the Commune about this are perfectly clear. The committee may be in possession of details about you and it is proper for you to show your face to the persons charged with proving your identity."

I had to get out. This conversation was already boring the coachman, who whipped up his horses ill-temperedly and swept off carrying with him my hopes, the price of my seat which was never returned to me and to crown everything, my parcel of clothes which in my confusion I had forgotten to take out of the coach.

This time, as it was already day, I was received in a furnished lodging house where I said I would stay until the following morning when I promised myself that I would not miss the next coach. I at once asked my hostess to tell me in what section she was located so that I could go and have my passport visa-ed by the revolutionary committee of the ward. She told me the name of her section and where the committee was sitting and warned me not to come back without having completed this formality, failing which she would not be able to keep me for the night.

I then set out. Daylight and the sight of many people moving freely in the streets restored my nerves to some extent and I walked boldly on my way when suddenly I was struck by a curious medley of colours which I had not been expecting. All the doors and all the windows carried a flagstaff on which floated the Tricolour. A few patriots, more republican in spirit than their neighbours, or wishing to be thought so, had hoisted this banner and from that time onwards, as it was dangerous to be less patriotic than anyone else, everyone had decorated his windows with tricolour streamers and large, coloured inscriptions on which one read the words: "Unity, indivisibility, liberty, equality, fraternity or death." Another notice posted up everywhere bore the inscription: "Charity, justice and humanity are part of our daily duty." A stranger arriving in Paris without knowing what was happening there, when reading the words "fraternity or death" might well imagine that he had only to enter the house of any citizen and make himself at home and that anyone refusing him hospitality would be led off to the scaffold as a base creature unfit to mix in human society. This high-light of hypocrisy reminded me of a phrase let fall by the philosopher of Geneva: "There is nowhere so much talk of liberty as in a state where it has ceased to exist."

As I was mentally comparing the fraternity of the notice boards with that displayed by my former friend, I arrived at the headquarters of the revolutionary committee of my section. I easily recognized the place by the notice on the building, the size of the tricolour flag which floated above the gate and the proportions of the red bonnet with which it was crowned, not to mention the hang-dog appearance of the men on guard at the entrance. My heart beat, but I walked in.

I could have imagined myself in the cave of Cacus. After crossing a little courtyard, narrow and dark, flanked with high walls, in which were collected an assortment of cut-throats armed with swords and pikes, I went up a squalid staircase at the top of which was an anteroom, leading into the room in which the Committee held its meetings. This anteroom was crowded with creatures even more hideous than those whom I had seen in the courtyard. It reeked of pipe-tobacco, brandy and meat, aggravated by the heat of a fiery stove, which had a sickening, suffocating effect on anyone coming into the room out of the fresh air. "What do you want?" said one of these horrible individuals as he gulped down a cupful of wine. "I have come to get my passport visa-ed." "Go into the room then," he said. It was the room in which the members of the Committee were sitting. I went in. It was worse than the anteroom. There was the same foul stench, the same bunch of brigands, but those in the Council room were more insolent than the others. They wore the rags of a feigned poverty, but they had hearts of steel and the mien of tyrants. From top to toe nothing could have been more disgusting than their personal appearance. As sans-culottism had been promoted to a virtue and as the people, so far from displaying the trappings of luxury, had thrown themselves into the opposite extreme, these individuals affected a squalid poverty. At that time in Paris dirtiness was a sort of passport and most certainly no one could have surpassed in this respect the persons before whom I was appearing. Long and dirty beards, greasy, filthy hair, stockings with holes, worn out sabots, red bonnets, ragged coats, hands sticky with filth, bare necks and shirts open to the waist, such were the characteristics of these ignorant, impudent bullies, brutes raised out of the slime, where they had won notoriety by their deeds of violence. To crown it all, they assumed in the midst of their filth a veneer of antiquity and gave each other Greek and Roman names which they disfigured grotesquely as soon as they began to address one another. They paid no attention to me when I approached them, for they were busy giving orders to policemen to put seals on the property of the persons they had arrested during the night. One of the members of the Committee (he seemed to be the chairman) was saying to the head policeman: "That's a job for you, Manlius; you're a clever cove, you're one of ours." "You can count on me, here's my hand on it." "It's what I say. You've got to stick on the seals—There's dibs there, you follow me."

After these honest fellows had whispered together for a while and the stickers-on or removers of seals had gone off on their mission with one of the members of the Committee, the chairman graciously took notice of me. "What do you want?" he said. "A visa for my passport." "Where do you come from?" "From Blanktown." "Full of aristocrats." "You are mistaken, citizen." "Who are you calling 'vous'? It's easy to see that they aren't in step in your community. It's only Pitt and Coburg who use the 'vous'. In a free country one has to say 'tu'." "Citizen, next time I shall not fail to do so." "What have you come to Paris for?" "To get some money from a gentleman of my acquaintance and go home again." At the word "gentleman" which I had let slip in my confusion there was such an uproar in the Committee that

I seriously thought I was done for and that they were going to imprison me. "Ah, you have come to see a gentleman. So you must be a gentleman yourself. Just look at this fellow, Brutus; hasn't he just the build of a federalist?" "I, citizen?" "You be quiet and bring us your witnesses so that we may see if they look as suspect as you do." "What witnesses do you want me to bring?" "How d'you mean, what witnesses? Monsieur is pretending to be an idiot, or is God dead? Make up your mind to it that we are a tough lot of b——rs and that we are not easily duped. Now go: leave your passport here and unless you want something worse to happen to you, don't let us see your ugly mug here until you're in order."

I bitterly regretted my visit to Paris and the mess I had got into and now, full of shame and despair I went back to ask my land-lady to explain what they meant by asking for two witnesses before granting me a visa. As she was familiar with the situation on account of the many strangers she lodged, she told me that two witnesses were indispensable to answer for the good citizen-ship of the owner of the passport. She added that if unsatisfactory reports were to hand about this person and he could not be located when the Committee sent to find him, the two witnesses who had answered for him would be put in prison until he was found.

I realized that it would not be easy to find witnesses and that in Paris where there were forty-eight revolutionary committees, each more eager than the other to clap people in jail it would hardly be possible, even in such a great city, to discover persons who would be prepared to take risks on behalf of people they did not know.

Nevertheless, I begged my landlady to tell me of someone who might render me this service. The woman had an honest appear-ance. She said, "But, citizen, you seem to have lived in Paris—do not you know anyone here?" "Yes, indeed I do," I said, "but it is nearly eighteen months since I left and I should be loth to go to the quarter where I was known. I should be taken for a fugitive and I am particularly anxious to leave this city before being spotted by any person of my acquaintance and especially by a former servant of mine, who must surely be a member of some revolutionary committee as he possesses all the qualities required to perform this honourable function." "Silence, you bad man," she said with an anxious gesture: "if someone were to hear us!" She continued: "But listen, I know a man who will do this for you. Of course he will have to be paid, for that is his profession." "Never mind," I said, "that's all I want." "He lives near here in the second little shop on the left in the Rue de la Loi." "And where is that?" I said, "I have lived for ages in Paris without ever having heard the name." She began to laugh and told me that all the street names had been changed, that Paris now had a Rue de Jean Jacques Rousseau, a Rue d'Helvétius, a Rue de Beaurepaire, a Rue d'Egalité, a Rue de Marat, a Quai Voltaire, a Place de la Révolution, a Section called after Mucius Scaevola and so on and so forth and that the Rue de la Loi of which she had spoken to me was the former Rue de Richelieu.

I was now *au courant*. I think it an excellent thing to honour the memory of great men and to hallow the memory of great events by giving to streets names, which being daily on the lips of men recall to them those great events and those illustrious personages. But it seems ridiculous, to say the least of it, to change in a moment most of the names, which had already been given to streets, and thus to cause confusion and inconvenience to citizens and especially to strangers. However, these were trifling considerations and, thinking less about these innovations than about the problem of procuring witnesses, I walked on until I found the shop which had been indicated to me.

When I entered this little hole of a place, I found a woman sitting by a sort of counter, waiting, it seemed, for customers to whom to sell salt and tobacco, the only articles in which she dealt and of which she kept a very small supply. I asked her where her husband was as I had to speak to him. She replied that he would soon be back and that I would not have long to wait. He had only gone to the Place de la Révolution to see a score and a half of aristocrats "sneezing into the sack". That was the phrase with which Hébert, Chaumette's assistant, described in a foul rag entitled *La Grande Colère du Père Duchêne*, the amputation of heads, which, severed by the blade of the guillotine fell speedily one on top of another into a kind of basin, where they floated in blood, which splashed up as the heads dropped, and flooded the pavement of the place dedicated to these daily butcheries. "I told him," she said, "that it wasn't worth while going over there for such a small number and advised him to stay in the shop."

As she had promised, her husband returned very soon. I explained to him the object of my visit. He appeared perfectly willing to act as my witness, and merely added that I should need another, adding, "Oh! I shall find one soon enough. Perhaps you have not dined." "No," I said. "Well sit down on that stool; we'll have a drink and after that I'll settle your business." "Gladly,' I said, "but on condition that I stand the wine." "Very good: I'll send the wife to fetch us something to eat." As he ate, my tobacconist, who had witnessed "the sneezing into the sack" reproached his wife for having tried to keep him at home and said that if he had listened to her he would have missed a great pleasure, as he had never laughed so much.

From the story which he told us and to which I had to listen without flinching, I learnt that the individuals who had provided the comedy were none other than one of the executioner's valets and the coachman of the member of the revolutionary tribunal who went every day to the place of execution with the persons condemned by the tribunal in order to witness their death and provide legal proof of the same. Now, as the guillotine was always ready from a quarter of an hour to an hour before the arrival of the condemned persons one of the executioner's valets who had been helping to set it up, amused himself by dancing round the instrument as soon as it was in position and by his capers, antics and grimaces entertained the crowd before providing them with the more substantial pleasure of seeing heads fall. As for the coachman he was not a whit less comical than the other fellow. The judge's carriage always preceded the carts carrying the condemned. The coachman announced to the crowd by his gestures that the aristocrats were coming, that they were here and that they would soon be putting their heads into the noose. The coachman, grotesquely arrayed in a red bonnet and a carmagnole of the same colour, leapt down from the box and sprang back again with a single bound. When the condemned were numerous he showed great pleasure and it appears that his gaiety was proportionate to the number of heads to be lopped off.

However, although on this occasion there were only thirty, he seemed to be in particularly good form, as my companion kept exploding with laughter at the recollection. "By God," he said, after concluding his narrative, "these dogs died very bravely. It's unfortunate that the aristocrats die like that. In this batch there was a little pullet of from seventeen to twenty, as fresh as a rose, who climbed up on to the platform as gaily as if she was going to dance a figure from a quadrille." "Seventeen to twenty was she?" I remarked: "that's early to start being an aristocrat." "You're right," said my companion, "but those people drink federalism with their mother's milk."

❧

An arrest under the Terror.
Lawyer Beugnot is also a deputy. He has his enemies. One day an inspector of police with an escort of sans-culottes carrying pikes and followed by a gendarme, bursts into his dwelling.

I can only attribute to a strong bias, aggravated by too much food and drink, the stupid and barbarous fashion in which this gendarme introduced himself to me. He came into my apartment carrying an unsheathed sword and after a string of oaths which lasted for some minutes asked me where and who I was. The inspector pointed me out to the man whose eyes, bloodshot and swimming with brandy, had failed to notice me. "Ah! that's him!" he cried, "I recognize him now. I've been looking for him for days, but couldn't find him. It's a good case. We'll tie his feet and hands and then off to the Conciergerie! Another bird for the guillotine!" The fellow was stalking proudly about my apartment making passes in the air with his sword and mouthing quotations from *Père Duchesne* (a political journal written in slang) which he from time to time applied to me to the amusement of the honourable company. I waited coolly until his lungs could no longer keep pace with the efforts of his memory. When that moment arrived I took occasion to ask to see the warrant for my arrest. The gendarme objected and began to repeat his favourite lines about binding me hand and foot and taking me to the Conciergerie. I insisted and the inspector supported me. At last I was allowed to read a warrant signed Soulès and Morino ordering me to be taken straight to the Conciergerie. The reading of this sentence of death revived my courage and I displayed the spirit of a man who has only a few days to live. I raised my voice and asked who among them was the civil officer, the representative of the law. No one replied. "Very well," I said, "as you do not seem to know let me instruct you. It is you, inspector; you who have been playing the part of an officious lackey to the gendarme, you are the representative of the law. That being so I request you to rid me of this impudent fellow who has been insulting me outrageously for the last half hour. His place is not here. It is at the door, where he should be waiting for your orders, in case I should resist arrest. But you have a certain guarantee of my submission in the fact that you out-number me by twenty to one." I then demanded to be taken before a properly constituted authority on the ground that I did not recognize myself in the warrant. "Have a care, now, about what you do," I said. "This is not an ordinary arrest, but one designed to clear up the point whether I am a state prisoner or not." This little speech, pronounced with vigour and in particu-lar the words "state prisoner" succeeded in upsetting the three men. The gendarme who, a couple of minutes before, was all for sending me without ceremony to the guillotine, gazed at me stupidly as though I was a rare specimen, which he was now looking at for the first time. He seemed to be saying to himself, "So that's what a man looks like who is a state prisoner." The inspector of police protested that he would take no responsibility and the member of the committee, hugging his body with his arms, directed his glance to the ceiling to show his embarrassment. They sent him back to the section from which he returned with these precise instructions: there is nothing to be done except to affix the seals and take away the citizen. "What then," I resumed, "am I not to be heard?" "No, citizen." "But what an atrocious violation of the dictates of reason and humanity! Have they then stuck up at every street corner a declaration of the rights of man just in order to be able to tear it up at their leisure?" "Citizen, it is not that at all." "Well, if so I must be wrong. Affix the seals and take me away. Your profession is to make of men what you will. It's you who are right."

They shut the doors of my apartment and affixed the seals. After the windows had been sealed we were ready to depart. Then the gendarme, who had become prejudiced in my favour since he had learnt that I was a state prisoner and also since I had proposed that he should be relegated to the door, pointed out that I had not made up a parcel of clothes. "Why?" I said. "Do you think they will keep me hanging about for long in the place I am going to?" "Citizen," said he, "your case will last six weeks or two months." "And on what do you base your calculation?" "I heard what you have just been saying. Isn't your case just like that of Custine (a general who had recently been executed)?" "Not precisely," I replied with a smile, "but the outcome might be the same." More fuss. My wardrobe had been sealed. The seals had to be removed. They argued about their right to do this. I lost my patience, went up to a seal and tore it off— "Come now, gentlemen," I said, "the question is settled. Give me some linen and let us be off."

They hastened to comply with my wishes. Encouraged by this initial success I asked if I might take some books with me. They agreed but said they must know what books. "I shall take, if you do not regard them as suspect, Epictetus, Marcus Aurelius and Thomas à Kempis." These authors were admitted readily enough, being comparatively unknown, but when I put my hand on a volume of Tasso, I was clumsy enough to mention the title of the work rather than the name of the author. "Will you allow me," I said, "to add *Jerusalem Delivered*?" "I am afraid that is impossible," said the inspector. I could not guess what connection Tasso could have with the party in power in Year II of the Republic, so I insisted. The gendarme then approached me, laid his hand on my shoulder to show his friendly interest and said in a low voice, "Citizen, believe me you will do well to leave that book behind. At this moment everything coming from Jerusalem has a bad smell." "You are right," I said to the oaf, "let us be going."

We got into a hackney cab which my intelligent gendarme had taken the precaution to summon. We were surrounded by pikemen, who crowded into the cab and on to the box. This degraded competition enraged me. I expressed my indignation loudly and succeeded in getting them to reduce my escort to five persons thereby creating a good number of malcontents.

I reached my destination about noon. The steps of the Palace were crowded with women looking like the spectators in an amphitheatre awaiting a popular performance. And, indeed, the car of death was at the door waiting for two unfortunate victims destined to be thrown to the beasts on that day. When I got out of my carriage all the occupants of the amphitheatre rose to their feet and uttered a long cry of joy. The clapping of hands, the stamping of feet and bursts of convulsive laughter expressed the savage pleasure of these cannibals at the arrival of a new victim. The short distance I had to traverse on foot was long enough for me to receive on the face filthy tributes which rained on me from all sides and I was able to judge by my reception on entering the prison, how I would be greeted when I left it.

The prison door was, for the moment, a haven of refuge and I was glad to see it open. There I was, then, swallowed up in that huge antechamber of death still called la Conciergerie. I crossed a kind of lobby and came into a room on the left which was used as the registry. The room was cut in two by a kind of openwork partition. The registrar's armchair, his office and the registers occupied the part looking out on the courtyards of the palace. That is where newcomers were received and registered. The other part was reserved for the use of condemned prisoners during the endless delay between sentence and execution. A new arrival could see them and speak to them, if he had the courage and the thin partition which separated them might seem to him a presage of the short distance that separated them from the scaffold.

On the day I arrived two men were already awaiting the executioner. They had been stripped of their coats and their hair had been cut and their necks prepared. Their expression was not altered. Either by accident or design they were holding their hands in a position of readiness to be bound and they were assuming proud and disdainful attitudes. They aimed glances of contempt at all who approached them and I judged from the few words they let fall from time to time that they were not unworthy of the fate that was to befall them. A sort of municipal officer had the insolence to try to console them and to ask them if they knew the name of the President of the court which had tried them. "No," said one of the condemned men, "but do not tell me. I do not wish to carry with me to the tomb the name of such a scoundrel." On which the second man said in a gentler tone, "I hope this President is not a Frenchman." Unhappy man, so you still loved your country. Ah! I salute your shade for this heroic love and this noble hope. You were right. These monsters to whom nature gives birth in a moment of aberration belong to no country. The man who delivered you to death was born and died in our midst, but France, torn by his impious hands would scorn to number him among her children. The room in which these unfortunates awaited their last hour presented a truly moving spectacle. Mattresses spread out on the floor showed that they had already passed the night there, a long night of torment. One could see the remains of their last meal. Their clothes had been thrown hither and thither and two candles which they had forgotten to blow out resisted the daylight but only added a funereal light to the scene. I was examining the horrors of this living tomb, when the door opened noisily and I saw gendarmes, turnkeys and executioners appearing. I saw no more, as I had a sudden seizure and it seemed as though all my blood were congealing in my heart. I sank down on a bench in the registry haunted by the machinery of death.

The departure of these two unfortunates had occupied the registrar and soon there were four of us newcomers waiting to be taken to our destinations. I remained on my bench, sunk in gloomy dreams. It was only when a certain time had passed and I had been jostled more than once that I noticed among the new arrivals an elegant gentleman, whose manners had lost nothing of their pristine impertinence. His clothes, his coiffure and his shoes bore witness to his respect for the most absurd extravagances of the fashion. There was very little room to move about in, but he did so freely, treading on his neighbours' toes and apologizing profusely when he had done so. Then he started again and all the time he was humming an Italian air. Even in the foyer of the Opéra he would have attracted attention as a perfect specimen of an idiot. His name was very like mine but that was all we had in common. He had been arrested for forging assignats and I as a measure of public security. The registrar, a man who made no mistakes, on this occasion got things wrong, perhaps for the first time in his life. He exchanged our warrants giving mine to this light-hearted, elegant fellow and his to me. One must be fair. Perhaps my sombre and miserable appearance helped to confuse him. We were put in the charge of turnkeys, who led the dandy to the cell which I was meant to occupy in that part of the prison which is called the Infirmary, while I went to take his place in a cell which was still, I believe, under the patronage of St. Charles. . . .

. . . . Immediately after the trial, or should I rather call it the scandalous scene, which preceded the death of the Girondin deputies, Bailly made his appearance on the same stage. He displayed the calm worthy of one of the first men of his century. No reproaches, no complaints fell from his lips during the six days of his trial before this mockery of a tribunal. He gave his answers up to the last with presence of mind, precision and dignity, though the questions put to him would make the least concerned of men boil with rage on reading them. They would have possessed some point had they been addressed to Mandrin, Collot-d'Herbois or any other of these brigand-chiefs. But who can refrain from indignation at the thought that this tissue of atrocious lies was prepared for one of the first philosophers of the age, one of the warmest-hearted humanitarians and one of the most distinguished scientists who have done honour to France? No doubt special orders had been given to force him to drain drop by drop the bitter draught that had been brewed for him, for inside the prison, in the cells to which he formerly brought consolation and relief and where he used to appear in all the glory of his spotless reputation, he was now treated with a refinement of barbarity. The process of dragging him to the court provided the turnkeys with a quarter of an hour's recreation. They would call him with an indecent affectation of geniality and when he hastened to obey in order to put an end to these repeated cries, the turnkeys would push him back and throw him from one to the other shouting, "Hallo! here's Bailly! Over

to you, Bailly! Catch Bailly, now", and bursting into fits of
laughter at his sober mien in the midst of this dance of cannibals.
Yes, I have seen this Bailly, saintly and glorious, who for his age
alone deserved respect, fouled by the hands of warders paid to
be brutal, staggering as he was pushed by one and roughly picked
up by another, and become the plaything of these demons, as a
drunken man becomes the butt of a crowd that has gathered
round him. The sight of such things saddened me more than if
I had witnessed his death, however cruel, for there is something
grand and holy in the death of a just man in the midst of torments.
One feels that the executioners are frustrated. They can only
consign him to immortality, and if one's heart is torn with pity
one's spirit is consoled.

.... Our common misfortune had brought me in contact with
Mme Roland, the Egeria of the Girondins. Her arrival at the
Conciergerie was an event and I was anxious to make the acquaintance of this woman, unknown fifteen months before, who
had in so short a space made numerous friends, more numerous
enemies, and acquired a high position and great celebrity, leading
only to chains and death. Mme Roland was aged between thirty-
five and forty. Her face did not possess the regularity of beauty,
but was very attractive to look at, with her lovely fair hair and
large blue eyes. She had a graceful figure and perfectly formed
hands. Her look was expressive and even in repose her face had a
noble and winning quality. One suspected that she was witty
even before she began to speak, but no woman ever spoke with
more purity, grace and elegance. It was to her familiarity with
Italian that she owed her talent for lending a genuinely new
rhythm and cadence to the French language. To a musical voice
she added gestures full of nobility and truth and a glance that
acquired animation as she spoke. Every day I experienced a fresh
delight in listening to her, less, perhaps, for what she said than
for the magical way in which she said it. To these rare gifts she
united a fund of natural wit and a wide knowledge of literature
and political economy. Such was my impression of Mme Roland
against whom I was prejudiced before I knew her.

.... Detached from the Revolution, Mme Roland was a different person. No one fulfilled better than she the ideal of a wife and

a mother or was able to show more eloquently that it is only in the accomplishment of her sacred duties that a woman can achieve happiness. Domestic joys, as depicted by her, took on a ravishing, tender aspect. The tears came to her eyes when she spoke of her daughter and her husband. The party politician disappeared and in her place one found a sensitive, gentle woman who commended virtue in the style of Fénelon. I did not know Mme Roland well enough to be sure that in practice she lived up to her sublime theories. Speaking of the union of virtuous hearts and the force that it engenders she said to me once: "The coldness of the French astonishes me. If I were free and it was my husband they were leading to execution, I would stab myself to death on the steps of the scaffold, and I am persuaded that when Roland learns of my death, he will drive a dagger through his heart." She did not deceive herself.

I must add, in further praise of her, that she had created for herself an honourable realm in the cells below. The authorities flung without distinction on the same straw and behind the same bolts the Duchesse de Grammont and a stealer of handkerchiefs, Mme Roland and some wretched streetwalker, a nun and a denizen of the Salpétrière. This lack of discrimination was a cruel infliction for the women of good class in that it exposed them to the daily spectacle of disgusting and horrible scenes. Every night we were awakened by the screams of women trying to tear each other to pieces. The room occupied by Mme Roland had become a haven of refuge in the midst of this hell. When she came down to the courtyard, her presence was enough to restore order and the women, whom no known power was able to master, refrained from misconduct for fear of displeasing her. To the poorest prisoners she gave money, and to all advice, consolation and hope. As she moved about, these women clustered round her as though she were their tutelary goddess—very different from that dirty courtesan, the du Barry, who brought shame on Louis XV and his century, and who was then confined in the same prison. The common women treated her with ruthless equality, though she still preserved the wanton air and proud bearing of an august whore.

On the day on which Mme Roland was to appear before the

court, Clavières, the ex-minister, gave me a message for her.
I did not wish to deliver it, but Clavières insisted and added that
an interview between him and her might be harmful to both of
them. So I agreed, and waited for the moment, when she would
come out of her room, to join her in the corridor. She waited
at the barrier for her name to be called. She had dressed herself
with care and was wearing an English style costume of white
muslin trimmed with net and gathered up with a black velvet
sash. She had done her hair carefully and wore a simple but
elegant bonnet, from beneath which her beautiful hair flowed on
to her shoulders. Her face seemed more animated than usual, her
complexion was brilliant and her lips wore a smile. With one hand
she was attending to the train of her skirt, while she made over
the other to a crowd of women who clustered round her to kiss it.
Those who realized that she was going to her death sobbed and
commended her to Providence. It would be impossible to do
justice to the scene. One had to be there. Mme Roland addressed
each one with affectionate kindness. She did not promise to come
back, nor did she tell them she was going to her death, but her
last words took the form of touching appeals to them. She urged
them to be at peace with one another, to be brave, not to abandon
hope and to practise the virtues which accord with misfortune.
An old jailer named Fontenay, whose kind heart had survived
thirty years of his cruel profession wept as he opened the grill to
her. As she went through I gave her Clavières' message. She replied briefly and in a firm voice. She was beginning to say more
when two turnkeys called her to go to the court. At this cry,
terrible for anyone but her, she stopped, shook my hand and said,
"Adieu, Monsieur, let us be friends. It is time." As she raised her
eyes to look at me, she saw that I was trying to check my tears
and that I was deeply moved. She seemed to feel for me but only
added these two words: "Be brave."

Our favourite walk, and indeed our only one, was along the
corridor. We went down there as soon as they let us out of our
cells. The women joined us somewhat later, as the claims of
dress were overriding. In the morning they appeared in attractive
négligé the materials of which were matched with such freshness
and grace that to judge from the general effect it was impossible

to believe that the wearer had passed the night on a pallet or more probably on a heap of filthy straw. As a general rule the women of the world, who were brought to the Conciergerie, kept alive to the last the sacred fires of good form and good taste. After appearing in the morning in négligé, they went up to their rooms and at noon one saw them coming down again tastefully arrayed and with their hair elegantly dressed. Their demeanour, too, had changed. Their movements were marked by greater emphasis and a kind of dignity. In the evening they appeared in undress. I noticed that almost all the women who could do so stuck to the rule of three costumes per day. The others made up for their lack of elegance by a cleanliness facilitated by local conditions, for the women's courtyard possessed a treasure in the shape of a fountain which gave them as much water as they needed. Every morning I used to gaze at these unhappy creatures, who had brought with them no change of linen, busily engaged round the fountain in washing, laundering and drying their solitary garment in noisy rivalry. The first hour of the day was dedicated to these duties from which nothing not even the arrival of a warrant, would have deterred them.

I am convinced that at this time none of the promenades of Paris could present gatherings of women so elegantly got up as did the courtyard of the Conciergerie at noon; which resembled a flower-bed framed in iron walls. France is probably the only country, and Frenchwomen the only women in the world, capable of offering such singular contrasts and of displaying, without any feeling of strain, the most attractive, voluptuous examples of feminine charm in the most repulsive and horrifying setting the universe can provide. I preferred to look at the women at noon and to talk to them in the morning. In the evening I did not abstain from more intimate conversations, when I ran no risk of disturbing anyone's happiness. It was then that everything conspired to help—the lengthening shadows, the exhaustion of the warders, the withdrawal to their cells of most of the prisoners and the discretion of the others, and in this moment of peace before night came down one often had occasion to bless the want of foresight of the artist who designed the grille. And to think that the men and women who found themselves able to indulge

themselves thus had their death warrants in their pockets! A
woman, aged about forty but still fresh, with fine features and an
elegant figure, was condemned to death during the first ten days
of Frimaire together with her lover, an officer in the army of the
North, a young man who seemed to combine a fine mind with
a charming face. They came down from the court at six o'clock
in the evening. They were separated for the night, but the woman
brought into play those weapons of seduction she possessed and
obtained permission to rejoin her lover. They gave up this last
night of their lives to love and drained once more the cup of
pleasure, only leaving each other's arms to mount the fatal cart.

. . . . I do not know what spirit it was that strengthened and
raised the hearts of all and inspired them with energy, but I do
know that I only saw one man show signs of cowardice and that
was M. du Châtelet, a former colonel in the French Guards.
He came from the Madelonnettes in a pitiable state of drunkenness. They threw him down on a pallet where he passed the
night. By the next day, he had recovered his senses but was none
the better for that. He went about confiding his grievances, woes
and regrets to all and sundry and seemed astonished to find that
no one was in sympathy with him. He went to the women's
partition and there, too, wept and snivelled. A girl of the streets,
but what a girl! looked at him as if he were a new and curious
specimen and asked who he was. When she was told, she went
up to him and said, "You should be ashamed of your tears. Let
me tell you, Monsieur le Duc, that those without a name acquire
one here, and that those who have one should know how to live
up to it." One would guess that the person giving this candid
piece of advice was an aristocrat, and in a sense nothing could be
truer. And if one asks where to look for the spirit of aristocracy,
the answer is in a poor street-girl who played her part to the end
with a kind of heroism which none of the shining lights of the
salons of Coblentz could have rivalled.

Her name was Eglé and she was between seventeen and twenty
years old. For two years she had been living in Rue Fromenteau,
whither she had come from a garret in the Faubourg Saint-
Antoine. This poor girl was, like so many others, the victim of our
debased morality and had become a very lively exponent of it.

She preserved a fine spirit in a body tarnished with countless stains. Eglé hated the new order of things and did not conceal her feelings. She voiced her opinions in the streets and supported them with subversive talk and seditious slogans. The police had arrested her and brought her to the Conciergerie with one of her companions whom she had inoculated with her aristocratic poison and a desire to propagate it. Chaumette had planned to bring these two poor girls before the court at the same time as the Queen and to send them all to their death on the same cart. Nothing could have been more in tune with his famous indictment and it must be admitted that this criminal, who had become Procureur of the Commune of Paris, observed a certain consistency. However, the government committees, finding the suggestion in bad taste, decided that Marie-Antoinette should go to the scaffold alone and reserved Eglé for a more suitable occasion.

Three months had passed since the death of the Queen and it is probable that Eglé and her companion might have been forgotten, if the former had behaved with ordinary restraint. However, she would have found it shameful to dissimulate or even to restrain the expression of her thoughts and she gave utterance to them in a manner so violently seditious in the middle of the Conciergerie that Fouquier determined to make an end of her.

The court did not take the trouble to draw up a new indictment against these two girls. They hunted up the one that had been prepared at the time of Chaumette's plan and it was served on them in its original form, so that Eglé and her companion found themselves accused in so many words of complicity with the widow Capet in a conspiracy against the freedom and sovereignty of the people. I read the charge and can vouch for it.

Eglé was proud of her charge sheet but indignant at the grounds on which it was based. She could not conceive that anyone could tell such stupid lies and, while talking to me, indulged in coarse sarcasms at the expense of the court which in her mouth had a ring of truth. I interrupted her in the middle of one of her tirades and said: "After all, my dear Eglé, if they had taken you to the scaffold with the Queen, there would have been no difference between her and you. You would have appeared as her equal." "You think so?" she replied, "but I should have known how to get the better of these devils." "How would you have done that?" "How? Why, as we were driving along, I should have thrown myself at her feet and neither the executioner nor the devil would have got me to move." One must not blame the unhappy girl for this extravagance. She was born in the midst of ignorance and poverty. The distractions of her deplorable profession did not leave her time to think or to reason. It is therefore not astonishing that she had never raised herself to the level of thinking of kings as nowise superior to the common run of mortals. And in any case it is hard to think of Rue Fromenteau as a suitable school of republican morals and thought.

Eglé admitted to the court that she had used the words and slogans in favour of the royalists which were attributed to her, but when they came to the charge of being the Queen's accomplice, she said: "Congratulations on your common sense! You suggest that I was the accomplice of her whom you call the widow Capet, and who was indeed the Queen for all you may say. I, a poor girl, who earned her living at the street corners and who would not have dared to approach one of the Queen's scullions! There's an accusation worthy of a pack of wasters and imbeciles like you." In spite this sally, Eglé obtained the clemency of the court. One of the jury observed that the accused was probably drunk, seeing that she had now lost her self-control, and some of the other jurymen, who had known the accused before, were of the same way of thinking. Eglé resisted with the same assurance her protectors and the arguments they used. She urged that if any member of the honourable company was drunk it was not she and in order to prove that she had used intentionally and in cold blood the words imputed to her, she thought it her duty to reproduce them textually and the court had to take serious steps to reduce her to silence. Finally they forced her to sit down and the court proceeded to deal with her companion. This girl found the jury equally disposed in her favour, no doubt because they had known her too. Being less determined than Eglé, she hesitated and admitted the charge of drunkenness, which was to save her life. Eglé indignantly broke her silence and called out to her companion that her weakness was a crime and that she was dishonouring herself. She tried to restore her courage and make her tell the truth. The girl, more confused and frightened by Eglé than by her judges, recanted and declared that she too had committed in cold blood the offence ascribed to her. The tribunal justly discriminated between the two accused and sent Eglé to the scaffold as an incorrigible aristocrat while condemning her companion to twenty years reclusion in the Salpétrière. When the sentence was read out Eglé listened with a smile to the clauses which declared her guilty of the crime of counter-revolution and condemned her to death. When they came to the confiscation of her property she said to the President, "Ah, you thief, I wish you joy of my property. I warrant it will not be enough to give you indigestion." When she came down from the court she blamed her companion for her conduct, but was not dissatisfied with herself. She only feared she might have to go and sleep with the devil—I quote her own words. The prisoners' guardian angel, good M. Emery, reassured her and she leapt on to the cart with the lightness of a bird.

. . . . The hour had come for locking the cells. We—Lamourette, Clavières and I and the two priests—were shut up in ours and the conversation turned as usual on the miseries of our existence. Lamourette interpolated some reflections on the brevity of life to which the fury of our persecutors was adding little in length. Then we each went to bed and to sleep—for we slept even there. The first nights one passes in a prison cell are sleepless, unless one is endowed with great force of character, but nature soon reasserts her inalienable rights. For my part I have noticed that since the day when I was put in prison, I have dreamt about places in which I was completely free. Probably when I come out, if I do come out, I shall dream of prisons and cells. An hour after we had gone to sleep, I was awakened by Lamourette crying out: "Clavières! Ah, poor fellow, what have you done!" Then I distinctly heard two sounds equally horrible—the death-rattle of a dying man and the dripping of his blood from the bed on to the flags. I jumped out of bed and Lamourette and the others also. But what could we do! It was useless to call for help from outside, we could not get any light, beyond what was thrown on the scene by a street lamp in one of the passages of the Palais de Justice opposite our window. Its feeble rays sufficed to indicate the tragedy, but not to reveal the details. The two priests threw themselves on their knees and asked us to join them in praying to God for the soul of the unfortunate man, whose passing we witnessed. After half an hour we could hear nothing but the sound of drops of blood falling on to the floor. We returned to our beds, but as we had been walking in the blood with which the stone floor was covered, we smeared our beds with it and next morning when they opened up our dismal retreat, the room looked like a slaughter house. . . .

. . . . I had great difficulty in persuading myself that my wife would ever be able to rescue me from the doom which befell my comrades, one after the other. I was called once more to the door and henceforth I shall no longer go down with lagging steps but with the glad hope of seeing my guardian angel. I looked round for my wife, but could only see several working women who were acting as messengers. These women were authorized by the head-jailer to do errands for the prisoners, to bring them food and render them small domestic services, which they all carried out in precise and loyal fashion. A few young ladies who were anxious to see the prisoners and could not obtain permission to do so, conceived the idea of dressing themselves in the clothes of these errand-women and coming to the prison with their baskets in disguise. The original errand-woman was rewarded with a money order for 10 francs and the door-keeper was given the same amount for agreeing to be deceived. Moreover, the lady in disguise was obliged to empty and fill the basket just like the woman she replaced. My wife had put on this contraband costume and at first I did not recognize her in it. I was merely astonished to be greeted so familiarly by a servant. "On this occasion," she said, "I hope you won't complain of my smartness. How do you like me?" At the sound of her voice, I recognized my mistake: I looked at her and my answer was to burst into an uncontrollable fit of laughter to which she replied no less merrily.

After we had had a good talk she said: "I'm not only here for you. I am also taking the place of the errand-woman of a certain M. Ducourneau. I have to give him his clean linen and take away the dirty. I have letters, tobacco and books for him. I don't know him at all, but the errand-woman told me, that if I sent for him he would come down at once." Ducourneau came down. He was a Bordelais, belonging to the party of the Girondins, a young man full of wit, with a wonderful knack of writing verse. The "errand-woman" accosted him with some embarrassment. "I am," said she, "the woman who usually does your commissions." "Don't go on to anyone else," said Ducourneau in lively tones. "This gentleman has explained everything. He says you are a brave and a charming woman and something of an aristocrat. That's how I like women to be and I am at your feet. Do not let us bother about these household details and let us talk about something more interesting. I congratulate citizen Beugnot on having the good fortune to know you." "There is some reason for that," I broke in: "Today's errand-woman is my wife." Afterwards, thanks to this masquerade and Ducourneau's wit, we engaged in a conversation so gay, that I warrant that nowhere in Paris at the same hour, was lighter-hearted laughter to be heard. When he returned to his room, Ducourneau composed for my wife a charming set of verses entitled "*La Messagère Révolutionnaire*". They did not give this lovable child of the Garonne time enough to climb the foothills of our Parnassus. A week later he had swelled the number of men who had died with laughter on his lips.

✤

The last letter of the condemned prisoner, Camille Desmoulins.

From the prison of the Luxembourg—the second day of the first decade of the month Germinal at five o'clock in the morning.
Kindly sleep gave respite to my sorrows. One is free while one sleeps and one does not feel one's captivity. Heaven had pity on me. I saw you in a dream and I embraced you all in turn—you, Horace, and Durousse who was in the house. But our little boy had lost an eye by reason of an evil humour which had attacked him, and the pain he suffered woke me up. I found myself in my cell. It was beginning to be light but, when I opened the windows, the thought of my loneliness and the dreadful bars and bolts which separate me from you, got the better of my fortitude. I

dissolved into tears, or rather I sobbed and cried from my tomb:
"Lucile, Lucile, dear Lucile, where are you?" (Here one **can** see
the trace of a tear.) Yesterday evening I had a similar experience
and my heart was split with pain when I perceived your mother
in the garden. Unthinkingly I fell on my knees before the bars.
I clasped my hands to implore the pity of her who, I doubt not,
weeps on your breast. Yesterday I recognized her grief (here is
another trace of a tear) by her handkerchief and by the way she
lowered her veil. When you come, make her sit nearer with you
so that I can see you both better. There is no danger in that, I
should think. My glasses are not very good. I want you to buy
me some like the pair I had six months ago with steel frames, not
silver, and with two stalks attaching them to one's head. Ask for
number 15. The salesman knows what that means. But before
everything else, I adjure you by my undying love, send me your
portrait. Let your painter have some pity for me who am only
suffering for the pity I have given to others. Let him give you
two sittings a day. I have discovered a crack in the wall of my
room. I put my ear to it and heard someone groaning. I risked
a few words and then I heard the voice of a sick man in pain.
He asked me my name. I told it to him and he cried out, "Oh,
my God" when he heard it and fell back on his bed from which
he had raised himself. I distinctly recognized the voice of Fabre
d'Eglantine. "Yes, I am Fabre," he said, "but what are you doing
here? Has the counter-revolution come?" We did not dare to go
on talking for fear that the hatred of our keepers might envy us
this slender consolation and that if anyone heard us we should be
separated and more closely confined. At present he has a room
with a fire and mine would be tolerable if a cell could ever be.
    . . . . They are calling for me. Just now the Commissioners of
the Revolutionary Tribunal have been questioning me. All they
asked me was: "Had I ever conspired against the republic?"
What a mockery! Is it possible that the purest republicanism can
be so insulted? I foresee the fate that awaits me. Adieu, my
Lucile, my darling Lolotte, my own wolf: say adieu to my father.
    . . . . I was born to write verses, to defend the unfortunate, to
make you happy, to create with your mother and my father and
a few persons of our way of thinking a new Tahiti. I had dreamt

of a republic which everyone would have adored. I could never believe that men were so cruel and so unjust.

I see the shores of life retreating before me. I still see Lucile. My arms embrace you still and I hold you with my fettered hands, while my severed head rests on your lap. I am going to die.

Note. This letter was not sent from the Luxembourg. Camille, after being transferred to the Conciergerie handed it to citizen Grossé Beauregard, one of his fellow prisoners, whom he had met in the house of Paré, the Minister of the Interior. As Camille's wife had already been immolated, the letter was delivered to citizen Paré, who remained in possession of it.

✤

The Death Cart

The Abbé Carrichon has promised to give absolution to certain noble ladies, if they are sent to the scaffold. He keeps his promise.

Mme la Maréchale de Noailles with the Duchesse d'Ayen and her daughter, the Vicomtesse de Noailles, were detained in their town-house from September 1793 until April 1794. I knew the first of these ladies by sight only, but the other two more intimately as I generally saw them once a week. The terror and crime increased simultaneously and its victims became more numerous.

One day when we were talking of these things and they were exhorting one another to prepare for death, I had a kind of presentiment and said: "If you go to the guillotine and God gives me strength, I will accompany you." Taking me at my word they replied in lively tones: "Will you promise us to do that?" I hesitated for a moment before saying: "Yes, and so that you may recognize me easily I shall be wearing a dark blue coat and a red waistcoat." After that they often reminded me of my promise.

. . . . On the twenty-second of July which was a Tuesday and the feast of Saint Mary Magdalen I was at home. It was about eleven o'clock and I was going out when I heard a knocking at the door. I opened and found the Noailles children and their tutor. The children were as gay as usual, though I know they felt the continued detention of their parents. They were going for a walk to take the country air. The tutor was pale, pensive and sad, his features convulsed by emotion and I was struck by the contrast between him and the children. "Let us go into your bedroom," he said, "and leave the children in your study." We did so and left the children playing. We went into my room and he threw himself into an armchair. "It's all up, my friend," he said, "the ladies have been summoned to the court. I have come to ask you to keep your word. I shall now go to Vincennes with the children to see little Euphémie. As we walk through the wood I shall prepare the children for their terrible loss of which at present they know nothing."

Though I had long been prepared for such an outcome, I felt disconcerted. The whole of this dreadful situation comprising the mothers, their children, their worthy tutor and Euphémie, the little four-year-old—it all seemed graven on my imagination in letters of fire. . . . I soon recovered myself and after a few questions and answers I said, "Go now. I must change my clothes. What a duty I have to perform! Pray to God to give me strength to go through with it." We got up and went into my study where we found the children amusing themselves, as cheerful and contented as possible. The contrast between their happy aspect and what they were going to learn and what we felt already wrung my heart. But I bade them a cheerful farewell. Left to myself I felt terrified. Have pity on them, O God, and on me, too! I changed my clothes and went out to do some business with a heavy weight on my heart. I interrupted my business to look in at the Palais between one and two. I tried to get in but it was impossible. I got some information from someone who was coming out, as though I still doubted the truth of the public announcement. The illusion of hope is the most tenacious of all, but from what I was told I could no longer doubt. I continued my rounds which took me to the Faubourg Saint-Antoine. You can judge of my thoughts, of the storm that raged within me, of my secret fears—all aggravated by a splitting headache! As I had business with a person I could trust I gave her my confidence. She encouraged me to fulfil my promise in the name of God. To dispel my headache I begged her to make

me some coffee, which did me good. I returned to the Palais very
slowly, thoughtfully and irresolutely, as though I did not want to
get there or to see those who had called me to their aid. I arrived
there before five. There was no news of the departure of a condemned convoy. I climbed very slowly up the steps of the
Sainte Chapelle and then walked in the Great Hall and round
about it. I kept sitting down and getting up again. I spoke to no
one. I concealed my agitation and grief under a mask of gravity.
From time to time I glanced into the courtyard to see if the
departure had been announced. Then I came back to my seat.
All the time I was saying myself "in two hours, or an hour and a
half, they will be no more". Never has an hour seemed longer to
me than that which dragged from five to six. My mind was full
of thoughts, which crossed and clashed, and eliminated one
another and caused me to swing from the illusions of an empty
hope to the realities of a too well-grounded fear. At last the sound
of movements below persuaded me that the victims were on the
point of leaving the prison. I went down and posted myself near
the little iron gate by which they came out, as it has not been
possible for the last fortnight to go into the courtyard.

The first cart filled up and advanced towards me. It contained
eight very worthy ladies, seven of whom were unknown to me,
while the eighth was la Maréchale de Noailles. The absence of her
daughter-in-law and her granddaughter provided a last feeble
ray of hope. But alas! the mother and daughter were riding in the
second cart. The latter was dressed in white, which she had worn
continuously since the death of her parents-in-law (Maréchal and
Maréchale de Mouchy).

She did not look older than twenty-four at the most. Her
mother, who looked about forty, wore a blue and white striped
négligé. Six men were attached to them, the first two of whom
stood a little farther from them than was usual as if to allow them
more liberty, and maintained a considerate and respectful
attitude for which I felt grateful.

They had no sooner got on to the cart, when the daughter
began to show towards her mother that lively, tender interest
which was characteristic of her. I heard someone say near me:
"look at that young woman, how she's fussing about her mother

and how she's talking. She does not look sad. . . ." I noticed her looking round for me and I seemed to hear everything they were saying. "He's not there."—"look again, Mama, I assure you he's not there." They had forgotten that I had told them that it would be impossible for me to be there. The first cart stopped by me for at least a quarter of an hour. Then it started again. The second was coming up to me and I prepared myself. It passed, but the ladies did not see me. I went back to the Palais, made a great détour and posted myself at the entrance to the Pont au Change in a conspicuous position. The Noailles ladies looked round in every direction. They passed without seeing me. I followed them along the bridge, separated from them by the crowd, but not very far off. Madame de Noailles kept looking for me and failing to find me. Her mother was beginning to look very anxious and the daughter redoubled her efforts to pick me out in the crowd. I was tempted to give up. I had done all I could. Everywhere else the crowd would be even denser. There was no way of attracting their attention. I was worn out and decided to go away.

It suddenly clouded over. Thunder grumbled in the distance . . . I changed my mind and resolved to try again. Following back streets I reached Rue Saint-Antoine, almost opposite the notorious prison of La Force, before the carts. Then a violent wind began to blow and the storm burst. Flashes of lightning and claps of thunder followed swiftly on one another. It began to rain in torrents. I retired to the entrance of a shop, which is always present in my mind's eye and which I shall never see without emotion. In a moment the street was swept clear. The only people to be seen were crowded into doorways, shops and windows. The procession had lost its discipline. The cavalrymen and the foot-soldiers were marching faster, as best they could, and the carts likewise. They had reached little Saint-Antoine, and I was still irresolute.

The first cart passed by in front of me. With a hurried and almost involuntary movement I left the shop in which I was sheltering and found myself quite close to the ladies. Young Mme Noailles caught sight of me and with a smile seemed to say: "Ah! here you are at last! What a relief! We have been looking for you everywhere. Mama, here he is!" At that moment Mme d'Ayen came to life again and all my hesitation ceased. I felt myself filled with extraordinary courage. Drenched with sweat and rain I had no more misgivings and continued to march beside them.

On the steps of the Church of Saint Louis I caught sight of a man who had the utmost respect and attachment for them and was seeking to render them the same service as I was. I grasped his hand firmly, with a rush of affection saying: "Good evening, my friend." A few steps distant from where we were there was a square into which several streets led. The storm was at its wildest, and the wind was blowing strongly. The ladies in the first cart were greatly inconvenienced especially the Maréchale de Noailles. Her bonnet turned over on her head, showing her grey hair. She staggered on the wretched floor with no hand-rail, her hands tied behind her back.

At once many of the people collected there recognized her and paid no heed to anyone else. They added to her torment by their insulting cries which she endured patiently. "There she is, look at her! That's the marshal's wife who used to run such a fine show and drive in her grand carriages. Now she has to drive in the cart just like the others." Nothing could be more insulting to a sensitive person than these cannibal cries. The unhappy should be treated as sacred objects, especially when they are innocent. The cries continued and the rain fell, more heavily than ever.

We had just reached the square before you come into the Faubourg Saint-Antoine. I went ahead, took my bearings and said to myself: "This is the best place to grant them what they most desire." The cart had slowed down; I stopped and turned towards it, making a signal to Mme de Noailles, which she understood perfectly. She said, "Mama, M. C. is going to give us absolution." They immediately bowed their heads with an expression of piety, repentance, joy and tenderness, which was balm to me. I raised my hand and with covered head pronounced the complete formula of absolution and the words which follow, very distinctly and with intense concentration. I felt that they were at one with me more than ever. I shall never forget this scene worthy of a Raphael's paint-brush.

From that moment the storm began to abate and the rain to decrease. It seemed to have been sent expressly by Providence to further the success of our plan. I thanked God for it and so did the ladies, whose faces now expressed only contentment, serenity and cheerfulness.

After we had passed the Abbey of Saint-Antony, I noticed near me a young man, a priest, whose sentiments I suspected for various reasons. His presence embarrassed me and I feared he would recognize me. I retreated and then advanced, but luckily he did not recognize me. He moved on rapidly and I did not see him again. At last we reached the fatal spot. What I felt cannot be expressed. The moment was overwhelming. The idea of parting was too poignant. I could still see them full of health and able to do so much for their families, and in a moment they would be gone for ever. The carts halted before the scaffold and I shuddered as I looked. The horsemen and footsoldiers at once surrounded it and behind was a large circle of spectators, most of them laughing and ready to be amused by the tragic spectacle. I was in their midst, but how different my feelings! . . . I saw the chief executioner and his two assistants. He differed from them in looking much younger and resembling in his gait and his costume an unsuccessful dandy. One of the two assistants was remarkable for his size, his rotundity, the rose he had in his mouth, his coolness and the leisurely nature of his movements. His sleeves were turned up and his hair plaited and frizzed and he had strikingly regular features, unmarked, however, by nobility, which could have served as a model to the great painters, for their portraits of executioners in their records of the martyrs.

One must admit that, either owing to a sub-stratum of humanity or by custom and the desire to get it over quickly, the sufferings of the victims were definitely mitigated by the business-like promptitude of the executioners, the care they took to get all the condemned persons down from the cart, before the executions started and to place them with their backs to the scaffold, so that they could see nothing. I felt they deserved some gratitude for this and also for the decorum they observed and their constantly serious expressions, which contained no trace of mockery or insult for the victims.

As the assistants were helping the ladies in the first cart to get down, Mme de Noailles looked round to find me. When at last she had caught sight of me, what messages did not her eyes now raised to heaven, now lowered to the ground contain with their sweet, animated, heavenly expression. Sometimes they were fixed on me so purposefully, that they might have drawn attention to me had the tigers by whom I was surrounded been more observant. I pushed my hat over my eyes without losing sight of her and I heard her say in thought: "My sacrifice is accomplished. I leave my dear ones behind. But God has called me, as I firmly hope. I shall never forget them. Bid them a tender farewell from me, and receive my thanks. Adieu, adieu!"

These expressions of her lively piety, her touching eloquence caused my tigers to say, "Oh, look how happy she is! How she raises her eyes to heaven and prays! But what good does it do her?" Then after a moment's reflection: "Those rascals of priests!"

After the last farewells had been spoken, they came down. I left the place where I was standing and went across to the other side, while they were getting down the other condemned prisoners. I now found myself facing the steps to the scaffold against which, the first for execution, a tall old man with white hair was leaning. He had a kindly air and they said he was a farmer-general. Near him stood a lady of pious aspect whom I did not know: then came la Maréchale exactly opposite me. She was dressed in black and was sitting on a block of wood or stone with wide-open staring eyes. All the others were lined up below the scaffold on the side facing the Faubourg Saint-Antoine on the west. I looked for my two ladies, but could only see the mother standing in a simple, noble, resigned attitude with her eyes closed. She seemed no longer disturbed but looked as she did while receiving the Communion. The impression she made on me is indelible. I often see her with the eyes of memory. I trust, with God's help, to have profited by her example. Now all had come down and the sacrifice was due to begin. The noisy merriment of the spectators and their ghastly jibes add to the sufferings of the victims, insignificant from a physical point of view, but aggravated by the three successive bangs one hears and the sight of so much blood. The executioner and his assistants climb on to the scaffold and

arrange everything. The former puts on over his other clothes
a blood-red overall. He places himself on the left, the west side,
while his assistants stand on the other side, looking towards
Vincennes. The big one is the object of much admiration and
praise on the part of the cannibals, who think he looks so capable
and thoughtful. When everything is ready, the old man goes up
the steps with the help of the executioners. The chief headsman
takes him by the left arm, the big assistant by the right and the
other man by the legs. In a moment they lay him flat on his face
and his head is cut off and thrown with his body into a great
tumbril, where the bodies swim in blood: and so it goes on. What
a horrible shambles! The Maréchale was the third to go up.
They had to make an opening in the top of her dress to uncover
her neck. Mme d'Ayen was the tenth. How glad she seemed at
the thought that she would die before her daughter! And her
daughter, too, looked happy to be following, not preceding her
mother. The chief executioner tore off her bonnet. As this was
fastened by a pin which he had not bothered to notice, her hair
was pulled violently upwards causing her pain which was
reflected on her features. When the mother had gone, the daughter replaced her. The young woman dressed all in white provided
a touching spectacle. She looked much younger than she really
was, as she offered herself like a gentle lamb to the slaughterers.
I felt as though I were witnessing the martyrdom of one of those
holy women depicted in the paintings of Correggio or
Domenichino.

She had the same experience as her mother. The executioner
once more failed to observe the hat-pin and caused her a similar
twinge of pain. Alas for the bright red blood which flowed in
streams from her head and neck! But in my heart I said "now she
is happy", when they threw her body into the gruesome coffin.
I was going away when I was arrested for a moment by the
features and the stature of the man who came after her.

He was a man well above middle height and broad in proportion with an imposing face. I had noticed him standing below the
scaffold. He had moved away, while they were immolating the
others in order to see what was happening. His height had
helped to satisfy his curiosity. He went up the steps unfalteringly

and looked at the executioners, the plank and the instrument of death with an intrepid glance. If anything, he looked too proud. "O God," I said, "grant that he is a Christian and not merely a philosopher."

The man whom they had just executed was Gossin or Gossuin who had done so much to divide France into departments. After his execution, I went right away, beside myself with emotion. I noticed that I felt icy cold. I walked faster, my mind wholly occupied with this heartrending spectacle, which was none the less grand, beautiful, comforting and touching. I said to myself then, as I have many times repeated since, "No, not for a hundred thousand crowns would I have missed this edifying experience."

When I left it was nearly eight o'clock. In twenty minutes they had brought forty or fifty persons to the scaffold and executed twelve.

Soon I reached Rue Saint-Antoine, where I entered the house of a respected family of my acquaintance. "Is it you?" they said. "Where do you come from so late and so far from home?" "Ah!" I said, "I have just witnessed a scene by which only the most soulless of men could fail to be encouraged to work more strenuously for his salvation." And then I told them the whole story in detail. I had supper and left very late. My night was greatly disturbed. My fitful slumbers were haunted by the sights and sounds of the day. I had felt no fatigue at the time, but on the following days I was overcome with exhaustion, with, thank God, no ill effects.

On the following Friday, July 25th, I was dining with friends. There was a knock on the door and a worthy friend of mine, who had twice warned me that he wished to see me, came into the room. "What brings you here?" said I. "I have been looking for you for two hours, then I took a chance and came here." "What for?" "To induce you to render the same service to the aunts of the Noailles children, Mme de Duras and Mme Lafayette, as you did to their mother. They are being taken to the scaffold." "Oh, my dear friend, what are you asking me to do? I hardly know these ladies and I am not sure that they will recognize me." He redoubled his entreaties, I resisted. My friends supported him, till I gave way and started on my sad journey to the Palais. I was just in time. The first carts were leaving—then they stopped to wait for the others. On the first one there were some ladies, none of whom I recognized. I examined them, looked them over carefully, turned away and turned back to look again. No, unless I was quite mistaken, the aunts were not there, God be praised! May the Almighty and All-merciful One, who has deigned to preserve them for their families pour upon them all the blessings for which I pray for my own people. May He unite us all with those who have gone before in a realm where there will be no revolutions to fear or to hope for: in this country which will have as Saint Augustine says truth for its king, charity for its law, and eternity for its measure of time.

⚜

The Executioner demands a rise of pay.

Paris.
August 6th,
1792.

Monsieur,

It is with great respect that I have the honour to submit to you the situation in which I find myself. It is of such a nature that I implore you, Monsieur, to spare me a moment of your attention.

The method of execution practised today costs at least three times as much as the former method, irrespective of the increased cost of living.

The number of criminal courts which I serve compels me to employ various persons capable of carrying out the orders which I receive. As I, personally, cannot be everywhere at once, I must have trustworthy helpers, for the public insists on decency. It is I who pay for them.

In order to get proper people for this task, I have to pay them twice as high wages as they got in previous years. Last Saturday they warned me that if I did not raise their wages by a quarter at least, they could not continue to work for me. Circumstances obliged me to promise this increase.

The abolition of class prejudices I thought would make it easier for me to find assistants but, on the contrary, I see that it has merely caused the disappearance of the persons of a certain class whom I could have employed, by making it easier for them to take service with individuals or to change their way of earning a living.

In order to keep one's employees, it is necessary to attach them to one by the lure of gain.

I have fourteen persons to feed every day of whom eight receive wages. Then I have three horses, three carters and the accessories.

Besides I have to pay a huge rent; though in former times the executioner was always lodged by the crown. I have to meet the unforeseen expenses of executions, of common occurrence, other family expenses like having to look after one's parents and old infirm servants, who have sacrificed their lives to this service and who have a right to decent treatment.

My present submission is that I have now for eight months been giving to the judicial accounts department statements of my expenses, which used formally at all times to be paid to me in accordance with the figures furnished, but which now are not being paid, though I have only asked for the amounts specified in the tarif and even, in some cases, reduced the charges.

On the 11th June last I had the honour to submit to you a petition to which I have had no reply. My means are straitened, indeed I am substantially in debt which prevents me from making such considerable advances and I know of no source from which to procure funds. I cannot go on borrowing money from the persons to whom I am already in debt and I cannot pay them as long as I am not paid.

I can only address myself to you, Monsieur, and beg you to order the payment of the money due to me. If this is not done in spite of all the sacrifices I have made to perform the duties of my office punctually, my life will be inevitably ruined and I shall be forced to abandon my post and my family after forty-two years of faithful service.

As the situation is urgent, I beg you, Monsieur, to cause some person of confidence to enquire into the truth of this my petition.

Your very humble and obedient servant

Sanson—
The executer of criminal
judgments in Paris.

THE SOLDIERS OF YEAR II

*T*HE COUNTRY *is in danger. At all the cross-roads they are recruiting volunteers to go and defend the frontiers.*
The force which the Convention is entrusting to its generals is an army of revolutionaries.
The soldiers elect their own leaders.

Extract from the regulations governing national volunteers.
The administration of battalions.
Art. 2. The officers, non-commissioned officers and volunteer members of the council of administration shall be elected by the entire battalion according to the number of votes by each individual. They shall be elected for one year after which they shall be subject to re-election.

By the same process an officer, a non-commissioned officer of each grade and four volunteers shall be chosen as substitutes for those members of the Council who may be sick or absent.

The national volunteers hardly consider themselves as soldiers.
Here is a contribution from one of them, Thiébault, later to become a General:

On October 1st 1792, when I heard that the Prussians were marching on Paris, I joined as a volunteer grenadier in the first battalion of the Butte des Moulins regiment and left for the front.
I marched for several days with the battalion but marching

wearied me and I lagged behind. I stopped first at Châlons and then at Sainte-Menehould.

On October 11th I procured a passport at Sainte-Menehould and, proceeding by easy stages in a carriage, I rejoined the battalion at Condé on October 25th.

They were bivouacking in Bon-Secours wood. It was clear that my health would not permit me to pursue this career so I returned to Condé and took up my quarters in one of the inns of this town. However, as I continued to spit blood, I left on November 30th for my father's house at Epinal, leaving with one of my comrades a written declaration that I was leaving the service. This document was signed by the battalion chiefs and then presented to General Dampierre who signified his approval. It was then returned to me stamped with the General's approval, which, in fact was of no practical value.

I should mention that service in the battalion of the Butte-des-Moulins was in no sense obligatory. Two hundred young men had already left this battalion before it reached Belgium. Among these were M. Odiot, the goldsmith, who only proceeded as far as Châlons and who was a lieutenant in the Grenadiers. Bertaux, the engraver: Grasset, at present conductor of the orchestra of the Bouffes (Italian Opera) and a captain in the Grenadiers, as well as Messrs. Lafargue, Lecoq, Devismes, de Vigearde and others, who left the battalion soon after I did. Moreover, there had never been any question of fighting except for the express purpose of driving the enemy out of France and for my part I was so anxious to be considered not as a soldier but as volunteer, in the fullest sense of the word, that I consistently refused to receive either pay or rations and provided my own arms and equipment. In addition, when I left Paris, I had reserved for myself the post which I occupied under M. Dufresne de Saint-Léon, when the business was temporarily wound up, and my right to return to it was I believe actually guaranteed by decree.

The above facts go to show that even in the battalion none of us was regarded as a professional soldier.

❧

*When senior officers appear unworthy of their positions, their men
dismiss them, as this note addressed to the Army Commission attests:*

Citizen Moulin, assistant-adjutant to the Officer Commanding
the Troops warns the Commission that the battalion due to go
into camp tomorrow has today dismissed its staff. This circumstance may delay its departure for the camp.

⚜

*There are women in the Army of the Revolution. Here are two
documents proving this, the one taken from the War Archives and the
other from those of the Convention:*

Army of Belgium—1st. battn. of Saint-Denis.
FINAL LEAVE OF ABSENCE

Having been apprised by Félicité Duquet, known as Vade-
boncœur, whose zeal had induced her to take up arms when the
country was in danger and who has since then been serving in
our battalion, that she is of the female sex and that she demands
the privileges due to her as a woman now that the hardships she
has endured in the camps no longer permit her to continue in
the service, and, whereas the law is silent on the subject of female
soldiers, I, therefore, the lieutenant-colonel commanding the first
battalion of Saint-Denis declare that I have taken into consideration the just request of the said Félicité Duquet and now grant
her a final leave of absence and permission to retire to any
locality she may select.

We, therefore, request all civil and military officers to permit
the said Duquet to pass freely and to grant her the assistance and
protection which the law accords to all French subjects and
particularly to the defenders of the country.

At the same time I declare publicly that the said Duquet conducted herself with valour and courage in all the actions in which
the battalion was engaged during the recent campaign.

Tirlemont, February 19th 1793, Year II of the Republic.
Sᵈ Maréchal St. Firmin.

⚜

The National Convention, taking into consideration the petition of citizeness Bourgès, who took part in various actions in the Vendée and who has rendered service to the Republic by succouring wounded soldiers and carrying them on her back to the ambulance waggons, decrees as follows:

The National Treasury will pay to citizeness Bourgès the sum of three hundred francs as financial assistance.

Furthermore the National Convention having heard the report on the petition of citizeness Bourgès, who has already received an indemnity on account of the valuable services rendered by her to our brave brothers-in-arms wounded in action, when she stripped off her own underclothing to provide bandages for their wounds, thus combining courage with humanity and benevolence, decrees that the National Treasury shall make a final payment, by way of relief, of three hundred francs to citizeness Bourgès in view of her important services to volunteers wounded in action against the rebels in la Vendée.

(13th of Pluviose. Year III.)

※

Citizeness Favre who was made a prisoner of war on March 1st 1793 and taken to Tirlemont describes her captivity (speaking of herself in the third person), in a deposition which she made on April 1st 1793 before the Commissioners of the Contrat Social.

She was first relieved of all her possessions including a sum of 860 francs in assignats and 50 francs in cash, as well as her watch, her clothes, and, generally speaking, everything she had, even her cravat, after which she was led away to the dungeons of Tirlemont to be put to death in the same way as the other prisoners, whom the enemy slaughtered by slicing them with their swords, being unwilling to waste gunpowder on them. While she was waiting to be butchered, they tore off her vest and saw that she was a woman. The Captain of Uhlans, who commanded the enemy detachment took her under his protection and had to threaten the others with sword and pistol to save her life. Afterwards she was sent to the enemy army headquarters at Tongres, where she was put in prison. . . .

☙

Citizeness Favre took advantage of her appearance before the Convention to call the High Command to account.

They leave our brave defenders without arms, without clothes and without boots. The gunners of the company are so badly equipped that they have not got a single pistol between them and most of them have no swords. Many of the soldiers have no muskets, and those which the others have are in very bad order, often lacking triggers or locks, although very good ones have been given to enemy soldiers who have infiltrated into our armies. There are whole battalions without breeches, the men being dressed only in capes so ragged that they are held together by pins. Why, the 7th battalion of the Paris army went on parade in this absolutely denuded state under the eyes of citizens Danton and Lacroix, who could not refrain from saying, "Oh! this lot are really and truly sans-culottes." When this battalion asked Dumouriez for arms, he merely replied, with an impatient gesture: "Ah, very well. We shall look into that." In conclusion most of the gunners have only their fists to defend their pieces with.

☙

The soldiers do not hesitate to report directly to the Minister of War on the progress of operations, nor do they refrain from saying hard things about their generals. Here is a letter from a grenadier elected to command his battalion.

Citizen Minister, Let me take advantage of a moment of leisure to send you an account of the unfortunate battalion which I command.

The third Paris battalion, with which you are acquainted, was in the forefront of the fighting since the campaign started. It was for a long time under your orders. It was present at the battle of Jemappes and unquestionably had a substantial share in this celebrated victory. This battalion, made up of true republicans has just been destroyed in defending the freedom of our country.

I draw your attention, Citizen Minister, to the fact that owing to sickness, desertion and leaves of absence its effectives were reduced to three hundred fighting men.

General Stengel had quartered us in a village called Brakal, some seven leagues distant from Aix-la-Chapelle. The battalion was obliged to split up into two parts in order to guard another place called Hirfak and to keep under observation a region more than four miles long on the farther bank of the Ruhr. The enemy were on the other side of the river and almost daily we exchanged shots with them. Our position was unquestionably well guarded. For some time past we had suffered so severely from the hardships of war which involved constant bivouacking in the open, that I had been obliged to ask General Stengel to send us to quarters, where we could rest and rehabilitate. My solicitations were in vain, and the general went so far as to insult me by asking if I was afraid. Incensed at this reply I answered that we should soon disprove the aspersion and, since he ordered it, remain at our posts, if it cost us our lives.

. . . . I heard the sound of musketry and at the same time perceived a body of cavalry advancing towards us, which everyone took for French cavalry. The battalion was marching in column with a piece of artillery at each corner. Leaving the battalion on my right at a distance of some three hundred yards, I approached the advancing horsemen. When I was within a hundred yards of them, I saw they were the enemy, and I also perceived another large column debouching behind the first one. I signalled to the battalion to move to the right, where they could take cover in an adjacent village. Meantime I anticipated the arrival of reinforcements, but in vain. We were abandoned. The Commandant of the first enemy column sent me a trumpeter summoning me to surrender. I paid no attention. Then the Commandant rode up to within twenty paces of me and said: "Commandant, will you surrender?" "To whom?" I said. "To the Austrians." My reply was to gallop at full speed towards the battalion, shouting to the gunners to have at them with grape-shot. They had only time to fire three rounds and the infantry to fire a volley, which must have caused heavy losses at that very short range. But in a moment we were surrounded on all sides and what could 250 footsoldiers do against two large columns of horse, especially in the middle of a plain? None of my men would surrender. In a moment I saw the enemy seize our colours and begin to cut down my brave comrades. I remained at my post till the end.

And then, Citizen Minister, in this terrible situation, it only remained for me to die. And I was prepared for death and wished to die, but I was resolved to sell my life dearly to my enemies so I charged them, holding my pistol in one hand and my sabre in the other. I was attacked on every side. Pistols and carbines were fired at me and horsemen went for me with their swords. I defended myself and only received a bullet through my head-dress. However, if my horse, terrified by the numbers that were hemming me in, had not carried me away through their squadrons, I should inevitably have been killed. My escape indeed was a miracle.

. . . . In the midst of my deep distress, I cannot refrain from making a number of comments on this disaster. Why was the General unaware that the enemy had crossed the river? Why had not the posts along the river been reinforced as the water was going down? Why was a garrison of 6,000 men (at most) considered adequate to guard fifteen leagues of country? Why were we abandoned by the rest of the force at a distance of only six leagues from headquarters? Why were isolated battalions left exposed to attack? . . . I appeal to your experience, Citizen Minister: cannot the person or persons responsible for our advanced positions at least be blamed for criminal negligence? I beg you to communicate this letter to the National Convention. I am sending a copy to the Citizen Commissioners.

Signed and certified by
Beauge—Grenadier
Boulinois—Grenadier.

✠

The Generals, for their part, consult their comrades, the soldiers.
Extract from Le Moniteur. *From a correspondent at Lille,*
November 14th 1792.

The positions of Mont Panisel, Quaregnon and Jemappes,
which covered Mons, had already been subjected for several
hours to cannon-fire, which had caused only insignificant damage
owing to the strength of the enemy's entrenchments. Then
General Dumouriez summoned all the grenadiers in his army and
addressed them more or less as follows: "Comrades, we are
fighting for the freedom of the nations. You know that the
soldiers of the despots are afraid of cold steel. I have called you
to my side to ask you if we could not capture this post (Mt.
Panisel) by sheer force of arms. If we can do so, we shall soon
be masters of Mons." The General had hardly finished speaking,
when the grenadiers cried out unanimously, "Yes, General, let's
be at them." On which they threw down their muskets, pouches
and belts, and, sword in hand, climbed like lions up the moun-
tainous entrenchments, forced their way inside and, after a killing
seldom equalled in the history of war, captured this outpost. The
two other outposts and Mons, itself, were soon evacuated.

✤

Nevertheless an iron discipline is maintained in the Army of the
Revolution.
From Gunner Bricard's diary:

Thermidor—Year II. For the last six days it has been raining
from morning to night but, in spite of that, we have been in
bivouacs.... On the 26th, six little drummer-boys of our battalion
went on a raiding party. The little rascals got into the house of an
old woman and took out of a drawer some silver rings and other
little bits of jewellery. When the old woman tried to take them
back they beat her and brought back their spoil to the camp. In
the evening they started quarrelling about the share-out. The
adjutant hearing the altercation put all six of them in the guard-
room. He was going to administer a severe thrashing to them

when the old woman came to complain to the General. The latter insisted that the drummers should be brought before a court martial. On the next day the Court pronounced sentence and condemned the two eldest boys to be shot, while the four others, too young to receive the death penalty, were sentenced to assist at the execution of their comrades.

On the 28th these unfortunate little fellows were shot before the assembled troops. The elder of the two was eighteen. He died bravely enough, but the younger boy kept calling for his mother to come to his help. The other four youngsters made the plain re-echo to their cries. The tragic scene brought tears to the eyes of all the soldiers.

※

The Army Commissioners supervise the good behaviour of the troops. Saint-Just is one of them.

The representatives of the People with the armies of the North, the Moselle and the Ardennes: whereas it has been established in a report submitted to the above by divisional-General Kléber, that the second battalion of Vienne fled ignominiously before the enemy, while the flags of the other battalions floated victoriously onward; and whereas the whole battalion cannot be blamed for this dereliction, seeing that valour and the hatred of tyrants are implanted in the hearts of all Frenchmen and when a battalion quits its post, the cause must be ascribed to the cowardice of the officers or to their failure to maintain discipline and to inculcate in their soldiers the love of glory, which consists in braving the dangers of war and conquering or dying at their posts, hereby decide that the senior officers of the battalion and all the captains of the 2nd battalion of Vienne are dismissed from their posts and placed under arrest.

Done at Montigny-les-Tignen, the 29th Prairial, in the Year II of the French Republic, one and indivisible.

Signed: Saint-Just, Gillet et Guyton.

※

Here is a picture of the soldier-citizen of the Year II, as seen by one of his generals.

Brigadier-General Bernadotte to Divisional-General Kléber.

5th Messidor (23rd June)

Your presence at yesterday's affair, my dear General, relieves me of the necessity of sending you a report, but I feel I cannot leave you in ignorance of the dash and gallantry of the four companies of grenadiers under my command. It would be difficult to describe the fire with which they hurled themselves into the wood on receiving my orders. The companies of the 47th regiment and the first battalion of the Seine-et-Marne behaved with rare courage. They carried out a bayonet charge against the enemy at the bottom of the village where the engagement took place, while the two companies of the 71st half-brigade attacked their left flank. The enemy battalion had already been thrown off balance by the two companies, before being attacked on the flank. More than two hundred casualties remained on the field and the remainder were in flight when reinforcements reached them. The fighting recommenced and became so close that the grenadiers were literally at grips with them. Citizen Levasseur, a captain in the Seine-et-Marne, threw himself on three Austrians, who had felled a grenadier in his company. He pulled his comrade free, killed one of the assailants, put another out of action and the third fled. I should add that this officer has distinguished himself by his intelligence and his professional keenness. Citizen Couvène, a grenadier in the 47th regiment, charged single-handed a squad of Austrians, fought his way through them, killing two, and on being rejoined by his comrades put the rest to flight. Citizen Alexandre, a captain in the 71st half-brigade when attacked by seven or eight Tyroleans, was on the point of succumbing, when Citizen Evrard, a volunteer in his company called out to him: "Captain, don't surrender. I'm coming to help you," on which he fired at and killed one of them and then charged the others with his bayonet and put two of them out of action. The others fled. I am extremely pleased with my grenadier officers and N.C.Os. They have certainly lived up to their reputation. The first battalion of the 71st half-brigade also deserve commendation.

I should be glad if citizen Levasseur could be rewarded for his activity and courage. Citizen Gindonné, a hussar of the 4th regiment, served me excellently yesterday. He is extremely intelligent and wide-awake. May I have your permission to keep him as my orderly and secretary until further notice.

You will find here a statement showing the losses of the 71st half-brigade, the 47th regiment and the 12th regiment of light cavalry together with the exploits performed by their members which have been brought to my notice.

Fraternal greetings
Bernadotte.

❧

The renown of the soldiers of the Year II remains with them since Victor Hugo. But their first great victory was Jemappes, in the first year of the Republic. This success opened the road to the Netherlands. Here is an account of this victory by Maréchal-de-camp Dampierre:

The entire infantry of our advanced troops was entrusted with the attack on the redoubts on the left and the high ground near the windmill of Jémappes.

I was ordered to attack with the infantry. We marched in a solid column to within a quarter of cannon-range and then, as we were losing men, Generals Dumouriez and Beurnonville ordered me to advance in open order. I must say that it would be impossible to envisage a better execution of this manœuvre, carried out as it was under the intense and short-range fire of forty pieces of artillery. The movement was performed with the precision you might expect on a field-day. I gave the orders from a position two hundred paces ahead of my men, under the guns of the enemy. As soon as the eight battalions had finished deploying, I ordered them to advance, as the drums beat the charge. We took the first line of trenches with the bayonet, but the enemy struggled desperately to hold the other redoubts. Cannons firing grape-shot, musketry, cavalry charges, every form of attack was employed but all failed before the invincible valour of the French. The gallant Whirl at the head of the 6th battalion of

the Grenadiers and my old and worthy friend des Ponchets leading the invincible 19th, formerly the Flanders regiment, carried
the first redoubt. The three first Paris battalions were on the left
of the 19th and all of them acquitted themselves with the greatest
distinction. The first of these, commanded by the brave Balland
repulsed a squadron of Coburgers supported by hussars and piled
up in front of them an honourable rampart of dead men and
horses. The battalion of Saint-Denis wavered for a few moments,
but soon its two chiefs got it back into action, and it behaved
perfectly till the end of the engagement. The 71st, formerly the
Vivarais, the heroes of Bannes, sustained three charges by the
Coburg dragoons, on whom they inflicted heavy losses. The 10th
and 14th battalions of light infantry commanded by citizens Le
Pescheux and Queissac behaved irreproachably.

The last system of trenches was the most difficult to carry. It
was defended by the Hungarian grenadiers, the pick of the
imperial troops, supported by the dragoons of Coburg and the
hussars of Blankenstein.

The heroic Dumouriez, together with Generals Beurnonville,
Egalité (the Duc de Chartres and future Louis-Philippe) and
myself charged at the head of our squadrons. The leaders of the
three mounted troops—the brothers Frégeville and Nordmann
displayed courage and a grasp of the situation. The troops were
raked on several occasions by grape-shot at pistol-range. That
was the enemy's last effort. After our charge they fled in the
greatest disorder. I planted several guns on the gorge of Cuesmes.
Stephan, the fiery Stephan, also brought up a few field-pieces and
we must have inflicted in this locality alone losses of nearly 1,000
men. Citizens Barrois and Hanicque distinguished themselves in
this engagement. Beurnonville was to be found in all parts of the
field, displaying his usual gifts and qualities—chary of the blood
of the men committed to his care and lavish of that of his enemies.
Citizen Saluces displayed great activity and courage. Citizens
Belliard and Lahoussaye, assistants to the adjutants-general,
followed the example of their chief Félix, carrying in all directions
Beurnonville's orders and mine with rare intelligence and
outstanding courage. Citizen Vannotte, an officer of the 6th
Hussars and my aide-de-camp, the son of a rich merchant of

Paris showed that he preferred the dangers of the field to the sweets of domestic felicity. But if I say this of him, should I not say it of all the volunteers? Of the soldiers from Paris and other towns of the Republic, who for more than two months have been sustaining incredible hardships, sleeping in bivouacs, frozen with cold and drenched with rain.

Before I close I must recall this feat of a veteran, Jolibois, my old comrade. Shortly before the battle of Jemappes, he learnt that his son had deserted from the Paris battalion. On the morning of the battle he turned up and took his son's place. At each round which he fired at the slaves of the despots, a tear dropped from his eye and he said: "O my son, is it possible that such a splendid day should be spoiled by the memory of your cowardice!" At the end of the day Balland and my brave comrades of the battalion brought him to me. I recognized him as I had already had the honour to serve with him and rushed to embrace him, shedding tears of admiration as I did so. I have written to the bravest of the brave, General Dumouriez, asking him to apply for an officer's commission for this gallant veteran.

Note. I must not omit to mention that two of the brave young volunteers in the Paris battalion, Conseil and Cardinal, who had taken a sword and pair of pistols from an officer in the Austrian hussars, offered me these trophies as a present. I accepted them from my gallant young friends.

Songs to celebrate victory. Verbal report of a Commissioner with the armies to the Convention.

Three times our infantry had been driven back: the cavalry began to waver and the success of our arms appeared uncertain when citizen Baptiste whose gallantry you have so justly rewarded, ran up to Dumouriez and said to him: "General, take your sword in your hand and charge and victory is ours!" These were his own words and hardly had he spoken them than he rushed off, rallied five squadrons of horse and four battalions of infantry and led them to victory. Meantime, Dumouriez at the head of several detachments of dragoons, chasseurs and hussars swept into the ranks of the enemy, while officers, generals and aides-de-camp sped hither and thither collecting dispersed detachments and bringing them up to take part in the charge. One of them, a certain Dufresse, aide-de-camp to General Moreton, found himself in the middle of a battalion of volunteers in retreat. He started singing to them *"Amour sacré de la Patrie"* and they all stopped and joined him in singing this sublime song. Then they faced about, climbed the slope, rejoined our forces and charged with fixed bayonets at the positions of the enemy, who alarmed at their spirited attack began to slacken their fire. Our pressure continued from all sides and the enemy was soon in flight. Only the dragoons of the Tower of Coburg continued to resist till the hussars of Berchigny and Chamboran charged them and the fighting proceeded hand to hand.

At this moment the inhabitants of Mons must have enjoyed from their post of vantage on the ramparts a truly consoling spectacle. The whole French army was arrayed in perfect order on the battlefield—A hundred fire-breathing mouths covered the uplands which dominated the valley by which the Austrians had fled. One heard only the occasional discharge of cannon as the division on the right fired on the fleeing enemy. Now the chiefs, the soldiers and all embraced one another. Some wept for joy, and others threw their hats into the air as they sang *"Ça ira"* or shouted *"Vive la République Française! Vive la liberté des Belges!"*

A disappointment, which the Austrians had not foreseen, was provided by the help the "Patriots" received from the population. This was at once a surprise and a source of irritation.

Notice to the Inhabitants

The Austrian soldiers to the French inhabitants of the frontiers of Luxemburg.

Remember, you dwellers in France, that on the 21st of last month, at a time when we were occupied in defending our own positions, we had to watch four of the villages in our territory being set on fire by the satellites of Robespierre. Remember also that up to now, though victors, we have always respected the peaceful dwellings of the inhabitants of a country which we are seeking to deliver from the hateful slavery into which it has been plunged by a regicide Convention, which, trampling underfoot the majesty of altar and throne, has been duping you by the illusion of liberty and equality, while it tears your children from your breast and sends them to be slaughtered in the bloody battles your enemies are losing every day, and robs you of the foodstuffs you need for your own consumption, and gives them to be devoured by your savage soldiers.

However, in spite of the execrable crimes committed by the scoundrels who obey Robespierre who, without the title, is your king or rather your tyrant; we have always disdained to employ even just reprisals and, persuaded that the inhabitants of the countryside are not their accomplices, have always observed the laws of humanity and honour, as well as the orders of our chiefs who, like ourselves, hold arson and pillage in horror.

If then, despite these sentiments which we shall not cease to entertain and if, despite our desire to spare an unfortunate country whose fate we deplore, we obeyed our first impulse to exact vengeance from the village of Tiercelet, do not be astonished and let the inhabitants of this place realize that they have only themselves to thank for the disaster that has befallen them. Why did they fire on us? Why should they want to defend themselves against us who have no quarrel with them?

Let this example serve as a lesson to show that if Robespierre's incendiaries can only make war with torches in their hands, the brave Austrian soldiers are quite capable of avenging themselves.

So now we declare to you, inhabitants of France, and indeed we swear to you, that weary as we are of the atrocities committed daily by your soldiers, we shall no longer observe moderation and that each and every time these scoundrels come and burn one of our villages, we shall reply by burning ten villages in your country, and every place from which we are fired on, during our peaceful passage, will be reduced to ashes.

A Prussian officer draws his conclusions from the unpleasant surprises experienced by the forces of the Coalition.

Extract from a letter found on a dead officer:

The French *émigrés* have deceived our good king and all the foreigners in the most infamous fashion. They had assured us that the counter-revolution would take place as soon as we showed our faces. They had also told us that the French troops of the line were a collection of riff-raff and that the National Guards would take to their heels at the first shot fired. Not a word of this was true. The *émigrés* have contributed nothing to our forces and the French troops resembled in no way the picture they had drawn of them. We found among them plenty of fine men and a well-mounted force of cavalry. Their discipline is as good as that of our troops and we have seen them performing evolutions which have compelled the admiration of our generals. Their artillery is very well served as we found to our cost on September 20th when we lost many brave men.

An inhabitant of La Haye witnesses the arrival of the victorious French.

In the Low Countries the Revolution is a *fait accompli* and the victorious French have planted everywhere the standard of liberty. The utter defeat of the Austrians at Jemappes and the capture of Mons have decided the fate of Belgium. History offers no example of a battle in which so much valour has been displayed and which has been so fruitful in results. The French Army has been estimated at 120,000 men. This is an exaggeration but it is true to say that the French had a formidable army, a well-served artillery and the will to conquer. After being driven back several times, they rallied and finally they carried the triple system of entrenchments covering Mons, in hand to hand fighting.

The great concentration of guns at Mons was carried by assault. To reach it the French soldiers had to climb over heaps of dead. Their guns had caused terrible carnage. Throughout the action they had been bombarding the Austrians with grapeshot which tore gaps in their ranks at every discharge. The Austrians defended themselves with great courage. They lost many of their finest men and their best regiments were destroyed. A battalion from Bender, another from Wurtzburg, the Coburg light-horse and the famous hussars of Blankenstein were annihilated. Count Hadik and Baron de Keim, who commanded the Bender battalion were killed and many other senior officers were killed and wounded.

It is stated that the French losses were only a quarter of those of the enemy. This decisive action should entail the conquest of the low Countries. Brussels is a prey to the most frightful confusion. The members of the Government have fled with all they could take away. At Ghent and Antwerp the people have pillaged the houses of all those who seemed to be attached to the Austrian Government. The latter and the *émigrés* can now only look for asylum in England and Holland. For days past the roads have been full of carriages loaded with refugees.

LA VENDÉE

LET US now consider the people of la Vendée, these truly
extraordinary men, whose political existence, whose
swift and astonishing successes and whose unexampled
ferocity were epoch-making features in the chronicles of the
Revolution—these people, who only needed an infusion of
humanity and a better cause to possess all the characteristics of
heroism.

*The above are the words of the republican general Turreau, and this
is how he sums up his adversaries.*

The Vendéans possessed a hitherto unknown style of fighting
and an inimitable one, in that it was solely appropriate to the
country and to the genius of the inhabitants. They were un-
shakably attached to their political ideals, possessed unlimited
confidence in their chiefs and kept their promises with a loyalty,
which could serve as a substitute for discipline. Their courage was
indomitable, proof against danger, hardship and privation. Such
were the qualities which made the Vendéans formidable enemies
and which deserve to place them in the front rank of warlike
peoples.

Animated at once by the spirit of religion and royalism, these
Frenchmen, who for long preserved a record of victory, could
only be conquered by French republicans.

The rebels, whom nature has conspired to favour, employ
their own peculiar tactics, which are admirably adapted to their
own position and to local circumstances. Assured of the advan-
tages derived from their method of attack, they never allow

themselves to be surprised. They only fight when and where they wish. Their skill in the use of fire-arms is such, that no known people, however warlike, however skilled in manœuvring make better use of their muskets, than the sportsmen of Loroux and the poachers of the Bocage. When they attack, their onslaught is terrible, sudden and almost always unforeseen owing to the difficulty in the Vendée of reconnoitring the ground and protecting oneself against surprises. Their order of battle is in the form of a crescent with the wings—the spearheads of their attack—manned by their best marksmen, by soldiers who never fire without aiming and who never miss their mark at normal range. Before you have time to know what has hit you, you find yourself overwhelmed by a rain of fire more massive than anything we can produce under our regulations. They do not wait for the word of command before firing, and have nothing like volley-firing by battalions, ranks or squads. Nevertheless, the fire to which they subject their enemy is as heavy, as well-sustained and certainly more deadly than ours. If you can stand up to the violence of their attack, they will seldom dispute the victory with you, but this will profit you but little, because they retreat so swiftly, that it is very difficult to catch them up as the terrain is almost always unsuited to the use of cavalry. Their forces disperse and they escape through fields, hedges, woods and thickets. They know all the paths, by-ways, gullies and ravines, and all the obstacles capable of impeding their flight and how to avoid them. Meantime, if you are obliged to give way before their attack, you will find it as difficult to carry out your own retreat as they find it easy to elude you when they are beaten. When they are winning they surround you and cut into your troops everywhere. They pursue you with inconceivable fury and speed. They run, when attacking or pursuing, as fast as they do when they are fleeing, but they continue firing all the time. They load their muskets as they march or even at the double and their constant movement does not detract from the briskness or the accuracy of their fire. Generally speaking warfare in the Vendée possesses such singular characteristics that it needs long experience to master them and the skilful general arriving with ten frontier campaigns to his credit, will find it very difficult to operate successfully in this region. I appeal to the generals, who, after having served on the frontiers, have been employed in this terrible Vendée, to support me. Let them say, if they could visualize this sort of war, before taking part in it. Let them say if the Prussian and Austrian soldiers formed and tempered by the discipline of chiefs like Nassau and Frederick, are as formidable fighters, as skilful, cunning and audacious warriors, as the fierce and fearless marksmen of the Bocage and Loroux. Let them say if they know of any form of war more cruel and more exacting for soldiers of every rank, and more bloody than this. Will they not agree with me, when I say that it kills order, discipline and subordination in an army and that the French soldier, speedily softened and debased in a country, whose pestiferous climate seems to taint the moral complexion of those who approach it, the French soldier, I repeat, disgusted with a war in which no glory is to be won, soon loses the energy, the constancy and the unconquerable courage which have brought him countless victories over the soldiers of England and Austria? Will they not admit that they would rather campaign for a year on the frontiers than fight for a single month in the Vendée?

✣

"*Cholet's little Kerchief*" (*a song by Théodore Botrel*). *Madame de la Rochejaquelein speaks:*

As to clothes, there were plenty of them—in the coarse local cloth, in linen, in duck and in Siamese material. There was a great output of red handkerchiefs. Many of these were already produced in the region and a particular circumstance had made them an article of general wear. M. de la Rochejaquelein usually wore one as a turban round his head, another as a scarf round his neck and several round his waist to accommodate his pistols. At the battle of Fontenay the "blues" were heard shouting "Aim at the red handkerchief." That evening the officers begged Henri to change his costume, but he found it suited him and refused to wear anything else. Then they decided to adopt it for themselves, so that it would no longer be a special cause of danger to him.

Thus red handkerchiefs became the fashion in the army: everyone wanted to wear them. This form of garb combined with the normal trousers and tunics of officers made them look like brigands, and that is what the republicans called them.

Before marrying M. de la Rochejaquelein (a kinsman of the Vendéan leader) the author of the following pages had been the wife of Lescure, the hero of la Vendée. She took part in some of the fiercest battles.

The generals hastened to assemble the main army at Chollet. It was from this side that Westermann, the republican general, expected to be attacked and he had taken precautions accordingly. However, our people crossed the Sèvre at Mallièvre and arrived near Châtillon, just when the unsuspecting Westermann was arranging for a Te Deum to be sung by the constitutional Bishop of Saint-Maixent. The Vendéans were present in force and were animated by a lively resentment against the enemy. Their feelings had been inflamed by the capture of Châtillon and the burning of houses by the Blues. The latter were encamped on high ground near a windmill. The peasants poured silently round them, and when they opened fire, the republicans, realizing with alarm that they were being attacked from several sides did not hold out for long. The position was carried and the gunners shot down beside their pieces. In a moment the rout and confusion were complete: the guns and ammunition waggons rolled helter-skelter down the steep descent into Châtillon. The reinforcements sent by Westermann were swept away by the tide of fugitives. He himself had no time to appear in action and was lucky to get away at the head of three hundred horsemen.

The fury of the peasants increased as the battle proceeded and, when the victory was won, they refused to give quarter to the enemy. Their chiefs called out to the republicans, "Surrender, we shall not harm you", but that was a vain hope; the soldiers took no prisoners. When our men reached the town, the slaughter became more fearful still. M. de Lescure, who commanded the vanguard had swept through Châtillon in pursuit of the flying enemy and he had ordered that several hundred of these should be locked up in the prison. The peasants, led by M. de Marigny, instead of obeying his orders, started to cut their throats. M. d'Elbée and others, who tried to stop them, had muskets aimed at them. Someone ran to tell M. de Lescure of these horrors and he soon arrived on the spot. Sixty men whom he had captured surrounded him, clinging to his garments and to his horse. He rode to the prison and the tumult ceased. The soldiers respected him too much to disobey him, but M. de Marigny beside himself with rage, marched up to him crying: "Get back, while I kill these monsters. They have burnt your château." M. de Lescure ordered him to cease this conduct, saying that if he did not, he personally would protect the prisoners. He added: "Marigny, you are too cruel: you will perish by the sword."

In that manner the massacre was stopped at Châtillon, but many of the unfortunate fugitives were knocked on the head in the farms into which they strayed. The burning of the village of Amaillou and our two châteaux, the first atrocities of this kind committed by the republicans had filled the villagers with a desire for vengeance. After that, they accustomed themselves to the violence of their enemies and recovered their natural good temper.

The women of the Vendée take a hand in the war. Mme de la Rochejaquelein:

It was after this engagement that the republicans picked up, among the dead bodies, that of a woman. The news-sheets made a great story out of this. Some said it was I and others that it was Jeanne de Lescure, the sister of the brigand-chief. It was thought that she was regarded in the Vendée as a saint, like Joan of Arc. This last guess was just as inaccurate as the others. All the generals had issued strict orders forbidding women to join the forces threatening to expel with ignominy the first woman found in the ranks and during the short period of recruitment not even *vivandières* were enlisted. A short while before the action at Thouars, a soldier had come up to me at la Boulaye, saying he wanted to confide in me. It was a woman, who wanted to change her woollen vest for one of Siamese cloth such as they served out to the poorest soldiers. Fearing to be recognized she had applied to me, begging me to say nothing to M. de Lescure. I found out that her name was Jeanne Robin from Courlay. I wrote to the vicar of the parish about her. He replied that she was a very good girl but that he had never been able to dissuade her from going to the war. She had been to communion before leaving for the front. On the day before the battle of Thouars, she went to find M. de Lescure and said to him: "General, I'm a girl. Mme de Lescure knows this. She also knows that there is nothing against me. Tomorrow there'll be a battle. Tell them to give me a pair of shoes. After you have seen me fight, I am sure you won't send me away." And in fact she fought without ceasing in sight of M. de Lescure, calling to him, "General, you won't get ahead of me; I shall always be nearer the 'Blues' than you." She was wounded in the hand, but that seemed only to raise her spirits. She showed him her hand and said, "That's nothing at all." At last she was killed in the hand to hand fighting into which she had dashed like a fury.

In the other divisions there were also a few women who fought in disguise. I saw a little girl of thirteen, who was a drummer in the army of Elbée and had a name for courage. She and one of her kinswomen took part in the battle of Luçon where they both were killed. In M. de Bonchamp's army there was a girl, who had got into the cavalry to avenge her father's death. She performed prodigies of valour in all the campaigns of the Vendée under the nickname of "the girl from Anjou".

Madame de Lescure sees in Kléber a young and formidable adversary confronting her husband:

The generals resolved to conquer or die in the coming engagement. The atrocities committed by the "Blues" had infuriated everyone. It was decided that no prisoners should be taken and that the soldiers from Mayence should be regarded as having violated the clause in the treaty by which they had undertaken not to fight for a year against the allies—a clause which implicitly included the Vendée, as that region provided the loyal and lawful army of the King of France and his contingent in the Coalition. Consequently it was forbidden to call for surrender or to offer quarter. The curé of Saint Laud celebrated Mass at midnight. Before the troops marched off he delivered a splendid sermon and blessed a great white banner, which I had had embroidered for the army of M. de Lescure.

The total number of the two armies was about forty thousand men. At first the men from Mayence occupied the village of Boussays and evicted a small detachment of Vendéans who offered no resistance. They then advanced on Torfou, carried this position and posted two battalions in front of the village. At the first discharge of firearms the Vendéans took to their heels, especially the soldiers of M. de Charette, whose previous reverse had discouraged them. Then M. de Lescure, dismounting with some of his officers cried out: "Are there four hundred men brave enough to come and die with me?" The people of the parish of Echaubroignes, who on that day numbered seventeen hundred armed men, replied with loud cries, "Yes, Monsieur le Marquis: we will follow you, wherever you will." These brave peasants and those from the neighbouring parishes were the best soldiers of his army. They had been nicknamed "the Grenadiers of la Vendée". Their commander was Bourrasseau, a local man. Thirteen hundred other peasants joined them and thus M. de Lescure at the head of his three thousand brave men succeeded in holding out for two hours against the attacks of the republicans. The nature of the ground which is bushier and more uneven than in any part of the Bocage prevented the corps from Mayence from seeing by what a small force they were opposed. Meantime M. de Charette and the other officers managed to rally their soldiers and to inspire them with fresh courage. Then our forces began to mass against the left wing of the republicans. The hedges and the broken ground concealed their movements from the enemy, who did not know on what points to concentrate their defences. Finally a fusillade was directed against them from the rear, where their guns were posted. Fearing to lose these, they got involved in manœuvres, which resulted in the utmost confusion. Their columns found themselves marching down deep and twisting lanes, where they were exposed to the fire of the Vendéans. They could not even save their cannons and their gunners were shot down beside their pieces.

General Kléber, who commanded the men from Mayence succeeded by his presence of mind and resourcefulness in re-establishing some order in his army and preventing an absolute rout. But in spite of the courage of the republican officers and the resolution of their men, they would probably have been annihilated in the end, had not General Kléber, after a retreat of about a league, during which he observed that the attacks of the Vendéans continued to disorganize his forces, placed two pieces of artillery on the bridge of Boussay and said to a lieutenant-colonel "Get yourself killed here, you and your battalion." "Yes, General" replied the brave man, who, in the event, perished. In the meantime Kléber had rallied the force from Mayence and put them in a position to arrest the further advance of the Vendéans.

A tide of defeat sets in. The Vendeans have lost their leader Lescure.

. . . . We left towards evening. They could not find a carriage for the wounded M. de Lescure, so they placed him in a cart whose rough joltings caused him to cry out with pain. When he reached Ingrande he was almost unconscious. We stopped at the first house where they put M. de Lescure on a ramshackle bed. I slept on the hay and there was hardly enough food for our supper. The confusion was so great that we had to beat the drum to get a surgeon to come and dress my husband's wounds. The Chevalier de Beauvolliers came to see us. He had learnt from letters which he had received by post that Noirmoutier had been taken by M. de Charette in a surprise attack. The next morning the main body of the army arrived and continued its march on Candé and Segré. We were at a loss to know how to carry M. de Lescure. He could not support the movement of the waggon and my aunt's barouche was too small. I went into the town with M. de Beaugé and M. Mondyou and we had a sort of stretcher made out of an old armchair. We had hoops put round it and placed sheets over them, so that the wounded man should be sure of getting air. I decided to walk by the stretcher with my maid Agathe and some of my people. My mother, my aunt and my daughter had gone on ahead. We moved in companies of families and friends. Each group had its protectors and defenders among the officers and soldiers. We all tried to keep together. The fighting men, having done their duty, now busied themselves in finding lodgings and provisions for the women, children, old people, priests and wounded, who had attached themselves to them.

When we started moving, M. de Lescure uttered heartrending cries of pain. For my part I was worn out with fatigue and discomfort. My boots hurt my feet. After half an hour I begged Forêt to lend me his horse. He had been appointed to command M. de Lescure's escort. We moved between two ranks of horsemen and were followed by a largish body of infantry.

Suddenly M. de Beauvolliers arrived with a coach he had succeeded in finding. They had taken the horses out of a guncarriage to put into it. They arranged mattresses in the coach and rigged up a sort of bed for the wounded man. M. Durivault got into the coach as well, while Agathe sat by M. de Lescure to hold up his head. The slightest jolt caused him to groan and from time to time he felt the most acute pain. A heavy cold added to his discomfort. Sometimes the blood flowed freely from his wound and then he experienced some relief and we took advantage of these moments to move on, only to halt when the pains recommenced. Then the rearguard caught us up and waited till the coach got going again. M. de Lescure was like a dying man. He seemed to feel nothing but pain: his character was changed. Instead of his unfailing composure and angelic sweetness, he suffered from continual fits of impatience and often flew into a violent temper. Agathe tended him with skill and patience, but my shortsightedness and my extreme emotion prevented me from serving him as well.

We advanced towards Candé. At about a league from this place we heard sounds which caused us to think that fighting was going on there. At the moment we were almost alone on the road. I was on horseback. We had gone ahead of the advance-guard. A moment later I heard someone shout: "There are the hussars." My reason staggered and my first impulse was to fly. But in the same moment I remembered that I was with M. de Lescure. Distrusting my own courage and fearing that the approach of the hussars would fill me with irresistible fears, I quickly got into the coach without saying why so that it would be impossible for me not to die with my husband. The cries and the tumult had recalled him to his senses. He sat up and drew himself to the window, called to the horsemen and told them to give him a gun. He wanted to be put on the ground and propped up. He would not listen to my protests and it was only his weakness that prevented him from leaving the coach. Several horsemen arrived at the gallop. He called them by their names and exhorted them to fight, but there was not a single officer among them. They had all ridden ahead, but at last he saw Forêt. "Ah! there you are," he said, "that's comfort! Now there's someone to take command." Then he calmed down and began to praise Forêt's courage and to express indignation at the cowardice of M. de S., whom he had seen hiding himself behind the coach.

The story of the hussars turned out to be a false alarm. Only three had been seen and these were flying from Candé at full speed. We reached that little town towards evening. It had been captured after a skirmish in which M. Després de la Châtaigneraie had been grievously wounded. We found ourselves fairly comfortable quarters and there was food to eat. The peasants came to me asking me to get the landlord of our lodgings to allow them to dig up potatoes in his garden. They showed less discretion in regard to the heaps of cider apples, which, in autumn, are placed before the door of almost every house in Brittany. Hunger made them throw themselves greedily upon this food, standing ready to their hands, which caused much sickness including an epidemic of dysentery which ravaged the army.

This march of the army of la Vendée provided a strange spectacle. The advance guard was fairly powerful and was provided with a few cannon. After them came the crowd, a disorderly throng, which filled up the whole road. In the confused mass one could pick out the artillery, baggage-trains, women carrying their children, old men helped along by their sons, wounded men dragging themselves with difficulty and a random assemblage of soldiers. It was impossible to prevent this confusion. The senior officers wasted their time trying to do so. Often as I rode through the crowd at night, I was obliged, in order to get across the stream of armed men, to swim through the bayonets, so to say, pushing them aside with both hands, as I could not make anyone hear me when I called out for room to pass. Behind them came the rear-guard, whose especial duty was to guard M. de Lescure.

This melancholy procession was usually strung out over a distance of four leagues. It was terribly exposed to the attacks of the enemy, who could have constantly profited by our unsound disposition. The hussars could easily have charged us and cut the centre of the column to pieces. We had no troops to protect the flanks of our army and our cavalry did not exceed 1,200 men. Our only reconnaissance troops were the poor peasants, who strayed off to the villages to right and left in search of bread. What preserved our army for so long from destruction was the mistaken habit of the republicans of always attacking the head or the tail of the column.

During the exodus of the army of the Vendée, another widow followed the troops with her children. She was Madame de Bonchamps, whose husband had been one of the first leaders of the royalist insurrection in the west. He had just been killed:

Messrs. de la Rochjaquelein and d'Autichamp told me that my husband, before he died, had placed me under their protection. They explained to me that I had better make up my mind to keep with the army the whole time, because that was the only way in which they could be sure of not losing sight of me and so remaining responsible for me. I agreed to this without hesitation.

Fighting continued and as I marched behind the army with my children in my endeavours to keep up with the rear-guard, I heard the distant sound of guns. I had often heard it when M. de Bonchamps was leading the troops because, when he parted from me he always left me in some house within range of the battle-field and then the terrible sound of the murderous guns used to give me a sensation transcending everything in horror. I kept saying to myself "My husband is fighting!" But when I had no longer to fear on his account, this same sound only revived the sad memories of the tears it once had made me shed and never, since my husband's death has this terrifying noise caused me the slightest pang of fear. I had already exhausted all the sensations of pain and terror.

We were obliged to follow the army, and the republicans, knowing that we could only follow one route, caused an enormous heap of wood to be transported on to the road we had to take. They then set fire to it. The whole road presented the aspect of a long avenue lined with trees felled and set on fire, which formed throughout its length a blazing river with no gaps in it. We were obliged to traverse this inferno with all our artillery at the risk of having our ammunition waggons blown up. The soldiers pre-ceding the guns tried, as best they could, to extinguish or throw aside the burning brands in order to clear a space through which the guns could travel. But these precautions, carried out hastily and without method, were hardly calculated to reassure the troops who looked with anguish at piles of gunpowder being dragged across smoking ground, blackened and starred with sparks on which at every moment red hot pieces of timber were falling and rolling. The passage through this hellish stretch was so terrifying that a deep and dreary silence reigned throughout the army composed of at least 60,000 men. However, thanks be to Providence, we came through unscathed.

I shared with the army the dangers and hardships of this terrible retreat and in addition I had an experience which caused me indescribable anxiety. During the bitter fighting my little Hermenée was missing for several hours. What I suffered during this period cannot be told or even imagined. At last I found him. When he saw me he was so full of joy that, wishing to jump into my arms, his impetus caused him to fall out of the arms of a servant, who was holding him up on a horse. He was all but trampled underfoot.

During the battle M. de la Rochejaquelein had told me to

withdraw and to take my children with me. My anxiety about
the missing Hermenée prevented me from obeying immediately,
and besides I feared that my sudden departure might discourage
the Vendéans. I put it off and this delay exposed me to very great
danger. I found myself in the midst of all the horror and the
confusion of a complete rout. Most of the horses were being used
to move the wounded and in certain places the road was so bad
that it was necessary to double or treble the number of horses
attached to the guns. In this confusion my strength was so exhausted that I could no longer hold my horse's bridle. The
"Blues" were firing grapeshot at us. I remained motionless and
would have been killed or died of fatigue, when some horsemen
of Bonchamps' army hurried to the aid of their general's widow,
sword in hand, seized the bridle of my horse and rescued me from
what seemed to promise inevitable death. After this bloody
battle, the army moved towards Ancenis and I followed. Like my
children, I was wearing the clothes of a peasant. Being wholly
concentrated on their safety and desirous of placing them out of
the way of persons who might be in pursuit of me, I thought
that my best plan would be to find a shelter for them among the
peasants with whom I could deposit them in case I were forced to
flee. Accordingly, I left the army in search of a suitable farm.
On my way I had to cross an arm of the Loire. I managed to get
hold of a boat but, when we were starting, a republican post on
the other side of the river forced us to retire on Ancenis. The
servant who was carrying Hermenée was struck by a ball and the
child fell on the deck. Luckily I was near him and picked him up.
But very soon we were once more in grave danger. The boat was
full of Vendéans, who in order to get out of range of the "Blues"
rushed to the side in order to jump out on to the opposite bank
with such violence that the boat upset and sank. We slipped into
the water, without suffering any harm, but the feelings I experienced as I was sinking are beyond me to express. I thought
that all three of us were lost. I held my children firmly by their
little hands, thinking at first mechanically that nothing would
save us, but my mood changed suddenly and I thought that,
delivered from this painful existence, I was going to appear in the
presence of God with these two angels for whom I was dying

and who would be my safeguard in that hour. However, some kindly men saved our lives by picking us out of the water and carrying us to the bank.

After this accident I took the advice of M. de la Rochejaquelein and M. Stofflet and went to Ancenis, where, in order to escape from the fury of the "Blues" I was obliged to hide in the house of an old woman employed on the family estate who had received many benefits from my family. I counted on her to show her gratitude for past favours all the more because she had already given asylum to our servants and I addressed myself to her with full confidence. What was my horror, when, having admitted her to the secret of my plans, I learnt from her own mouth, that when the enemy had threatened to burn her house, she had delivered to them my unfortunate servants who had all been massacred. She told me this story with a cold simplicity that made it sound the more atrocious justifying herself by saying that she was compelled by "the times". These two words which she repeated ceaselessly provided an excuse for all her crimes. As I was now in her power, I had to conceal my deep indignation. She offered to shelter me for one night only. It was late and I had no other shelter. I was forced to accept her offer, feeling sure that if the "Blues" came, she would not fail to deliver me into their cruel hands. However, they were not obliged to come on that particular night, so I did not think there was a great risk in accepting the shelter she offered for eight or ten hours. But when I was alone in my bed, given up to my own thoughts, a host of morbid fears filled my imagination. I got up in the middle of the night to listen at the windows, which looked out on the yard: I thought I heard a mysterious noise in the house, which raised my fears to the highest point and it was only when daylight came that I began to be reassured. I hastened to dress in order to leave without delay this house in which I had passed such a ghastly night.

However, when I saw the old woman again at eight o'clock as I was getting ready to go, she looked so simple and so peaceful that my suspicions vanished. In reassuring tones she advised me to leave in the afternoon of that day and make for the village of Saint-Herbelon, which was not far from Ancenis. She added that she had kept awake the whole night so as to be able to warn me if there were any rumour that the "Blues" were coming. There is something persuasive about truth. This woman spoke in good faith and I believed her. She brought for me, my children and a servant I had with me, some milk and butter and some excellent bread and we breakfasted very peacefully. Afterwards I prayed to God to protect my flight. I told my beads on a little rosary that I always carried with me and when I had done that I felt in the depths of my soul as much confidence and assurance as I had felt terror during the previous night. As I had a great need for sleep, I threw myself on a bed in my clothes and fell into a deep slumber. At five o'clock I was suddenly awakened by the mistress of the house, who came to warn me that the "Blues" were expected in the neighbourhood. I only just had time to clear out with my two children and the girl who was with us and to set out for Saint-Herbelon. It is only four leagues from Ancenis to Saint-Herbelon. Nevertheless, though I left at five in the evening, I did not reach this village till six in the morning. It is true that we were walking and that I was carrying Hermenée on my back, while the girl carried my daughter. We caught sight of the "Blues" in the distance several times and then were obliged to retrace our steps. I am sure that we covered six or seven leagues that night. At last we arrived at Saint-Herbelon, after running countless risks. There we received hospitality in a farm. On the same day a burning fever obliged the three of us to go to bed. My daughter and I found our bodies were covered with pustules: it was the small-pox, very mild in the case of my daughter and myself, but the rash did not come out properly on Hermenée for whom I felt the most piercing anxiety.

We had not thrown off this horrid disease when the neighbours came and told the farmer who had taken us in, that if he had any Vendéans hidden in his house, he would do well to send them away at once, because a detachment of "Blues" was on the way and they would burn the place down, if he was harbouring any-one. In this extremity the farmer took us into a cattle-shed open to all the winds and hid us there under the straw. There we re-mained the whole night. The excessive cold, added to all that he had gone through during the crossing of the Loire, prevented

Hermenée's small-pox from coming out and on the following day my darling child died in my arms. I do not know what would have happened to me in this dreadful situation but for the support of religion which is all-sufficing and all-enduring. I thought of this beloved child in heaven and I only wept for myself. I wrapped him in a great white kerchief and held him dead in my arms for forty-eight hours, being unwilling to be parted from him till I could lay his body in consecrated ground. At last I succeeded in having him buried secretly in the graveyard of Saint-Herbelon. This cruel event caused it to be known that we had taken refuge in the cattle-shed, so we had to leave. An excellent man from the village, a certain Drouneau, came to take us away and led my daughter and me to la Hardouillière, half a league away to the house of one of his relatives. We were still covered with small-pox. I felt distressed at leaving my faithful servant, but it was a consolation to know that as she was no longer with us she was in no danger whatever.

Later the republicans came from Nantes to make a round-up in the neighbourhood of our new refuge, so we were quickly made to leave the house and placed in a hollow tree, forty feet high. We climbed up the hollow trunk by means of a ladder and there we remained for three whole days and nights with the small-pox still on us. Besides that I had a gathering on my knee and one on my leg, from which I suffered greatly, but I believe they helped to save my life as all the evil humours came out in them in abundance.

The kind peasant put a little jug of water and a piece of bread near us in the hollow tree. Who could express what I suffered in this miserable situation, after the first moment of relief I experienced at the possibility that I and my daughter could hold out in the hollowed trunk? At the end of an hour I was so exhausted by the constrained attitude I had to adopt in my narrow prison and could not alter, that I thought it would be impossible for me to get a moment's sleep. My daughter suffered less than I did because I was holding her on my knees and she was able to turn round, which she never did without rubbing against my injured knee. This caused me acute pain, but I took care not to complain. I passed a terrible night and discomfort and anxiety completely prevented me from sleeping. My little girl slept a little, but she kept moaning in her sleep and her moans pierced my heart. Whenever she awoke she asked for something to drink. I, too, suffered from a burning thirst, which I did not dare to satisfy for fear of exhausting our little supply of water. At last at dawn our peasant brought us some brown bread and some apples. This visit was in itself a consolation for me, as it made me realize that we were not entirely deserted and that we still had someone on whom to lean. I had no appetite, but I ate the apples greedily because they relieved my thirst, but soon I felt that this unwholesome diet was affecting my health and my daughter's as well. Our fever increased and in spite of the wintry weather we both were burning hot. In this dreadful situation it seemed impossible that we should escape a speedy death in view of the multiple ills from which we suffered. But this prospect gave birth in my mind to one of the most extraordinary sentiments that can ever have distracted a mother's mind. I conceived the ardent wish to survive my daughter, if only by an hour. I could not bear to think of what would happen to her or of her feelings when I ceased to answer her, when I could no longer caress her or hold her in my arms, when she would see me motionless, inanimate, frozen and heedless of her tears and cries. My spirit was being swept away by these thoughts, which would surely have cost me my life, had I not been fortified by my religion and raised above myself. I prayed with confidence, ardour and resignation and after each prayer proceeding from the bottom of my heart, I felt myself strengthened and revived. The blood in my arteries beat with lessening violence and my fever sank. My eyes, heavy with fatigue, closed and I slept, sometimes for two or three hours at a stretch, enjoying a sweet and peaceful slumber. My child also began to recover her strength and I ceased to fear for her life. Early on the third day they brought us some milk, all of which I saved for her, and which did her much good. At last they discovered our refuge or at any rate suspected it. A peasant who had passed one night by our tree heard me coughing several times. He must have guessed that there was someone hidden there for he talked about it when he reached his village. A man who had formerly been a soldier in M. de Bonchamps' army heard him tell the story. This soldier was staying in the village with his old father, but as he had formerly served in the royalist army he used to hide himself when the republicans came into the village. He knew that I was a fugitive and at once guessed the truth, which he scrupulously concealed from the other villagers. That night he pretended he was going to bed but, instead, he came straight to the spot where I was concealed, having learnt from the peasant where it was. Suddenly, the night being nearly over, I heard my name being called. The lateness of the hour and the sound of a man's voice which I did not know caused me much apprehension. I did not answer, but the soldier did not give up. He told me his name, which did not reassure me particularly, because I did not remember him. He persisted, adding in a low voice. You must trust a soldier from the army of Bonchamps. This dear name influenced me as he had hoped. I burst into tears and thanked God for sending someone to free us. He climbed on to the tree and helped me to scramble up to where he was. Then he invited me and my little girl to get on his shoulders, which we did. We made a heavy burden, but by skill and good luck he carried us safely down until, as he reached the ground, his foot slipped and we all three fell into the hedge. I was terrified for my child, but was promptly reassured for, completely unhurt, she started laughing at our adventure. The sound of her laughter, so strange considering where we were, and now so unfamiliar to my ear caused me surprise, joy and a deep emotion. The soldier took us to the house of his father, not far distant. This good old man received us with a touching cordiality. They lit a great fire, which affected me so much that having warmed myself for a moment, I fainted away. These good people, terrified, thought I was dead and my little girl uttered piercing cries, but after they had worked on me for a while I recovered consciousness. Then they put me and my daughter into a bed and, though the mattress was a bad one, I found it wonderful. The possibility of stretching my limbs was a godsend. I have never passed a better night.

. . . . However, the enemy hussars came on several occasions to search house. I had to hide myself sometimes behind cupboards and sometimes under beds. Very often their swords passed close by my head. One evening I was surprised by a hussar and had no time to hide. I did not lose my head, but, as it was rather dark, I started peacefully to spin by the fire. The lamp had not been lit and one could not see very well. The hussar took me for the farmer's wife and asked me a lot of questions. I replied shortly. Suddenly I told him that I heard the brigands coming and said that we knew some bands were likely to arrive, whereupon he took to his heels and mounted his horse, thus relieving us of his presence. In spite of the welcome we had received from our hosts and the generosity with which they treated us, I clearly saw that I was compromising them.

. . . . Although I was dressed as a peasant and passed as a local inhabitant the enemy arrested me. The name I had assumed was immediately recognized as false by the people who supplied them with intelligence. However, they did not know my real name and the description they had received of my features, which dated before my small-pox, could not betray me. This description featured a fresh and lively young woman, while I was bent and lame. My face was still covered with the red blotches of the small-pox: my features were swollen and I looked like a woman of forty at the least.

By this time I was so exhausted and so miserable that a prison appeared a welcome refuge to my eyes.

. . . . At last they came to tell me that I had obtained my pardon. What joy I experienced then in kissing my daughter! What unmixed happiness I felt as I looked at her! The assurance of my life restored us to one another and it seemed as though I was once more becoming a mother.

. . . . However, the court at Nantes did not send me the order of my pardon and on the second day I received an unsigned note in which I was urged to apply for the order with insistence so as to preclude the possibility of a fatal revocation. This note alarmed me greatly and the more so because, having no servant, I did not know how to send my claim to the court at Nantes. I confided in the gaoler, the kindest-hearted man imaginable. He thought it over for a while and then suggested that I should send my daughter to the court to be accompanied by his servant-maid. "The court," he said, "will be sitting for two or three hours longer, so we must send her at once." There was nothing else I

could do, so I agreed to his proposal. We had to coach my
daughter, who was rather afraid of the court, though she did
not exactly know what it was, but did not hesitate to carry my
message. I made her repeat a dozen times the words she had to
say and she left me full of vague but heavy misgivings. Arriving
at the Tribunal, she entered the court-room with suitable gravity
and addressing the judges in loud and clear tones said, "Citizens,
I have come to ask you for Mama's order of pardon." After this
speech the servant said who I was. The judges found the child
very attractive and one of them, turning to her, said that he knew
she had a voice which had charmed all the prisoners and that
he would give her the order of pardon on condition that she sang
her prettiest song. The child wanted to please the court, and she
thought that the loudest of her songs would be the best and that
the whole gathering would be delighted by the splendid song
that she had heard so often sung in enthusiastic unison by sixty
thousand voices, so, summoning all her strength, she sang
fortissimo

"Long live the King and down with the Republic."
If she had been a few years older we should both have been sent
to the guillotine next day. Heroism would have exasperated this
sanguinary tribunal, but her ignorance and ingenuousness disarmed them. They smiled and made a few patriotic observations
on the detestable manner in which the unfortunate children of
fanatical royalists were brought up, but they gave my daughter
the order of pardon which she brought back to me in triumph.

I came out of prison and remained for two or three months
longer at Nantes, after which I obtained a passport to go to
Paris, where I finished off some business. I then returned to la
Baronnière, my late husband's property which I was obliged to
sell in order to pay back certain loans he had contracted to meet
the expenses of the war. I now had scarcely enough to live on,
but it was consoling to know that our ruin was due to honourable
causes.

※

*The underground movement in la Vendée was kept alive for some
years longer. Its last members fell one after the other as they shared the*

wild adventures of their leader Charette, who, with his plumed hat
continued to elude the Blues. Madame de Sapinaud speaks:

Charette, formerly so humble and modest, was now un-
recognizable. He wore a plumed hat, a lace cravat and a violet
suit embroidered with green silk and silver braid. Several young
and pretty women formed his escort. In the first war he had been
a model of all the virtues and had been noted for his exemplary
piety. They used to say when Monday came round: "Today is
Charette's day of triumph", for it was on a Monday that after
saying many masses, he had won a complete victory at Quatre-
Chemins.

This general's rearguard was less brilliant. It contained a number of women who had come from the marshes and who had
escaped the fire and sword of the enemy. For the most part they
were barefooted and in rags, as were their little children. Their
husbands had been killed and their farms burnt. The future held
out no hope for them and they could look for no shelter save in
an army which at any moment might fall a victim to the enemy.
I felt much pity for them, and thought perhaps that my daughter
might be sharing their lot, if she was still alive. The peace which
I had enjoyed at Château-Mur was soon at an end. At Whitsun
the "Blues" returned. Before they arrived, a large number of the
inhabitants including myself left the place. It was a time of
affliction. The unhappy mothers took with them their dearest
treasures. Their children kept up with them painfully and did
not cease to cry as they stumbled along, while some of the mothers
carried their little ones in their arms, who, too young to understand what was happening to them or realize the sufferings of their
mothers, replied with a smile to their tender caresses.

My servants and I were dressed as peasants. We carried in our
wallets brown bread and butter which we shared with these unfortunates. Learning that things were quieter at Saint-Laurent,
where I always longed to be, I finally managed to withdraw to la
Barbinière. But how my heart sank at the sight of these empty
rooms where I had so often embraced my daughter and her little
ones!

In several of his battles Charette had won almost miraculous victories. At the moment when he was reckoned to be destroyed he would reappear with redoubled audacity. His name struck terror into the hearts of an enemy that outnumbered him by six to one. After exhausting and weakening his foes, he caused them to retreat, while he withdrew into the forest of Galins. His first care was to provide his troops with supplies. At his command was created a multitude of corn-mills out of barrels at the bottom of which large flat stone slabs were placed. A kind of crusher, which a man turned on an axis ground the wheat into flour. But two bushels a day was the maximum output. The women worked as hard as the men and used wooden shovels to crush the ears. This was their principal occupation during the daytime. In the evening, after they had put their children to bed, they worked by the light of candles made of resin at mending garments worn-out on service. Whenever there was an alert, they left everything to look after their children, whom they held pressed to their bosoms until calm was restored.

These women had built with their own hands little huts for themselves and their families and near them sheds for their cows. These they changed continually in order to avoid the snakes, who crawled in, attracted by the smell of the milk which the women heated in order to make cream. These creatures are very common in la Vendée. A dressmaker who came to see me at la Barbinière had passed three months in the forest. She told me that she had several times seen as many as six of them round the milk basins, but she had never heard of anyone being bitten.

THERMIDOR

✤✤✤

*P*ARIS IS *celebrating the festival of the Supreme Being. The Convention, indeed, has by decree informed the world that it believes in the immortality of the soul. The Parisians propose to burn with due solemnity an image symbolical of Atheism—a hideous doll. The inspirer of the festival is Robespierre for whom the celebration is to be a personal triumph. A provincial, Cassanyès, deputy for the Eastern Pyrenees takes part in the fête and notes how brittle Robespierre's triumph is:*

On the day of the festival an immense concourse of people had gathered from all sides. The members of the Convention in costume appeared on the terrace of the Château of the Tuileries. They had built there an amphitheatre sloping down into the garden and in it they had set up a pyre on which to burn the symbols of atheism and superstition. At a given moment the President, a torch in his hand was to go down and set fire to all the emblems of irreligion from whose ashes would spring the symbol of that philosophy which recognizes the existence of the Supreme Being.

When Robespierre went down to light the pyre, he was followed by seven or eight members who were doubtless personally devoted to him. There were murmurs of "here come his lictors" among the other members of the Convention. At last the procession started for the Champ-de-Mars, where the great ceremony was to be enacted. As they entered the Champ-de-Mars Robespierre took his place at the head of the Convention. He had doubtless given his instructions to the ushers of the Chamber, as the latter made every effort to induce the members of the Convention to march in regulation military fashion. But their efforts were unsuccessful as everyone wanted to walk with his equals indiscriminately. I remember that I offered my arm to my friend Férand, member for the High-Pyrenees. Like me he had been in the army. Throughout the march we talked of what had happened in our respective armies without paying the slightest attention to the ceremony. As we came into the Champ-de-Mars, we found ourselves, Férand and me, the two right hand men of the procession. An usher came up to tell us to march in line. We pretended not to hear what he said to us and did the reverse. We observed that everyone else followed suit. After this we left the ceremony and went to a café in the town to refresh ourselves. So it is that I really have not anything special to say about this festival, except that it created ill-feeling against Robespierre among the members of the Convention.

"A shy man": that is the impression that the Swiss, Etienne Dumont, formed of Robespierre.

I had two talks with Robespierre. A sinister-looking man, he never looked one in the face and was continually blinking his eyes in a painful manner. Once when a question arose connected with Geneva, he asked me for some explanations and I pressed him to make a speech on the subject. He told me that he was as shy as a child, that he trembled whenever he went up on to the rostrum and felt absolutely nothing when he began to speak.

One of the judges of the Revolutionary Tribunal, Vilate, watched the procession from his window. Robespierre had luncheon in his house and made it clear to his host that he alone had no inkling of the menacing atmosphere which surrounded him.

The feast of the Supreme Being coincided with a day of radiant sunshine. It seemed as if the Divinity were at once calling on mankind to render homage and coming down among them to relieve their sufferings. Barrère and Collot-d'Herbois had invited themselves to breakfast with me in order to have a good view of the ceremony. Mme Dumas, the wife of the President of the Revolutionary Tribunal had come unexpectedly very early with the same object. I went down about nine o'clock. Returning from a stroll in the garden, I met near the esplanade Barrère, Collot-d'Herbois, Prieur and Carnot. Barrère seemed put out. He said, "We expected to breakfast with you, but we didn't find you in your room." I pressed them to come back with me, but they refused and urged me to come and share their meal at a neighbouring restaurant. I left them, and as I was walking through the Hall of Freedom, I met Robespierre dressed up in the costume of the People's Representative, holding in his hand a bouquet composed of flowers and sheaves of corn. He looked radiantly happy—for the first time. He had not breakfasted. With a heart full of the sentiments inspired by the splendid weather, I pressed him to come up to my quarters. He accepted my invitation without hesitation. He was astonished to see the immense gathering which filled the garden of the Tuileries, with every face reflecting hope and gaiety. The women added to the beauty of the scene by the elegance of their costumes. All felt that they were celebrating the Feast of the Author of Nature. Robespierre ate little. His glance was constantly directed towards this magnificent spectacle. He seemed to be intoxicated with enthusiasm.

"Behold the most interesting portion of humanity! Here is the universe assembled before us! Nature, how sublime is thy power and how full of sweetness! How the tyrants must grow pale at the thought of this Feast!"

That was the extent of his conversation. Who would not have been deceived by the tyrant's hypocritical utterances?

Maximilien waited until half-past twelve. A quarter of an hour after he had left, the members of the Revolutionary Tribunal appeared in my rooms with the idea of watching the fête from my windows. A moment later there arrived a young mother, brilliantly attractive and in crazy high spirits, leading a charming child by the hand—a portrait of Venus and Cupid. She felt no shyness at finding herself in such formidable company. When they began to move out, she seized hold of Robespierre's bouquet which he had left on an armchair. Readers, forgive these frivolous details!

✤

The ninth of Thermidor. The sound of the tocsin is suddenly heard. It is the last tocsin of the Revolution. Beugnot hears it from his prison:

On the ninth of Thermidor, at four o'clock in the afternoon of a lovely summer's day, I was walking in the courtyard with Dupont (de Nemours) and Admiral Latouche-Tréville. Dupont was having a heated discussion with the Admiral on the question of introducing free instead of slave labour into the sugar islands, when he suddenly stopped and said: "My dear comrades, I hear the tocsin. Yes, by Gad, it is the tocsin all right. We had better look out for ourselves!" The Admiral immediately left the group and went up to his room, where he barricaded himself in. We did not hear a word from him for twenty-four hours. He afterwards told us that his policy, when a revolutionary crisis was in progress, was to sit tight until it was decided who was right and who was wrong, and then to go and salute the victor. We then went up into the council chamber, which soon had its full complement of prisoners. There Dupont made a speech and explained to us the dangers which threatened us: "As soon as the tocsin sounds," he said, "it is possible that they will want to recommence in the prisons the scenes of last September." For his part, he said, he was resolved to sell his life dearly. He exhorted us to do likewise and developed his plan of defence. There were twelve of us, who could arm ourselves more or less with the fire-irons, which luckily they had not removed, two daggers which we possessed, our pocket-knives and the legs of chairs. We should adopt the old order of battle, according to which the most powerful man should head the group, having two others behind him, three in the third row and four in the last. The fighting force would thus consist of ten men, while the two remaining men would stand in reserve on the right and left flanks, ready to spring to the rescue whenever help was required. It would further be necessary to think of our retreat and we should establish a strong barricade of beds, behind which we could withdraw and

wait for relief from outside. The situation was certainly disquieting, but it was impossible not to laugh at the seriousness
with which Dupont worked out his order of battle. He was
determined to fight and tried to induce us to have a rehearsal.
This we refused to do, but we unanimously elected him our
military dictator for the moment of danger, should it come.
Towards midnight we heard an extraordinary noise in the prison.
The turnkeys, who were keeping a good watch on us, with the
object of defending us if we were attacked or throwing open the
doors for us to come out, came and told us that it was Robespierre,
who had been brought into la Force. We remained dumb with
fear. Half an hour later, there was another outbreak of noise.
It was Robespierre being set at liberty. The turnkeys had mis-
informed us without meaning to. It was indeed a Robespierre
who had been introduced into the tower of la Force, but it was
not the great Robespierre; it was his brother. Our fears increased.
It was clear that fighting was going on somewhere and it appeared as if Robespierre, beaten at first, had regained the upper
hand. A fresh incident confirmed this view. A fortnight previously a member of the Revolutionary Tribunal named Villate
had dropped into our midst. This man was Robespierre's great
friend and acted as his spy in the Tribunal. The government
committees had accused him of some dereliction in the performance of his noble duties and arrested him. This little gentleman
who was less than thirty years old had an attractive, gentle
appearance, matched by his manners and demeanour, together
with an affectation of exquisite sensibility.

This little beast was in what was called the bandits' den, a safe
member of the jury—that is to say that during a whole year he
had not voted for the acquittal of a single accused person. When
he arrived in the prison, they wanted to smash him up. Ferrières
had even suggested that this could be done with impunity and
I believe they would have done it, had not Duquesnoy and I
opposed them. At the moment when they set the young Robespierre at liberty, they had called Villate to go out with him.
From that moment we thought that the victory of Robespierre
senior was complete. However, Villate, a very refined little
dandy, had been spending some time in dressing up, and at the

precise moment when he was stooping under the doorway leading to the street, he found himself face to face with Bourdon de l'Oise, the commissioner of the Convention, who pushed him roughly back and had him locked in a cell.

These contradictory incidents followed one another rapidly and produced a phantasmogorical effect on us. Our minds were in a state of flux, when, about two o'clock in the morning, they came to inform us that the Convention had triumphed and that Robespierre and his friends had been arrested and cut to pieces. Dupont solemnly resigned his position as commander-in-chief of the resistance and everyone went to bed as usual—but not to sleep, for when dawn came we were still engaged in endless discussions of the causes and probable consequences of the happenings of the night.

⚜

The Assembly revolted against Robespierre and arrested him and all his friends. However, the Commune de Paris under their General Henriot rebelled against the Assembly. The concierge of the council of the Commune records the events without knowing exactly what they mean.

Declaration of Michel Bochard, concierge of the Maison Commune, regarding what happened from the 9th to the 10th of Thermidor.

At about 6 p.m. the meeting of the General Council opened. I went up to the chamber to see that everything was in order and that nothing was missing like pens, ink and lights.

At that moment I noticed the lieutenant-colonel of the 32nd division, who had several gendarmes belonging to his corps with him and Captain Durand. They had all sworn to be loyal to the General Council. I did not know that the oath they had sworn was against the National Convention.

About half an hour later I was horrified to see an officer belonging to the gendarmery of the law-courts being disarmed, because he was carrying an order from the committees of public welfare and security. I do not know against whom the order was aimed. A little later I perceived that the General Council was in revolt. This had such an effect on me that for the rest of the night I did not know what I was doing.

At last about 7 p.m. the mayor ordered me to sound the tocsin immediately. I refused point blank. Seeing that I persisted in my refusal and would not obey the orders of the mayor and the agent, Charlemagne and nearly the whole Council called me a scoundrel and took a decision forcing me to obey.

Then I gave up the key, and the tocsin was sounded. I have the order of the General Council in my house, duly signed. I also know that a certain committee was formed about nine o'clock, but as I was not paying attention, I cannot say what for.

At ten o'clock I was ordered to put out Chinese lanterns to illuminate the square. I asked for a written order, and it was given to me.

I know that between 10 and 11 at night several deputations came to take the oath of loyalty to the General Council, but I did not pay much attention to them.

At two o'clock in the morning—I am sure of this—a gendarme called me and said he had just heard the report of a pistol in the Egalité hall. I went in and saw Lebas stretched on the ground and immediately afterwards Robespierre the elder tried to shoot himself with a pistol. The shot missed him and also missed me by a hair's-breadth. I might have been killed as Robespierre fell against me in the passage as he was leaving the room. Legrand, the deputy of the national agent, handed me his wallet and his watch to deliver to his wife, but I finally took them to the watch committee of the Maison-Commune.

On the 10th and 11th I was so busy answering questions and doing one thing and another that I had not time to hand in the wallet and the watch until the 12th.

✤

Merda: for a day this gendarme embodied the history of France.

On the 9th of Thermidor of the Year II at two o'clock in the afternoon, the gendarmerie squadron to which I belonged and which was known as "the Men of the Fourteenth of July" received orders in their barracks in the Petit-Luxembourg from General Henriot to proceed forthwith to the headquarters of the Commune.

At half-past two we were drawn up ready for action in the Place de la Commune. The people seemed excited. We enquired why and as they were serving us out with cartridges, which they had never done in previous riots, we were told we were to march against the prisoners in la Force, who had revolted. At that moment several battalions belonging to the different sections of the city arrived in the square. General Henriot, with his staff, was at their head. He harangued them but we were too far off to hear what he said. When his speech was over, there were cries of Long live the Republic! Long live the good patriots! and Long live Robespierre. Then Henriot left the infantry and rode up to us saying: "Come on, brave gendarmes, at the gallop: come and save the patriots."

We moved to the right and followed the general along the quays, knocking down a lot of citizens with our horses. I did not know what to think of this conduct, when a young citizen walking with his wife on the Quai de la Ferraille, who appeared to be familiar with the decrees just issued by the Convention, said to Henriot: "You are no longer a general. You're a brigand. Gendarmes, don't listen to him. He is under arrest." At this moment an aide-de-camp of the general struck him a blow with his sabre and ordered him to be taken to the guard-room of the Commune. Meanwhile, we pursued our course at the gallop by way of the Rue de la Monnaie and Rue Saint-Honoré, spreading terror round us.

When we reached the Place du Palais-Egalité (Palais Royal) Henriot recognized various members of the Convention. He insulted them and ordered us to arrest them. As the citizens in question sought to escape he hurried after them himself. Citizen Merlin de Thionville remained alone in my custody. One of my comrades wished to take him to prison, but I managed to prevent him by saying that this citizen was a representative of the people, that his person was sacred, and that we had to wait for fresh orders. When he rejoined us Henriot had citizen Merlin taken to the guard-room of the Palace and then led us to the Committee of Public Security. We were in two ranks and I was second man in the front rank.

Henriot rode into the courtyard and, dismounting with his

aides-de-camp, without giving any orders to our commandant, he tried to enter the offices. The grenadiers on duty refused to let him in, on which he marched up to us in a rage and said, "Dismount, my brave gendarmes, let us go and release the patriots, whom these fornicating beggars are holding in prison."

The men at the head of the column, who had entered the courtyard dismounted and six or seven of us followed the general and his aides-de-camp, with drawn swords in their hands. The grenadiers crossed their bayonets in front of us and the fight was going to start, when a big usher, belonging to the Convention— citizen Fontaine, I think—threw himself into our midst and said, "Stop, gendarmes: he is no longer your general: he is under arrest. Here is the law, obey it!"

These words checked Henriot and his followers. The grenadiers, taking advantage of this moment of uncertainty fell on the aides-de-camp. Henriot wanted to defend himself but I, outraged by his recent behaviour, seized him round the waist and advised him to surrender. This he did without a struggle and was immediately handcuffed, together with his aides-de-camp.

This man who a moment before had been insulting and riding down the citizens, suddenly lost his nerve and begged everyone to pity him. The deputy Amar went up to him and insulted him. Henriot, with a stunned air replied: "But Amar, I don't know what you are blaming me for. I have done everything you told me to do." "Silence, monster," said Amar sharply—"Guards, citizens, take him to the cells." And he disappeared.

It was then four o'clock. In the other committee-rooms they were interrogating Robespierre and the other conspirators, who had been arrested. I do not know what was happening at the Convention, but a great mistake they made was in not appointing another general to command the forces in Paris as soon as they had decreed the arrest of Henriot. It will become evident later on how this omission almost ruined the success of the day.

Nevertheless, all seemed calm at the Convention. The examination of Robespierre and his accomplices was concluded about six o'clock and they were then sent off in different carriages, some to Carmes and others to Saint-Lazare. But the carriages were stopped, the escorting gendarmes manhandled by the mob and the prisoners were released and conducted in triumph to the head-quarters of the Commune. When they had arrived there the conspirators formed themselves into an executive government committee to save the people, as was proved by different papers subsequently found on Robespierre, and they decided to send an armed deputation to the Committee of Public Safety to take over Henriot and his aides-de-camp.

It was then nearly eight o'clock. The tocsin was sounding at the Commune and the tumult round the Convention building was increasing as the members began to arrive. I went to report the situation to the Committee of Public Safety and told them of the rescue of the conspirators which I had learnt from some of my comrades, who had been in the escort.

The members of the Committee of Public Safety were much embarrassed. I joined in their discussions and told them there was only one thing to do and that was to march at once on the head-quarters of the Commune and arrest everyone found there with-out giving them time to realize what was happening. They agreed to this plan, but there was no officer to carry it out.

They proposed to put me in command. I said I was an ordinary gendarme with officers above me. "Well, if that is so, you will have all the greater merit" said citizen Carnot. Finally I accepted and was immediately given a written order to take command, under the Convention, to go and place under arrest all the members of the Commune de Paris and report on my activities every half-hour. I did not give them time to transcribe this order into the registers of the Committee. I tucked it under my hat-band and hurried off to the Committee of Public Security to show it to my officers and carry it out, cost what it might.

At the moment I reached the Committee, the deputation from the Commune, of which I have already spoken, also arrived supported by the gunners from the faubourgs and several thous-and persons, armed and unarmed. Coffinhal, the leader of the deputation entered the second hall with the gunners and, standing by the long table, said: "In the name of the sovereign people, we summon you to hand over Henriot and his friends, whom you are holding prisoners." The Committee had to give way and

Henriot, released from custody, appeared in a few moments. He leapt on to the table, embraced his friends and cried: "Long live Robespierre! Long live the good patriots! Long live the gallant gunners who have delivered their general!"

Being unable to do anything in the midst of this disorder, I went out into the courtyard. Seeing his horses, which were still with ours, he mounted and then asked where were the cowardly gendarmes who had arrested him at three o'clock. My comrades immediately cried out, "That was Méda, Méda—the interferring bastard." "Kill him", shouted the gunners, striking their guns with their sabres, "Kill him!" Thanks to the confusion and the darkness I escaped by ducking under the bellies of several horses and ran to the Committee of Public Safety to report what had just happened under my eyes.

I found no one at the Committee. The members were at the Assembly. I went there and found them assembled in the small hall behind the President's armchair. I informed them of Henriot's release—"You are a traitor," said Barère: "you should have blown his brains out." "But, citizen," I said, "one doesn't kill people like that." "You are a criminal," he pursued. "Grenadiers, arrest him." "No, no," said citizen Carnot, "it's our good gendarme." "Oh yes, so it is," said Barère: then he asked me for some more information and returned to the rostrum, where he caused the House to sanction a proclamation outlawing all the conspirators, appointing a fresh general to command in Paris (citizen Barras) and despatching twenty-four representatives to the different sections of the city.

During this time Henriot had spread disaffection among the few troops remaining in the neighbourhood of the Convention, telling them that his innocence had been recognized and that he had been reappointed commander of the forces in Paris, and adding that they should assemble at the headquarters of the Commune, where the chief danger lay. However, I arrived in time to lay my hand on a battalion from the Pantheon commanded by citizen Sans-Gêne, and the rest of my comrades whom Lieutenant Bruel had mustered and led to the Commune because, he said, one must always follow one's general. As Bruel wished to resist me, I arrested him and several of my comrades. who a few

moments before would have been quite ready to deliver me to
the fury of Robespierre's partisans, supported me till the moment
when the twenty-four representatives, whose despatch to the
different sections had been ordered by the Convention, had left
the Chamber. I then caused a number of gendarmes to dismount
and gave their horses to the representatives who mounted and
rode off to the different quarters of Paris.

.... The staircase of the Commune was filled with supporters of
the conspirators. We could hardly get by, marching three abreast.
I was very excited and reached the door of the assembly room of
the Commune long before the grenadiers. The conspirators were
in the secretariat to which all the approaches were closed. I got
into the council chamber, giving out that I was an orderly with
secret despatches. I then took the passage to the left where I
received several blows on the head and the left arm from the
partisans of the conspirators, who wished to prevent me from
getting by, in spite of my claim to be an orderly. However,
I reached the door of the secretariat. While I was knocking, these
people continued to strike me, but eventually the door was
opened.

I then saw some fifty persons in a state of great excitement. The
discharge of my guns had surprised them. I recognized Robespierre in the centre of the group. He was sitting in an armchair
with his left elbow on his knee and his head supported by his left
hand. I leapt on him pointing my sword at his heart and cried,
"Surrender, traitor." He lifted his head and said, "It's you who
are the traitor. I shall have you shot." At these words I took hold
of one of my pistols with my left hand and, passing it over to my
right hand, I fired. I meant to shoot him in the chest, but the ball
struck his chin and smashed his lower jaw. He fell out of his chair.
The report of the pistol scared his brother so much that he threw
himself out of the window. At this moment a tremendous row
started around me and I cried, *"Vive la République!"* My grenadiers heard me and echoed me, at which the conspirators were
thrown into the utmost confusion; they dispersed in all directions
and I remained in possession of the field.

While Robespierre was lying at my feet, someone came to tell
me that Henriot was escaping by a secret staircase. I still had one

loaded pistol, so I ran after him. I caught up a man who was escaping by this staircase but it was Couthon, the cripple, whom they were trying to get away. The wind had blown out my light and I fired at random, missing Couthon, but hitting the man who was carrying him in the leg. I went downstairs and sent to fetch Couthon whom they dragged by the feet into the council chamber. I looked for the unfortunate man I had wounded, but they had carried him off immediately.

Robespierre and Couthon were lying on the floor in front of the platform. I searched Robespierre and took his wallet and his watch, which I handed to Léonard Bourdon, who had just come in to congratulate me on my victory and to give instructions regarding the maintenance of order.

The grenadiers threw themselves upon Robespierre and Couthon, whom they thought dead, and dragged them by the feet as far as the Quai Pelletier. There they wanted to throw them into the water, but I stopped them and handed the two men into the custody of a company of the Gravilliers. When day came, it was seen that they were still breathing, so I had them taken to the infirmary at the Conciergerie. It would be hard to imagine greater sufferings than they had to endure during those eighteen hours.

Order being now established round the headquarters of the Commune, Léonard Bourdon took me to the Convention. He presented me to the members and House passed several resolutions in my favour, as you will note from this extract from the *Moniteur* and the quotations from the minutes of the House attached hereto.

Such, Citizen Minister, were the events of the ninth of Thermidor in which I figured as an actor or a spectator, and some of which appear to me worthy to be consigned to the pages of history. If any question arises regarding any of these incidents, it will suffice to refer it to me. I am sure that any of the citizens who were present and whom I have named in the report will hasten to confirm my statements with testimony which will substantiate my claim to a share in the success of the day.

⚜

The agony of Robespierre and his group.

Robespierre was carried on a plank to the Committee of Public Safety on the tenth of Thermidor between one and two in the morning by some artillery men and armed citizens. He was laid on the table of the audience room which is immediately before that in which the Committee holds its meetings. A deal box containing samples of ration bread sent by the Army of the North was placed under his head as a sort of pillow. He remained for nearly an hour in a motionless condition, which led one to think that he was on the point of expiring. At last he began to open his eyes. The blood was flowing copiously from the wound in the left of his lower jaw. His jaw was broken and his cheek perforated by a bullet. His shirt was covered with blood. He had no hat and no tie. He was wearing a sky-blue coat and breeches of nankeen silk with white cotton stockings, which had slipped down on to his heels. Between three and four in the morning, it was noticed that he had in his hands a little bag of white leather on which was printed the inscription: *Au Grand-Monarque, Lecourt, sword-cutler to the King and his troops, Rue Saint-Honoré and Rue des Poulies, Paris,* and on the other side of the bag the words: to *M. Archier.* He used this bag to wipe away the clotted blood which came out of his mouth. The citizens who surrounded him watched all his movements. Some of them gave him piece of white paper, in default of linen, which he employed for the same purpose, using his right hand alone and propping himself on his left elbow. Robespierre on several different occasions, was sharply rebuked by various citizens, in particular a gunner from his own country, who reproached him in the language of a soldier for his falseness and his villainy. Towards six o'clock in the morning, a surgeon who was in the courtyard of the National Palace was called in to dress his wounds. He took the precaution to put a key in his mouth. He found a fracture of the left side of his jaw. He extracted two or three teeth and then bandaged his wound and had a basin full of water placed beside him. Robespierre used this from time to time and raked out the blood which filled his mouth with bits of paper which he folded and refolded, using his right hand alone. Quite unexpectedly, he sat up, pulled up his stockings, slipped under a table and sat down in an armchair. As soon as he had sat down, he asked for some water and clean linen. During all the time that he was lying on the table after he had recovered consciousness, he stared at the people who surrounded him and especially at the employees of the Committee of Public Safety, whom he recognized. He often raised his eyes to the ceiling, but apart from a few convulsive movements his bearing was singularly imperturbable even while his wounds were being dressed which must have caused him acute agony. His complexion, normally bilious, was as livid as a corpse's.

At nine in the morning Couthon and Gobault, another of the conspirators of the Commune were brought up, each of them on a stretcher, to the foot of the great staircase where they were deposited. The citizens charged with their custody remained with them, while a police superintendant and an officer of the National Guard went to give an account of their mission to Billaud-Varenne, Barère and Collet-d'Herbois, then sitting in committee. These three immediately passed a decree to the effect that Robespierre, Couthon and Gobault should be transferred forthwith to the Conciergerie. This decision was carried out at once by the loyal citizens, who had been charged to take care of the three conspirators. It is stated that Robespierre, while he was being carried to the Conciergerie in an armchair, struck one of his bearers with his fist as they were going down the great stairs.

St.-Just and Dumas were brought to the audience room of the Committee of Public Safety and transferred immediately afterwards to the Conciergerie by the people who had brought them. St.-Just looked at the great notice proclaiming the rights of man, which had been put up in the audience room and, pointing to it said, "All the same, it was I who did that."

�֍

Two witnesses of the execution

It was about six in the evening when the tyrant and twenty-one of his principal accomplices left the Conciergerie to go to the scaffold. They rode in three carts. Henriot, drunk as usual, was beside the younger Robespierre, while the tyrant sat next Dumas, the instrument of his fury. Saint-Just sat by the Mayor of Paris. Couthon was in the third cart. Henriot and the younger Robespierre had suffered head wounds and were covered with blood. Couthon was bandaged and the tyrant had the whole of his head tied up except the upper part of his face, because he had received a pistol shot in the jaw. It is impossible to imagine a more hideous sight or a more cowardly specimen. He looked thoroughly broken down. Some persons compared him to a muzzled tiger others to one of Cromwell's lackeys, since he did not possess Cromwell's bold bearing. All the others round him had, like him, lost their assurance. Their lack of dignity added to the resentment of the people, who remembered that the conspirators who preceded them had at least known how to die. These people had not the strength to speak to one another or the courage to say a single word to the public.

The crowd was enormous. All along the road to the place of execution one heard cries of "Down with the tyrant!" "Long live the Republic!" and imprecations of every sort. The people were having their revenge for the flatteries commanded by the Terror and the hypocritical homage they had so long been forced to pay.

It was about 7.30 when the traitors reached the Place de la Révolution. Couthon was the first to go. Then Robespierre the younger. The tyrant's head was the last but one to fall and that of Fleuriot Lescot the last of all. The heads were displayed to the public, who greeted the spectacle with prolonged cries of "Long live the Convention!" and "Long live the Republic!"

Thus in less than twenty-four hours the most horrible plot ever devised against human liberty was discovered, foiled and punished.

✣

Second Version

On the 10th of Thermidor at four in the afternoon, the sinister procession issued from the courtyard of the Palais de Justice. No crowd of such dimensions had ever been seen in Paris. The streets were choked with people. Spectators, men and women of all ages filled the windows on all the floors, and men had climbed on to the roofs of the houses. There was universal jubilation with an admixture of fury. The long suppressed hatred against these criminals now exploded with redoubled force. Each one of the spectators saw in them his personal enemies. Everyone applauded madly and seemed to be sorry he could not do more. Most of the watchers fixed their gaze on the cart in which the two Robespierres, Couthon and Henriot were riding. These miserable creatures were all mutilated and covered with blood and looked like a group of brigands whom the gendarmes had surprised in a wood and had been unable to arrest without inflicting wounds upon them.

It would be difficult to describe the appearance of Robespierre. His face was wrapped in a bandage of dirty, bloodstained linen and, from what one could see of his features, was horribly disfigured. A livid pallor made it even more repulsive. He kept his eyes cast down and almost closed, but whether that was due to the pain caused by his wounds or to the consciousness of his misdeeds one cannot say. Just before arriving at the place of execution, he was shaken out of his lethargy by a woman, who forced her way through the crowd and rushed up to the cart conveying this cannibal. She grasped the railing of the cart and with the other hand threatened him, saying the while, "Monster, spewed up from hell. The thought of your punishment intoxicates me with joy." Robespierre opened his eyes and looked at her sadly as she added: "Go now, evildoer, go down into your grave loaded with the curses of the wives and mothers of France."

When the cart had reached the foot of the scaffold, the executioner's assistants carried the tyrant down and laid him out prone until it was his turn for execution. It was observed that while his accomplices were being beheaded, he appeared not to be taking notice. He kept his eyes shut and did not open them until he felt himself being carried up on to the scaffold. Some said that when he saw the instrument of death he heaved a sigh of pain, but before dying he had to endure a bitter pang. After having thrown down his coat which was crossed over his shoulders, the executioner roughly tore away the bandage and splint which the surgeon had put on his wounds. This unshipped his lower jaw from his upper one, and caused the blood to flow in torrents. The wretched man's head was now no more than an object of horror and repulsion. When at last it was severed from his body and the executioner took it by the hair to display it to the people, it presented an indescribably horrible spectacle.

Thus perished the fiercest of the savage beasts, the most monstrous criminal that nature ever conceived. On the two following days eighty-three other rebels were put to death, mainly members of the general council of the Commune or their outlawed accomplices.

❧

The Revolution is over. France has recovered her smile and her foreign visitors. Henri Meister was one of the first of the foreigners to arrive in Paris by the Geneva coach. This is what he saw.

It was on the 22nd September 1795, between eight and nine in the morning, that we arrived in Paris by the Faubourg Saint-Laurent without being stopped at any barrier, without experiencing the slightest difficulty and without being asked a single question. I shall not try to portray to you here, Monsieur, all the delightful memories, all the heart-searing regrets and all the presentiments of joy and grief that stirred my heart when I saw once more the place that I had so long idolized.

.... If one were to judge the population of Paris by the crowds one sees in certain quarters, in the promenades and most of all in the places of entertainment, one would be tempted to believe that it had rather increased than diminished. More accurate estimates prove the contrary and especially the figures for the consumption of articles of prime necessity. There are two classes of the former population, three-quarters of whom have clearly disappeared—the servant class and the luxury craftsmen. Some of the former have obviously been merged in other classes, and have become tradesmen for instance, utilizing the objects left by their masters to create the initial capital for their business.

.... There are some quarters of Paris which seem entirely deserted and you will easily guess that the most abandoned of all is that of the Faubourg Saint-Germain, where among whole streets flanked by Palaces, the only occupied mansions are those occupied by new government departments. If it occurs to you to go into one of those buildings on the front of which is written in large letters "National Property for sale" you will be horrified at the deterioration you will find. Most of these mansions have been stripped of their furniture, their mirrors, their panelling, their moulding. The search for lead on the roofs and saltpetre in the cellars has served as a pretext for ruining all the woodwork and even undermining the walls. In every house into which a revolutionary committee has found its way one seems to recognize the traces of an army of Huns or Vandals. Nor must one forget all the great houses transformed and laid waste by the forty-four sections of the Commune of Paris, who grabbed, one after another, the finest houses, which they found unoccupied in their quarters and set up in them their offices and guard rooms. There are several such houses, which not long since, could have been acquired for several millions—that is for a song—but a man of moderate means not in a position to risk a long-term speculation, would find in such a bargain an infallible way to ruin himself, for what could he do with a house of this sort, if he could not promptly resell it at a profit? Who would wish to rent it? And how could he live in it himself without having to spend on it at least twenty times the purchase price considering the price of foodstuffs, materials and labour?

.... It is when the entertainments are over, towards ten o'clock at night, that the stranger is especially struck by the gloom and the destitution of Paris, especially if he has known the city in happier days. Formerly one used to hurry off to supper and other entertainments, and the noise of thousands and thousands of carriages rolling by caused the streets to re-echo with the sounds of joy and folly emanating from a light-hearted, frivolous people, happy or seeming to be happy, who had no presentiments regarding the disasters and horrors, which later smeared their history and will leave their repercussion on the minds of remotest posterity. Today when people have come out of the theatres, the silence of the tomb reigns everywhere. It is quite an event to meet a carriage and even foot-passengers are rare, except for the patrols. The town is lit, as before, but only the patrols profit by it.

Since the ninth of Thermidor a few private carriages have re-appeared, belonging to foreign ambassadors, members of the Committee of Public Safety (who are provided with vehicles by the Republic), and a few contractors or their mistresses. But all these carriages together make no serious impression on an immense town like Paris. There are even very few hackney cabs. The persons who used to have carriages of their own are not yet inclined to pay 100 francs for a single journey, even though, at the present rate of exchange, these 100 francs only represent 24 sous in cash. Cabriolets have become common, since speculation has become the chief, if not the only occupation of Parisians. I counted some fifty of them at the gate of the old Louvre, where the Bourse is operating at present.

The extent and activity of this universal speculation exceeds anything you might suppose, if you were not on the spot. But you can't walk a yard in the streets without encountering some proof of it, unmistakable and depressing. In the first place almost all the house frontages and the broad alleys, at any rate in the most populous quarters, have become so many stores in which furniture, clothes, pictures and prints are being sold. One now sees almost everywhere the same exhibits as one formerly only found on the Pont Saint-Michel, the Quai de la Ferraille and between the pillars of the public markets. One might suppose that everything which was formerly to be found inside these houses and flats was now being exposed for sale in the streets. The capital of the world looks like an immense old clothes shop. One is tempted to believe that the whole of Paris is being subjected to a forced sale.

At every step you meet men and women of all ages and every condition of life carrying parcels under their arms. These contain samples of coffee, sugar, cheese, oil, soap or whatnot. Or sometimes it is the last piece of furniture or the last garment that an unfortunate individual has to dispose of, in order to get enough money to buy food for himself or his unfortunate family. . . .

Everyone is so afraid of not selling or buying early enough, that deals are transacted with a casualness which has to be seen to be believed. There is a large mansion in Paris which has been sold four times in a fortnight, probably without any of the purchasers having ever seen it. I, myself, made an offer of three millions for a property on behalf of a friend without even having succeeded in acquiring any positive information regarding the income from rents, though I endeavoured to obtain it from the two last purchasers and from the notaries by whom the deed of sale had been drawn up. Generally speaking the intending purchaser wants to know if the object of the sale is inherited property, the property of a monk or that of an *émigré* (because there is an immense difference in the estimated value of property between these three kinds), the price offered at the last auction, the acreage and so on. In a word the richest mansion in Paris or the finest property in France is bought and sold as casually as one takes a card at faro. . . .

Thus the man who leaves his house every day with his pockets full of assignats and without any plan except to buy anything which strikes him as a good bargain, may easily make a great fortune in a short time. That is what several persons have succeeded so brilliantly in doing. The Vicomte de Ségur is said to be one of these. In any case he has one of the most splendid shops in Paris and thanks to this fortunate circumstance, they have pardoned him for being the son of a Marshal of France and the recognized lover of a very great lady of the old régime, as well as being a dyed-in-the-wool aristocrat, who made no secret in his conversations and his witticisms of his political opinions. . . .

One of the things which struck me everywhere in Paris was an odd expression of uncertainty and estrangement visible on all faces. People looked uneasy, defiant and tormented and some of them haggard and hysterical. I fancy that if a man who had never seen nor even heard tell of Paris, were to come here for the first time, he would be tempted to use the same words as M. de Jussieu used to a certain individual, "Monsieur, I have not the honour to know you, but I find you greatly changed."

⚜

A Corsican, Parisian by adoption, is impressed by the domination which women have acquired over the French now that the shadow of the Terror has been removed.

Luxury, pleasure and the arts have regained their sway in an astonishing fashion. Yesterday they gave *Phèdre* at the Opéra for the benefit of a former actress. The house was full and there was a queue from two o'clock onwards, though the prices had been trebled. Once more there were lines of carriages and the men of fashion reappeared looking as if they had forgotten their eclipse and treated it as a prolonged dream which they would do well to forget. Women are to be seen everywhere—in the theatres, in the parks and in the libraries. In the savant's study, you will find the loveliest creatures. Here only, of all places in the world, they deserve to hold the steering-wheel. So of course the men are mad about them, think of nothing else and live only by and for them. A woman needs to come to Paris for six months to learn what is due to her and to understand her own power.

*

This adopted Parisian, who writes to his brother, is Napoleon Bonaparte—Here is an extract from another of his letters:

Things are quiet enough here. There is a little disturbance at the theatre when they play "*Le Réveil du Peuple*" and "*La Marseillaise*" which the young people do not seem to like.

. . . . We have had no great heat yet, but the harvest is as beautiful as one could hope for. Everything goes well. This great people is giving itself up to pleasure. Dances, theatres and the women, who are the most beautiful in the world, have become the great business of life. Ease, luxury and good form have all returned. The memory of the Terror is just a nightmare.

. . . . For my part I am satisfied. All that I am waiting for is a chance to take part in a battle, to snatch the laurel crown from the hands of fortune or to die on the field of glory.

SOURCES

The extracts published in this volume are taken from the following works or documents:

(B.N. = Bibliothèque Nationale)
(A.N. = Archives Nationales)

THE FOURTEENTH OF JULY

Pages

17, 24 etc.   *A Diary of the French Revolution by Gouverneur Morris, 1752-1816 Minister to France during the Terror*, edited by B. C. Davenport (2 vols.). Harrap, 1939.

20-1.   *Recollections of Mirabeau and the two first Legislative Assemblies*, by Etienne Dumont. Paris, 1832. B.N. Ln 14,263.

22 29.   *Memoirs of the Baron de Besenval*, Paris, 1821. B.N. La³⁰ 6A.

26.   Beffroy de Reigny (Louis Abel) known as "Le Cousin Jacques"—*History of France during three months from March 15th to August 15th 1789*. B.N. 8° Lb 2,218.

32.   *Histoire de la Révolution de France de 1789, par Deux Amis de la Liberté*. Paris 1790-1803. B.N. 8 La 32 17.

38.   "Relation de la prise de la Bastille le 14 Juillet 1789 par un de ses défenseurs", *Revue Rétrospective*, M. J. Taschereau. Paris, 1834, Tome IV. B.N. G 15,571.

45.   *Diary of Louis XVI.* A.N. Æ 11 1,281.

45.   Unpublished accounts of the Taking of the Bastille (Dorset), Jules Flammermont, Paris, 1885. B.N. Lb 11,355.

46.   Bailly (Jean-Sylvain), *Memoirs of an eye-witness of the Revolution or diary of events witnessed by him*. Paris, Year XII—1804, B.N. 8 La 7.

50.   *Memories of life as an émigrée* by Mme. la Marquise de Lage de Volude, Lady in waiting to Her Serene Highness the Princesse de Lamballe. Paris, 1869. B.N. 8. La 39.

51.   *Memoirs of Madame la Duchesse de Gontaut, 1773-1836*. Paris, 1891. B.N. Ln 33,189.

THE FIFTH AND SIXTH OF OCTOBER

56.   *Memoirs of General Thiébault*. Paris, 1898. B.N. 8° Ln 41,895.

59.   Etienne Dumont: *vide supra*.

61.   *Memoirs of the Marquis de Ferrières*. Paris, 1821. B.N. 8° La 56.

66. *Letters of Madame Elisabeth of France*, sister of Louis XVI, published by Feuillet de Conches. Paris, 1867. B.N. 8° Lb 6,204.

THE FLIGHT TO VARENNES

71. *Memoirs of the Duchess of Tourzel*, published by le Duc des Cars, Paris, 1883. B.N. La 572.

79. Choiseul-Stainville (Duc de), Narrative of the departure of Louis XVI, June 20th 1791, written in August 1791 in the prison of the High Court of Orleans. Paris, 1822. B.N. 8° Lb 5,051.

87. Story told by M. Drouet, Posting-Master at Sainte-Menehould, of the manner in which he recognized the King and effected his arrest at Varennes. Paris. B.N. 8° Lb 10,011.

90. *Memoirs of Pétion*, published by C. A. Dauban, Paris, 1866. B.N. La 154.

THE ÉMIGRÉS

108. Daudet (Ernest), *History of the Emigration*, Paris, 1904. B.V. 8° La 64.

108, 110 Lage de Volude and Gontaut: see above.

113, 121. *Ten years in the life of a woman during the Emigration*, by Vicomte de Broc. Paris, 1893. B.N. 8° Ln 41,430.

116. *Memoirs of a Royalist Officer*, by M. de R. . . . , formerly a colonel in the artillery. Paris 1824. B.N. 8° La 13.

LA MARSEILLAISE

123. Tiersot (Julien), *Rouget de l'Isle*, Paris, 1892. B.N. Ln 40,770.

124. *Chronique de Paris*, No. 122, 21st July 1793. B.N. 4° Lc 218.

124. Thiébault: see above.

THE TENTH OF AUGUST

126. *Memoirs of Lieut-Genl. Comte Mathieu Dumas from 1770-1836*, published by his son. Paris, 1839. B.N. La 19.

128. Roederer (Pierre-Louis), A chronicle of fifty days from 20th June to 10th August 1792. Paris, 1832. B.N. 8° Lb 6,099.

THE MASSACRES OF SEPTEMBER

142. Maton de la Varenne, *The Crimes of Marat and the other Murderers—or a Resurrection*. Paris, 1795. Year III. B.N. 8° Lb 6,147.

153. Interrogation of Jacques-Charles Hervelin, the drummer, accused of having taken part in the massacres at La Force from the 2nd to the 4th of September 1792. Proceedings of the Second Committee of Surveillance sitting at Rue Avoye, Section of the Réunion de Paris, on the 7th of Floreal in the third year of the Republic. A.N. F 4,743.

153. Letters of J. Ch. Hervelin addressed to the members of the Commission of civil police. A.N. F 3,299.

VALMY

160. Goethe (Wolfgang), *Campagne in Frankreich, 1792*. Paris, 1891. B.N. 8° 7,069.

162. *Gazette Nationale or Le Moniteur Universel*, No. 268, 24th September 1792. B.N. 099.

164. *Memoirs of Count R. de Damas 1787-1814*. Published by Jacques Rambaud. Paris, 1912. B.N. 8° Ln 58,163.

THE MISFORTUNES OF THE ROYAL FAMILY

174. Memoir written by Marie-Thérèse Charlotte of France on the captivity of her parents, the King and Queen, from 10th August 1792 to the death of her brother on 9th June 1795. Paris, 1892. B.N. Lb 5,130.

187. Cléry (Jean Baptiste Antoine Hanat), *Diary of events in the Tower of the Temple during the captivity of Louis XVI*. London, 1798. B.N. Lb 47.

201. Pinel, *Letters of Philippe Pinel*. Paris, 1859. B.N. Ln 16,343.

200. Chauveau-Lagarde. *Historical note on the trial of Marie-Antoinette*. Paris, 1816. B.N. 8° Lb 858.

203. Rosalie Lamorlière. *Account of Marie-Antoinette's captivity in the Conciergerie*. Paris, 1897. B.N. 8° L 354 (1, 4).

219. Le Moniteur: see above.

220. Prudhomme, *The Revolutions of Paris*, Vol. XVII. B.N. 8° Lc² 171.

CHARLOTTE CORDAY

222. *La Gazette Française*, No. 561 of 14th July. 4° Lc² 658.

224. "Memories of Charlotte Corday" by Mme. Loyer de Maromme, published in *la Revue Hebdomadaire*, January-March, 1898. B.N. 8° Z 13,581.

226. Anecdotes concerning certain persons and remarkable events of the Revolution by J. B. Harmaud (de la Meuse), Paris, 1820. B.N. La 122.

228. *Courrier Universel*, 23rd July 1793. B.N. Lc 764.
230. Letter from Roussillon in the *Chronique de Paris*, No. 122 of 21st July 1793. B.N. 4° Lc 218.
231. Extract from the minutes of the civic fête in honour of Citizen Marat celebrated by the Société des Sans-Culottes of Bourg-Régénéré. Bibl: Ville de Paris X, 42-718.

THE COLLAPSE OF THE ÉMIGRÉS

233, 237. Gontaut and Falaiseau: see above.
238. *Intimate correspondence between the Comte de Vaudreuil and the Comte d'Artois during the Emigration (1789-1815)*. Paris, 1889. B.N. La 51.

THE TERROR

242. *History of the French Revolution of 1789 by Two Friends of Freedom*. See above.
253. *Memoirs of Comte Beugnot (1785-1815)*. Paris, 1866. B.N. 8° La 7.
268. Desmoulins (Camille), Works published for the benefit of his sister. Paris, 1838. B.N. La 393.
270. "The Execution of the Noailles Ladies (1794)" by the Abbé Carrichon, a priest of the Oratory. *La Nouvelle Revue*, Vol. L. January-February 1888. B.N. 8° Z 1,287.
279. Letter from the executioner Sanson to Roederer, *Revue Rétrospective*, published by Taschereau. Paris, 1833-8. Vol. II. B.N. G 15,569.

THE SOLDIERS OF THE YEAR II

281. Most of the testimony quoted in this chapter is taken from Chassin and Hennet's collection—*The National Volunteers during the Revolution*. Paris, 1906. B.N. N 345.

LA VENDÉE

298. *Memoirs by General Turreau composed to serve as basis for the history of the war in the Vendée*. Paris, 1824. B.N. La 6 B.
300. *Memoirs of Mme la Marquise de la Rochejaquelein*. Paris, 1817. B.N. 8° La 21.
308. *Memoirs of Mme la Marquise de Bonchamps on La Vendée*. Paris, 1823. B.N. 8° La 24.
318. *Historical Memoir on la Vendée* by Mme. de Sapinaud de Boishuguet. Paris, 1824. B.N. 8° La 25.

THERMIDOR

320. Unpublished Memoirs of Deputy Cassanyès, quoted in the *History of the French Revolution* (chapters relating to Dept. of Pyrénées-Orientales by Pierre Vidal). Paris, 1885-9. B.N. La 593.

321. Dumont: see above.

321. The secret reasons for the revolution of the 9th-10th Thermidor by Vilate, an assessor in the Revolutionary Tribunal of Paris detained at La Force. Paris, 1825. B.N. Lc 805.

323. Beugnot: see above.

325. Statement of Michel Bochard. Paris, Year IV. B.N. Le 1,767 A.

326. Charles-André Merda, *Historical Summary*, etc. Paris, 1825. B.N. 8 Lc 805.

333. Details gathered regarding the last moments of Robespierre and his group from 9th to 10th of Thermidor. Paris, 1794, Year II. B.N. Lb I. 149.

334. Continuation of Perlet's diary from the 12th of Thermidor, Year II (July 30th 1794), Vol. XI, No. 675. B.N. 8° Lc 203.

335. *History of the French Revolution:* see above.

337. *Recollections of my last journey to Paris (1795)* by Henri Meister. Paris, 1910. B.N. O 513.

341. *Memoirs of Joseph Bonaparte.* Paris, 1853. B.N. Lb 273.

INDEX

Selective. Figures in italics denote quoted references.